ALASKA'S NATIVE PEOPLE

CHIEF EDITOR

LAEL MORGAN

Photos by Lael Morgan except as noted.

CONTRIBUTING EDITORS

John Active

Karl Armstrong

Mary Jane and Hugh Fate

Phil Kelly

Edna McCurdy

Lillie McGarvey

William Paul Sr.

Dorothy Jean Ray

Howard Rock

Fred Stickman

ALASKA GEOGRAPHIC®

Volume 6, Number 3, 1979

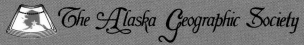

The Alaska Geographic Society

*To teach many more to better know
and use our natural resources*

Editors: Robert A. Henning, Marty Loken, Barbara Olds, Lael Morgan, Jim Rearden **Editorial Assistance:** Robert N. De Armond, Tim Jones, Betty Johannsen, Susan Hackley Johnson, Margy Kotick, Norm Bolotin **Design Editor:** Dianne Hofbeck **Cartographer:** Jon.Hersh **Illustrations:** Val Paul Taylor

Editor's note: *Spellings for villages and geographic points vary considerably. When we have found discrepancies, we have endeavored to follow local usage.*

ALASKA GEOGRAPHIC®, ISSN 0361-1353, is published quarterly by The Alaska Geographic Society, Anchorage, Alaska 99509. Second-class postage paid in Edmonds, Washington 98020. Printed in U.S.A.

THE ALASKA GEOGRAPHIC SOCIETY is a nonprofit organization exploring new frontiers of knowledge across the lands of the polar rim, learning how other men and other countries live in their Norths, putting the geography book back in the classroom, exploring new methods of teaching and learning—sharing in the excitement of discovery in man's wonderful new world north of 51°16'.

MEMBERS OF THE SOCIETY RECEIVE *Alaska Geographic*®, a quality magazine in color which devotes each quarterly issue to monographic in-depth coverage of a northern geographic region or resource-oriented subject.

MEMBERSHIP DUES in The Alaska Geographic Society are $20 per year. (Eighty percent of each year's dues is for a one-year subscription to *Alaska Geographic*®.) Order from The Alaska Geographic Society, Box 4-EEE, Anchorage, Alaska 99509; (907) 274-0521.

MATERIAL SOUGHT: The editors of *Alaska Geographic*® seek a wide variety of informative material on the lands north of 51°16' on geographic subjects—anything to do with resources and their uses (with heavy emphasis on quality color photography)—from Alaska, Northern Canada, Siberia, Japan—all geographic areas that have a relationship to Alaska in a physical or economic sense. (In 1979 editors were seeking photographs and other materials on the following subjects: shellfish and shellfisheries of Alaska; Aleutian Islands; Yukon River and its tributaries; Wrangell and Saint Elias Mountains; and Alaska's Great Interior.) We do not want material done in excessive scientific terminology. A query to the editors is suggested. Payments are made for all material upon publication.

MAILING LISTS: We have begun making our members' names and addresses available to carefully screened publications and companies whose products and activities might be of interest to you. If you would prefer not to receive such mailings, please so advise us, and include your mailing label (or your name and address if label is not available).

CHANGE OF ADDRESS: The post office does not automatically forward *Alaska Geographic*® when you move. To insure continuous service, notify us six weeks before moving. Send us your new address and zip code (and moving date), your old address and zip code, and if possible send a mailing label from a copy of *Alaska Geographic*®. Send this information to *Alaska Geographic*® Mailing Offices, 130 Second Avenue South, Edmonds, Washington 98020.

Library of Congress cataloging in publication data:
Morgan, Lael.
 Alaska's native people.
 (Alaska geographic; v. 6, no. 3 ISSN 0361-1353)
  Bibliography: p.
  1. Eskimos—Alaska 2. Aleuts. 3. Indians of North America—Alaska. I. Title. II. Series.
F901.A266 vol. 6, no. 3 [E99.E7] 917.98'008s
ISBN 0-88240-104-1 [970'.004'97] 78-10528

CONTENTS

THE COVER: Mary Snigaroff enjoys the crowberry picking season at Atka. As in most Alaskan villages, berry picking time is important for subsistence and it's also fun for youngsters, who eat as they go.

Harry Brower's whaling crew, based at Barrow, paddles their skin boat through an ice lead in search of bowhead whales.

Editor Lael Morgan visits Joe Mekiana's sod house
during a return trip to Anaktuvuk Pass, where she stayed for a
month during the winter of 1972. Upon returning she found
that only Mekiana — her former neighbor — still lived
in a traditional house rather than in the new housing project.
Note Mekiana's rooftop desk, a castoff from the village
school. (ART KENNEDY, REPRINTED FROM ALASKA® MAGAZINE)

This volume attempts to explain, in a few words, a few maps, and a lot of pictures, just who and where are the many vastly differing "Native peoples" of Alaska. The purpose is not scientific or academic and makes no pretense to so be. We just thought it was about time we got it together in a single volume — Eskimos and Aleuts and Indians — so that each of them might better know each other and we Caucasians might also better understand the differences, the cultures, and the locations of the various races, clans, phratries and tribes. Much scattered material has been published by others over the years — most of it too academic for the average reader — but we think it is a first time and about time for getting it all into one book.

To accomplish the job of describing all the Native peoples of Alaska, we have selected photos not necessarily at random, but to provide graphic explanation of how it was in this perhaps most important moment in Alaskan time. People in the photos will pass on. Titles and occupations will change. But the land and the relationships of Alaska's Native People to The Land will continue in one degree or another. It is as though it were the beating of a great heart. When you are with these people in their land it is a thing you can hear and feel.

The time is The Seventies. The future is many tomorrows.

It was inevitable that our Roving Editor Lael Morgan contributed the bulk of the pictures and copy. The bush is her beat. She knows Alaska's Native people as does no other writer. As Chief Editor, Morgan has provided us with an immense coverage from Prudhoe Bay to Saxman to Agattu Island. It has taken three years and thousands of miles of back country traveling. And we have also had a lot of help from scholars and Native friends. It is a good book. We hope you like it.

Sincerely,

Robert A. Henning

President
The Alaska Geographic Society

Introduction

Eskimo Jessie Ralph of Buckland, a Seward Peninsula village. After the death of her husband, a reindeer herder, and the disappearance of the family reindeer herd, Jessie depended on subsistence hunting to feed her children. The boots she wears are made from reindeer hide.

A few years ago I interviewed Claude Demientieff Jr., a young Athabascan who was reared in the traditional way in the bush and went on to Harvard. The topic of the times was the transition of Native Alaskans from a subsistence economy to a money economy, because the problems were many, alcoholism and a rocketing suicide rate among them.

"Why is this?" I asked Claude. "Why is it some Native people have such a hard time bridging the gap from subsistence living—village—to the city? Why can't they adjust?"

"It's the same problem you have, Mrs. Morgan," he said gently. And he had a point.

I had come to Alaska in 1959 in search of economic opportunity but was captivated by the lifestyle of the Native people. Like them, I was happiest out of doors and had a deep love of the land. Unlike them, I was raised with a stiff New England reserve toward Outsiders and was awkward in dealing with fellow human beings. The warmth of the Native villages, and the people's understanding and tolerance for the feelings of others, were especially valuable to me.

In those days there were few locks on the doors, hunters shared their meat, and "lonesome" was a word that didn't exist because when you lived in a village you had yourself one close-knit family. And upward mobility was no concern because there wasn't a chance of it anyway. The thing you did was outwit the weather and the seasons and the game—marvelous—the triumph of survival in the toughest and most beautiful country of them all.

Heady stuff, going Native, and I got so far into it I started talking in terms of "we" and "they" and occasionally had to be reminded that I was really a "they"—a Caucasian who was only a lucky guest in a chosen land. I enjoyed the advantages of being a Native—almost being a Native—without paying the price.

When I first came into this country, almost every family along the Yukon River and at Saint Lawrence Island had someone dying at home of tuberculosis. The infant mortality rate among Natives topped even that of India; the average life expectancy in the remote areas was 27.

Education, provided by the Bureau of Indian Affairs, was far below the standards of white schools and, for many, chances of attending even a bad school were

Left — David Akootchook, who hunts in the style of his ancestors, is from Barter Island, in the Arctic Ocean close to the Alaska-Yukon Territory border. Akootchook's forebears hunted along the Arctic Coast from Inuvik, Northwest Territories, to Barrow, Alaska, making the 480-mile trip several times each year.
Lower left — David Friday of Chevak, a Yukon-Kuskokwim Delta village, comes from a traditional Yup'ik background, which he is actively involved in saving. After getting a good education, David went to work for Yupiktak Bista, the region's nonprofit organization.

Flora Nacori, a Yup'ik Eskimo from Bethel, models an intricate Nunivak Island fur bonnet during a visit to the island as part of a cultural heritage program sponsored by the nonprofit arm of Calista Corporation. Flora traveled 150 miles from her home to take part in the program, organized to teach urban students traditional skills.

7

remote. Paying jobs for Natives were few—assuming one could qualify. And to add to the indignity, the Native nation was seen as a nation of squatters, for few Natives had any formal title to the land on which they lived.

Early, I fell in league with a small newspaper, the *Tundra Times*, which had been founded by Native people to prod government agencies into improving these statistics. What they wanted was more than a handout: They wanted control of their own destiny, and that began, they figured, with gaining title to the land on which their people had always lived.

It sounded quixotic. Few of us who undertook the Native land claims fight in 1966 ever thought we'd see a settlement in our own lifetimes. But in 1971 Congress awarded title to 40 million acres of land and a billion dollars to Alaska's Aleuts, Eskimos and Indians.

End of idyll, I figured.

I went back to my old job at the *Los Angeles Times* and the "real world." It lasted six months, until one day I noticed geese flying north over the freeway and got to wondering what was going on back in the bush, and I came home again.

It was not all good. Some who'd been sympathetic in the "good ol' days" when the Natives were downtrodden were suddenly leery of 70,000 aboriginal people with a power base. Although little of the land claims money had filtered down to individuals (roughly $100 per person at that time) it was widely held that all

Shemrose Apatiki of Saint Lawrence Island wears dance beads in her hair, as women in her family have done for many generations. Shemrose's people originally came from Russian Siberia and, although they are Yup'ik, as are the Eskimos of Alaska's western coast, their lifestyles and traditions are different from their relatives on the Alaska mainland.

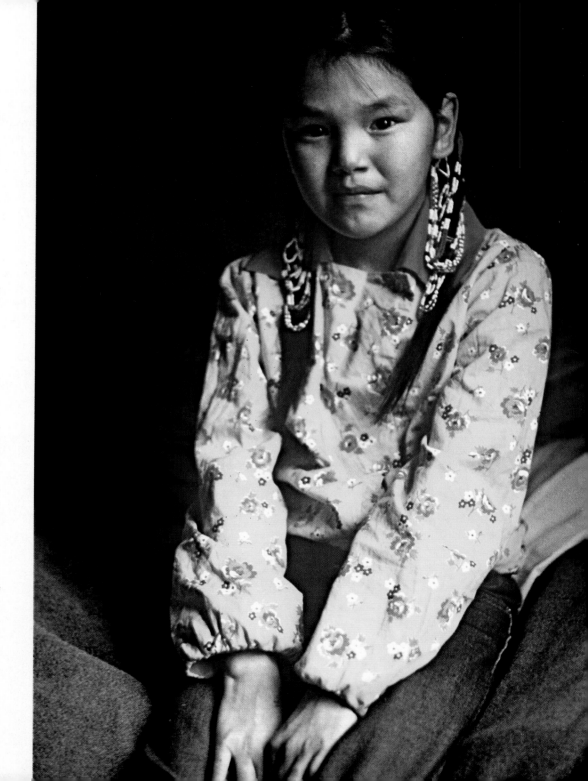

Natives were suddenly rich. Many Native leaders who had scrounged money or used the wife's grocery money to lobby Congress now had top-paying jobs as corporation managers; they could afford to buy a suit or two and maybe make car payments. Furthermore, everyone seemed newly proud of being Native. Native languages were now allowed in the public schools. All this made the establishment uneasy, and even reasonably tolerant Alaskans began to wonder aloud if the Natives were going to take over the state.

Most of the unrest, and the talk about white backlash, came from lack of understanding. The Native Land Claims Act was almost unfathomable, even to good legal minds, and little was known about the Native lifestyle. So on April Fool's Day of 1974, I undertook the task of traveling the state to tell it like it was for a series in *ALASKA®* magazine and ultimately to write a book.

Originally I'd figured it would be a short assignment.

Above — Molly Kudren is an Aleut from Atka, the most westerly village in the Aleutian Islands. Aleuts have always lived by the sea and even today, like Molly and her father Dan Prokopeuff, they spend much of their time afloat.
Right — Catherine "Caba" Chichenoff of Kodiak, whose father was a sea otter hunter, was educated at a Russian school that continued operations long after the United States purchased Alaska. Because intermarriage between Russians and Natives was common during the Russian era, many people had trouble qualifying as Natives after passage of the Alaska Native Claims Settlement Act. (To qualify, applicants had to prove they had at least one-fourth Alaskan Indian, Eskimo or Aleut blood.)
Mrs. Chichenoff helped many Natives prove their right to be enrolled by translating old records for her regional corporation, Koniag, Inc.

"Why don't you visit all the villages in Alaska?" my editor boss suggested with seeming innocence.

"Why not!" I said blithely, with practically no idea of the size of the job. Later I found a copy of the Land Claims Act and counted some 220 Native villages that qualified under its guidelines; most were without roads and many without scheduled transportation . . . which meant some rough sledding.

But it was good to be home and fascinating to watch what was happening in the bush, for perhaps nowhere else on earth could I have witnessed so much change in so short a time.

Andrew Isaac, traditional chief of the United Crow Bands, with his wife Maggie. Issac, an Athabascan from the Tanacross area, can remember the coming of the first whites to the area.

When I had lived in Anaktuvuk Pass in 1972, two-thirds of the people occupied sod houses. Two years later, all but one holdout had moved to modern houses—including my former landlord, a highly respected Eskimo hunter. I found him at ease, with a new wife and a French poodle named Baby, in the plywood house he'd once rented to me.

The Tlingit kids from Craig have visited Red China. The chief reindeer herder from Kotzebue has swapped notes with a Communist counterpart in Russia. An Athabascan and an Eskimo friend—both trappers—have gained membership in the Playboy Club in Chicago. The Atkan reindeer herder who taught me Aleut is respected as a linguist by scholars worldwide. And many homes that had no electricity when I first visited now keep up with international news via satellite television.

Yet surprisingly many things remain the same. The billion dollars from the claims settlement went mainly to corporations, most of which have yet to declare dividends and some of which have announced staggering losses. Although these corporations created many paying jobs for Natives in population centers, it is still possible to go hungry in a remote village when hunting is poor—to breakfast, as I did one morning, on one can of Spam with an Eskimo family of nine because

Claude Demientieff Jr. was reared along the Yukon River, where his father skippers a freight-carrying riverboat. Young Claude studied at Harvard but returned to Alaska to join the Native movement, working as an executive for the Tanana Chiefs, a regional organization.

Upper left — *Harry Marvin, keeper of the Killer Whale House at Hoonah, a Tlingit village on Chichagof Island in Southeastern Alaska, proudly models his tribal dress. Many Tlingit villages began to blend with the white man's world at the turn of the century, destroying traditional costumes and abandoning their language. Hoonah joined whites economically, but held fast to its Tlingit heritage.*
Left — *Irene Rowan comes from Klukwan, a Tlingit village near Haines. She was president of the Klukwan Village Corporation following the land claims settlement, later owned an advertising and public-relations firm, and went on to a top position with the Bureau of Indian Affairs in Washington, D. C.*

the ice was too poor to hunt seals and the old man was too proud to take welfare.

It is still possible to find a village where no one over 35 except the postmaster speaks English, still possible to find villages without house locks, and still possible to find villages where hunters share their meat.

Hearts are still open, even when times are tough. Never have I found myself without lodging in a Native settlement. Never have I had anything stolen. In some 200 villages I have only locked my door once—at the request of a health aide who let me sleep by her medicine chest. Never have I gone hungry, although I take only what I can pack on my back: sleeping bag, cameras and a couple of hunks of jerky.

To the modern way of thinking I have been negligent throughout this assignment in not writing letters of thanks for the kindnesses shown, but early on, when I began to know the languages, I heard Native people making fun of Outsiders because they said "thank you" so often when talk is cheap. If you really want to thank someone you must *do* something that shows appreciation, and to the best of my ability I have tried.

It has been my hope that, through my reporting, Outsiders with whom village people must deal in matters of health, economics and their very futures, would better understand the value of the Native ways, and that Native groups with their widely varying languages and traditions would better understand one another.

This book is dedicated to the late Howard Rock, friend and teacher, who sacrificed a promising career as an artist to edit the *Tundra Times* for the Eskimo, Indian, Aleut Publishing Company, because he really believed in Alaska's Native people and their remarkable way of life.

Lael Morgan

Chief Editor

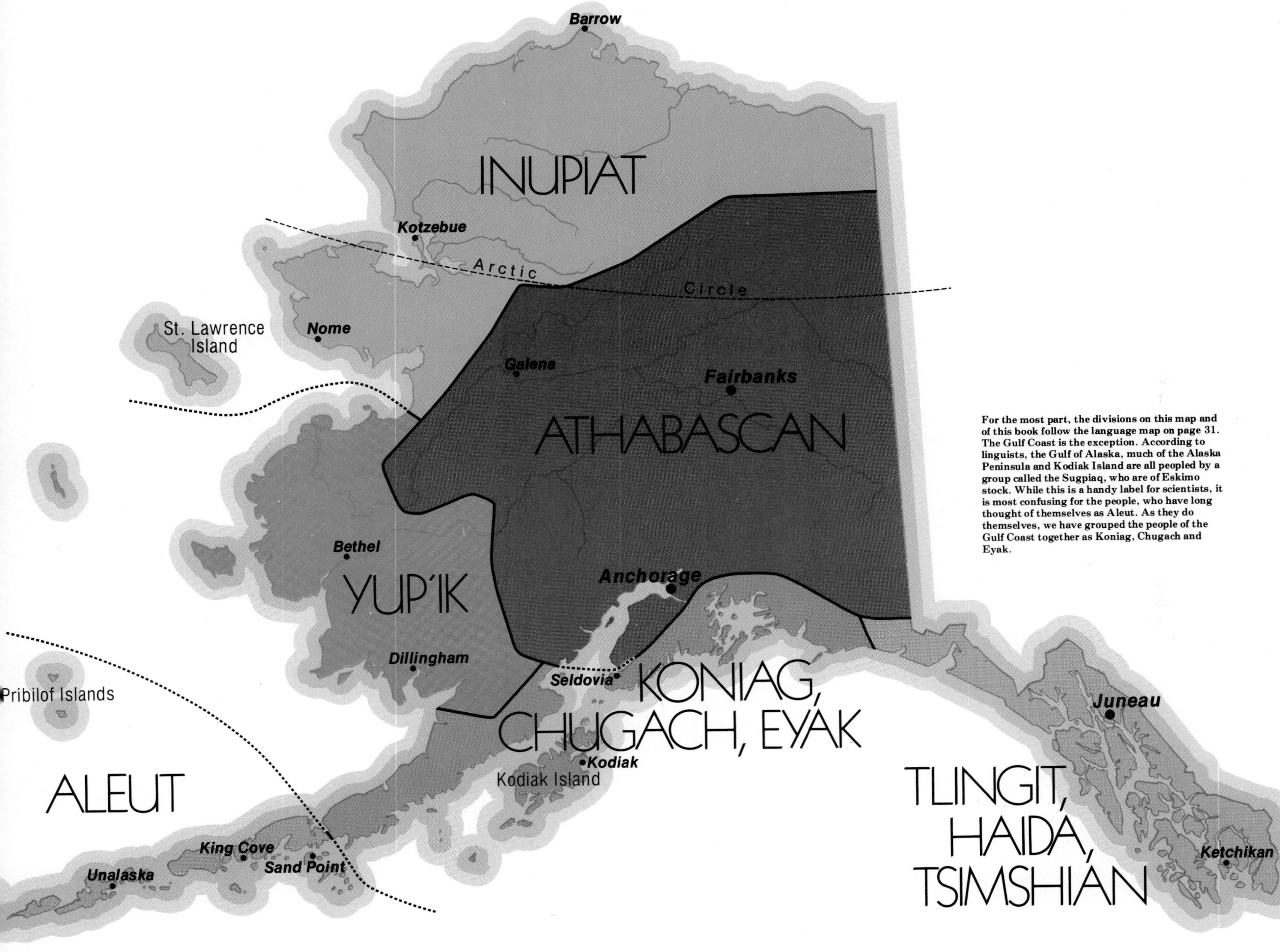

Barrow

INUPIAT

Kotzebue

Arctic

Circle

St. Lawrence
Island

Nome

Galena

Fairbanks

ATHABASCAN

Bethel

YUP'IK

Anchorage

Dillingham

Seldovia

KONIAG,
CHUGACH, EYAK

Pribilof Islands

Kodiak
Kodiak Island

Juneau

ALEUT

King Cove
Sand Point

Unalaska

TLINGIT,
HAIDA,
TSIMSHIAN

Ketchikan

For the most part, the divisions on this map and
of this book follow the language map on page 31.
The Gulf Coast is the exception. According to
linguists, the Gulf of Alaska, much of the Alaska
Peninsula and Kodiak Island are all peopled by a
group called the Sugpiaq, who are of Eskimo
stock. While this is a handy label for scientists, it
is most confusing for the people, who have long
thought of themselves as Aleut. As they do
themselves, we have grouped the people of the
Gulf Coast together as Koniag, Chugach and
Eyak.

The First People

By Dorothy Jean Ray

Three separate ethnic and linguistic stocks—Indians, Aleuts and Eskimos—lived in the territory later called Alaska when it was discovered by the expedition of Vitus Bering in 1741. At that time there were about 5 million inhabitants on the entire North American continent; of that number, between 60,000 and 80,000 lived in Alaska.

The Indians were of two general groupings, both of whom spoke languages classified as Na-Dene. One group, the Tlingits and Haidas, lived on the heavily wooded archipelago and mainland of Southeastern Alaska; the other group, the Athabascans, lived in the Interior. The population of the 14 Tlingit subdivisions was about 10,000, and that of the 7 Athabascan divisions was about the same, although distributed over an area about eight times larger.

The other two ethnolinguistic stocks, the Aleuts and Eskimos, spoke languages that had been derived about 4,000 years previously from one ancestral language: Eskaleut. The Aleuts lived on a long archipelago that included almost one-third of Alaska's coastline and consisted of 108 islands larger than a half-mile long. The Aleuts were the first Alaskan inhabitants to succumb to the ruthless actions of the Russian fur hunters, who killed whole families and overran their hunting grounds. The Aleut population in 1741 is estimated to have been between 5,000 and 16,000, but early Russian writers thought that in aboriginal times there might have been as many as 25,000 Aleuts.

Eskimos occupied almost the entire Alaskan coast from the Arctic Ocean to Tlingit country at Yakutat Bay. This area included Kodiak Island, the Alaska Peninsula and Prince William Sound in southern Alaska. During the 18th century, the Eskimo population was probably between 23,000 and 35,000. Traditionally at least 20 divisions or tribal groupings of Eskimos have been recognized, but there may have been more than 30 autonomous political groups during the early 1700's. The first Alaskan settlement to be seen by Europeans was the Eskimo village of Wales on Seward Peninsula, where, nine years before Bering's voyage of discovery, the Russian explorers Mikhail Gvozdev and Ivan Fedorov dropped the anchor of the *Gabriel*, but did not go ashore.

The recorded history of Alaska covers less than three centuries, but its prehistory goes back many thousands of years. Although the outline of prehistory is ever changing with new archaeological discoveries, a few facts will doubtless go undisputed. The ancestors of the North American Indians, Aleuts and Eskimos entered the New World from Asia via a huge continent called Beringia or the Bering Land Bridge, which included both

Dorothy Jean Ray lives in Port Townsend, Washington, and is a recognized authority on the art and people of Alaska. She has worked for many years as both an anthropologist and writer in Alaska, and was recently one of nine authors honored by the State of Washington. She was recognized for her publication, Eskimo Art: Tradition and Innovation in North Alaska.

Fog shrouds the abandoned Eskimo village of King Island, 40 miles off the west coast of the Seward Peninsula in the Bering Sea. Archaeological evidence suggests that man was on the Seward Peninsula at least 13,000 years ago, but early occupants were not necessarily ancestors of today's people. (RICHARD HARRINGTON)

This drawing of the King Islanders was published in 1887 in the Report of the . . . Corwin . . . in 1885. *It was not the* Corwin's *first visit to King Island, however. Earlier, in 1881, Edward William Nelson, on assignment for the Bureau of Ethnology, also stopped there, on the* Corwin. *In his account,* The Eskimo About Bering Strait, *published in 1899, he wrote, "From the vessel the village presented the appearance of a cluster of cliff swallows' nests on the face of the island, the* entrances to the houses looking like rounded black holes among the granite boulders. As the anchor chain went rattling out, the people who had been watching us from the houses gave a loud shout and ran down to the water, leaping from rock to rock and looking like pygmies, so dwarfed were they by the gigantic background." *In the 1960's, the King Islanders moved to Nome, but many still return in the summertime to hunt and fish.*

Alaska and Siberia. It was a thousand miles long from north to south, with a coastline that stretched from the Gulf of Anadyr in Siberia to the western end of Umnak Island. In Beringian times, today's coastal Eskimo villages would have been hundreds of miles inland.

Many hundreds, and probably thousands, of years passed as the people moved eastward and southward out of Asia, slowly changing their dwelling places. Ancestors of the American Indians apparently came to America through north Beringia in the Bering Strait area, retaining their habit of hunting land animals; the ancestors of the Eskimos and Aleuts, on the other hand, appear to have taken the southerly route along the Beringian shores to the Aleutians, establishing their homes on the coast for sea mammal hunting.

Recent discoveries have revealed that man was on Seward Peninsula by at least 11,000 B.C., and on the upper Yukon River more than 25,000 to 30,000 years ago, but in all probability these early occupants were not ancestors of the present groups. There is evidence, however, that ancestors of today's Aleuts lived continuously in the eastern Aleutians for over 8,000 years and that Na-Dene may have been present in Alaska since before 9000 B.C.

When Europeans arrived in Alaska there had been no migrations from Asia for at least 5,000 years. The general settlement pattern had been stable for some time and the numerous tribal groups were well established in territories as varied as the tribal ways of life. The land the tribes occupied ranged from sea level to the highest point on the North American continent (Mount McKinley—20,320 feet high), and from impenetrable forests in mild rainy climates to the desertlike tundra, with its biting cold and wind. But the languages spoken, the people's physical characteristics and much of their culture—social organization, religion, art—were not determined by the environment, although of course it played a part in use of local foods and raw materials.

For instance, Eskimos were mainly coastal people who hunted marine mammals, but some, like the Nunamiut people of the Brooks Range and the Kauwerak of Seward Peninsula, lived inland and hunted the caribou almost exclusively. The Tlingits and Haidas were also coastal dwellers who hunted marine mammals, but they were not Eskimos. Most of the Athabascans lived inland and built their homes on rivers, but Eskimos also lived in inland river settlements: on the Colville, the Noatak, the Kobuk, the Nushagak, the Yukon, the Kuskokwim. The Tlingits had magnificent cedar trees that they converted into huge plank houses and beautifully carved art objects, but Eskimos too used wood, making houses, boat frames, sleds and sculptures from wood that had drifted to their beaches.

Despite their cultural differences, the Alaskans shared a number of characteristics. The people were, first of all, what are known as hunting and gathering peoples. They had no agriculture and only one domesticated animal, the dog. Waterways were their principal highways and all had some kind of boat. And although many of these people traveled over large areas, few, if any, of the tribes of Alaska were nomadic. With the exception of the Nunamiut, the upper Noatak Eskimos and possibly a few of the Kutchin Athabascans, all groups lived in permanent dwellings in permanent villages and moved to their summer camps, also in permanent locations, for various summer occupations. The tribes generally had well-defined concepts of boundary lines and used various portions of tribal lands repeatedly from season to season. Almost all groups depended substantially on fish, and the women gathered as many berries and greens as their resources permitted. Religious beliefs were basically similar: there was only a hazy concept of a supreme being; the spirits of food animals were respected and honored with festivities; and the shaman, or medicine man, was the important interpreter of the supernatural and the doctor for nonspecific illnesses. Except for the Tlingits and Haidas, who practiced cremation, most groups recognized the existence of an afterlife by caring for a corpse and depositing personal goods with it in the burial. Ceremonial celebrations often inspired the carving and use of art objects and the composition of songs and dances. Everywhere the myths included tales of the Raven, usually as the creator of the world, and of warfare and raiding—especially among those Eskimos and Indians who lived near each other.

On that same 1881 trip to the Arctic, Edward Nelson discovered a trading camp near Kotzebue which had attracted from 600 to 800 Inupiat Eskimos; about 300 more were camped near Point Hope. This scene of Point Hope Eskimos tenting was sketched a little farther north at Cape Lisburne. The tents were conical, a patchwork of sealskin tailored around a cone of sticks about 10 feet high and 12 to 15 feet in diameter. Nelson also noted that the camps were methodically laid out, something rare in that casual society. (FROM NELSON'S "THE ESKIMO ABOUT BERING STRAIT, 1899")

THE ESKIMOS

The stereotype of a lonely Eskimo family huddled in a snow-block house in a land of perpetual snow is not typical of Alaska. To be sure, the flat coastal tundra often seemed limitless and bleak, but Alaskan Eskimos never lived permanently in snow igloos, and no family lived alone except at seasonal fish and berry campsites. The variations in Alaskan Eskimo life were very great. The Eskimos ranged from a truly arctic tundra people of the long winter night and long summer day to the Chugach and Kodiak Islanders of the fjords and forests of a southern climate less severe than that of Montana. The majority of Alaskan Eskimos lived on the coast of the mainland, but many also lived on rivers, as we have seen, and on large and small islands: Saint Lawrence, Kodiak, Nunivak, Little Diomede, Sledge and King. The Nunamiut, the "People of the Land," lived in and near the Brooks Range, but they often made visits to the Arctic Coast before they settled permanently at Anaktuvuk Pass in 1948.

The Eskimos spoke three separate languages (excluding the Aleut). Inupiat was spoken north of Golovnin Bay and across the North to Greenland; Yup'ik was spoken from Golovnin Bay southward; and Sugpiaq was spoken by the Pacific Eskimos. (The Saint Lawrence Islanders, who lived near Siberia, spoke a major variation, but it was not a separate language.) Inhabitants of each island, river and coastal settlement spoke a dialect that differed slightly from that of the adjacent group.

All Eskimos except the Nunamiut had a wide array of food products, which they obtained from their own tribal territories or through alliances with another tribe, a practice that provided an effective hedge against famine. Seals were generally the mainstay of Eskimo subsistence, but fish, eggs, birds and plant foods were also important. Some groups hunted beluga (white

whales) and *oogruk* (bearded seals) in special places, but
the large black whale was hunted by only a few,
including the Eskimos of Point Barrow, Point Hope and
Wales in the Far North, Aleuts along the Aleutian
Islands Chain, and the Eskimos of Kodiak Island and
Prince William Sound in the south. The Bering Strait
people captured walrus when the herds migrated twice a
year through the strait on the ice. The ivory tusks of the
walrus were both traded along the coast and carved by
the local residents into unique tools and sculptures. In
summer most Eskimos were able to get a few caribou in
the coastal mountains or on the coast, which the
animals visited to escape insects. The Eskimo diet also
included large quantities of greens, berries and roots
eaten fresh or preserved in skin containers or baskets for
the winter. Some of the food—for example small fish
and *muktuk*, the skin and top layer of meat from a
bowhead whale—was eaten frozen and/or raw, but
most of it was cooked in water heated with hot rocks or
seared directly over the flame.

All except the Nunamiut and upper Noatak people
lived in semisubterranean dwellings of driftwood
(sometimes whalebone) and sod in permanent winter
villages. (The Nunamiut and Noatak people made
domed structures of bent sticks and caribou skins or
sod.) Village populations ranged from a dozen to 50 or
100, but Wales, with a population of 500, was the
largest Eskimo village anywhere at the time of Alaska's
discovery. A focal point of each village was the
ceremonial house, the *kazgi*, where the men gathered to
work and where social functions were held. Some
villages, like Wales, had four such structures, each
belonging to one faction of the village. The Kodiak
Island variation of the word *kazgi* was used as *kashim*
by the Russians in their writings and subsequently
adopted by American writers.

The houses were small, averaging about 14 feet
square. The floors and walls of the one or two rooms

In exploring and mapping the arctic sound that bears his
name, Otto von Kotzebue in 1816 found local Eskimos
fiercely independent and able traders. Kotzebue's artist,
M. Louis Choris, captured their no-nonsense demeanor. The
two men at the left are shown with tonshured skulls, a fashion
favored by Siberian Eskimos, while the hooded man and
woman appear in parkas much like those worn in Alaska
today. (FROM KOTZEBUE'S "A VOYAGE AROUND THE WORLD, 1823,
1824, 1825," PUBLISHED IN 1830)

were often made of neatly trimmed driftwood planks
and contained sleeping benches and sometimes
cupboards. The houses were heated with seal oil or
wood, depending on the locality. A useful architectural
feature was a long entrance tunnel, which lower than
the house, trapped the cold. From one to three families
occupied a house. In the summer the occupants eagerly

Intérieur d'une maison dans l'île s'. Laurent.

One of the best things about Otto von Kotzebue's expedition to the Arctic in 1816 was the careful recording of his artist, M. Louis Choris, whose eye for detail was almost photographic. In an account of the trip, A Voyage Around the World, 1823, this illustration represents Saint Lawrence Island, where Kotzebue landed on July 28.

The boat was met by several "armed but friendly" Eskimos. "We saw no women; probably on seeing our approach they fled to the mountains. They informed us that two years earlier, or thereabouts, a large ship, having arrived amongst them, took by force one of their compatriots from whom they heard nothing further."

Kotzebue found the Saint Lawrence people dressed much like the Aleuts and he traded tobacco and iron utensils with them in return for walrus teeth and fox skins. He reported that these people also traded on the nearby Asian coast where they had friends, but that they apparently warred constantly with tribes on the North American continent.

moved out of their dark dwellings into shelters made of skin, brush or wood, usually at a campsite. The camps to which a family returned year after year were within the group's own territory, but by the early 19th century a family often combined fishing with trading at various distant fairs where they obtained Native and European products and met persons from other places.

One of the anomalies of Eskimo culture was the hospitality extended to non-Native travelers and the freedom with which the Eskimos themselves could safely go to other tribal territories through their alliances, kinship ties and trading routes, yet an Eskimo or Indian who could not explain his presence in foreign territory was supposedly killed on sight. In Eskimo folklore this tragic figure was known as *inyukutuk*.

Almost every Eskimo had considerable manual dexterity, which the men put to good use making tools and sculptures of wood, bone and ivory, and every object needed for living and transportation, and the women in making fur garments and baskets. Though many masks and figurines were conceived or carved by shamans for ceremonial use, there was no special group of artists such as often existed among the Tlingits. The women, especially among the Inupiat speakers, were noted for their carefully fitted tailored clothing made from complex patterns and decorated with fur and skin insets in geometric designs. A distinctive Eskimo garment with an attached hood and ruff is now called a parka, a word borrowed by the Russians from the Siberian Kamchadal language.

The large boat called the *umiak* was in greater use among the northern Eskimos than those in the south. Sleds pulled by dogs were probably not common until late prehistoric times, and L. A. Zagoskin, a Russian naval lieutenant who lived and traveled in Alaska between 1842 and 1844, said that the tandem technique of hitching dogs was introduced by the Russians, replacing a fan arrangement.

Festivals like the messenger feast and feasts to commemorate the dead were celebrated by almost all Eskimos. These festivities required a large outlay of goods for inter-village exchange, and although the food for entertainment and gifts demanded cooperation of a leader's kin, the primary aim was to reinforce alliances and interpersonal relations among groups, not to reinforce social position as among the Tlingits. The Eskimos did not recognize social classes, but there was a definite distinction between a poor man and a rich man. Leadership was based on hunting skill, which enabled a man to be rich, as well as on diplomatic skill in dealing with other tribes, especially on the western coast where boundaries of territorial hunting areas were important.

THE ALEUTS

The population of the Aleutian Islands had been drastically reduced by the time of the Russian-American Company's first charter in 1799, and comparatively little information has been recorded about the Aleuts' aboriginal life. In the 1740's, almost every livable island was occupied, and some like Unalaska had as many as 24 villages. The aboriginal settlement patterns were rearranged when the early Russian fur hunters relocated Aleut groups for better control and for more effective use of the men for hunting. From the beginning of organized fur hunting by various companies, Aleuts were hired or indentured to hunt on the open sea or to perform other duties. They were often taken long distances—particularly by the Russian-American Company—traveling to Kodiak Island, Prince William Sound, Cook Inlet, Sitka, California and even Hawaii.

Although the higher elevations of the rugged and treeless Aleutian Islands have scarcely any plant growth, the grassy and bushy vegetation of the lower coastal areas often presents a green, opulent

Captain James Cook visited Unalaska in 1778 on his third voyage around the world and noted in his log that the Aleuts there were "remarkably cheerful and friendly amongst each other and always behaved with great civility to our people."

They did not seem to be long-lived, however. "I nowhere saw a person, man or woman, that I could suppose over 60 years old and very few over 50."

They took their living from the sea, Cook reported, lived without dogs or other domesticated animals and buried their dead on the summits of hills. This sketch, of Unalaska, was published with Cook's account, A Voyage to the Pacific Ocean . . . Third and Last Voyage, *and was engraved by J. Hall and S. Middiman. Artist on the trip was Johann Webber.*

appearance. But winds, mists, and fogs are constant companions to the islands. The archaeologist Waldemar Jochelson said that during his 19 months' stay in the islands in 1910 the skies were clear only 9 days.

The Aleuts lived entirely on the coast, and recent surveys reveal that north and south sides of the islands were equally favored as sites for villages and camps. The people went to the interior of their islands for certain stone materials and for berries, greens and roots, but all else was obtained from the ocean and its beaches. A permanent winter settlement would be made at a location that provided a convenient supply of fresh water and a low, level area for launching boats and spotting enemies.

The ancient Aleut dwellings were apparently large communal structures built partly underground of logs, posts and sod. Some were said to be 240 by 40 feet, housing as many as 40 families, but the average dwellings in archaeological sites are usually about one-fourth as large. Entrances were holes in the roof; to enter, occupants descended notched logs. The interiors were partitioned with mats and heated with oil in stone lamps. After the Russian occupation, Aleuts lived in much smaller houses (*barabaras*).

Although only 10 per cent of the extensive coastline was low, safe and large enough for settlements, every small beach, reef, tidal pool and cliff of the islands was used for fishing, bird hunting and the collecting of mollusks, sea urchins and eggs. The coastal waters of the Aleuts' territory did not freeze; so there was none of the ice hunting that took place among the Eskimos farther north. To hunt sea otters, sea lions, porpoises and whales, Aleut hunters (and also the Kodiak Island Eskimos) struck out daringly into the open sea in kayaks, often out of sight of land and obscured by fog, with a skill unsurpassed by any others in the world. The smaller sea mammals were killed by means of a small spear thrown from a spear thrower, but whales were pierced with a lance smeared with aconite poison obtained from monkshood root. The whale died about three days after it was poisoned. Some whales drifted ashore to be claimed by the hunter, but many were never seen again. The Aleuts had no clay cooking pots and ate much of their food raw.

They did not use sleds, but had *umiaks* as well as the indispensable kayaks, called *bidarkas* by the early Russians. (The three-holed *bidarka* was a Russian invention.) Bows and arrows were rarely used for any purpose except warfare because land animals were scarce. The westernmost range of caribou, wolves, mink, weasels and wolverines was Unimak Island just off the Alaska Peninsula.

The tall wild beach rye grass furnished material for both the coarse household mats and bags and for the famous Aleut basket, one of the most delicate baskets known. To make the baskets the women shredded blades of grass until they were fine as silk, using their fingernails, which were grown long for this purpose. The main article of Aleut clothing was a long hoodless coat made from the skins of sea mammals or birds. One of the principal items for exhibiting the women's sewing talents was the gutskin parka, a kind of raincoat, which

In his Voyage Around the World, 1823 . . ., *Kotzebue reported arriving "happily" at the well-supplied Russian-Aleut settlement of Unalaska. During his lengthy stay there while he waited for warm weather, he noted that the village contained "a puny little wooden church, four wooden houses and beyond that thirty or more native huts made of earth." The population, he added, consisted of 16 Russians and perhaps 150 Aleuts.*

"The company [Russian-American Company] has charged the Aleuts with killing foxes and sea otters. The fox pelts are extremely beautiful; there are many black ones; sea otter pelts are equally well known; but these animals are rare. The company pays for these pelts with tobacco, brandy, nankeen [sturdy yellow cotton cloth], tea, sugar syrup and wheat, as well as brightly colored clothing."

Kotzebue's artist, M. Louis Choris, chose to depict the Natives in traditional garb, however, and was among the last to record their elegant Native craft.

Costumes des habitants des Îles Aléoutiennes

Naturalist Henry Wood Elliott was appointed U.S. Treasury agent at the fur seal rookery island of Saint Paul in 1872 and it is through his delicate sketches and straight-forward reporting that much Aleut history was recorded. For the most part he admired the Aleuts, writing, "In fact among all the savage races found on the Northwest Coast by Christian pioneers and teachers, the Aleuts are the only practical converts to Christianity so far, readily changing barbarous customs and wild superstitions for the rites of the Greek Catholic Church and its more refined myths and legends."

Later he went on to record a number of Aleut legends and he also did well by the seals on which the Saint Paul people depended, sketching them in endless antics and reporting their numbers as "almost fabulous." (FROM "OUR ARCTIC PROVINCE, ALASKA AND THE SEAL ISLANDS, 1886")

was ornamented with meticulously twisted and braided sinews and hairs sewn into the seams in complicated designs of tassels and loops. The men carved ivory and wooden figurines, wooden bowls, wooden hunting visors and masks.

Of all the peoples in Western Alaska, the Aleuts seem to have taken the greatest care in their funeral rites. Important individuals were embalmed and entombed in boxes with masks and other personal belongings. Unlike other northern peoples the Aleuts did not fear the dead. Neither the Aleuts nor the Chugach Eskimos had the community ceremonial house.

THE ATHABASCANS

The seven separate Athabascan groups of Alaska were the Ahtna (Ahtena), Eyak, Ingalik (Tena), Koyukon, Kutchin, Tanaina and Tanana, each of which was further subdivided into tribes or bands with its own territory. The vast and sprawling Athabascan land, containing a spruce and birch growth called taiga, was drained by long, mighty rivers and characterized by climatic extremes—from 100°F to -60°F, or colder. The Athabascans were Interior dwellers almost exclusively and were ringed by Eskimo groups everywhere except on Alaska's eastern boundary where the Canadian Athabascans lived. The only Athabascans who lived on salt water were the Tanaina on the shores of Cook Inlet and the now almost extinct Eyak Indians who had moved down the Copper River to the delta.

The Interior taiga did not provide the concentration of fish and game characteristic of the maritime areas. Hard times and famines were frequent, and some of the Athabascans had resorted to cannibalism under extreme duress. The constant search for food kept many Athabascans—for example the Tanana and the Kutchin—on the move, with little time to spend in their home villages. The great bounty of the ocean was not theirs and, despite fish in the rivers, the principal source of food was land animals, caribou, moose and rabbits.

The Tanaina and Ahtna, who lived in the more southerly regions, and, to some extent, the Ingalik had a less harsh life. Like the Tlingits, the Tanaina's basic food was fish, especially salmon, which was abundant in Cook Inlet and its tributaries. The Tanaina also hunted land animals and, unlike all other Athabascans, sea mammals. The Tanaina preserved both fish and meat by drying and smoking.

The Tanaina and the Ingalik lived in permanent villages of more than a hundred persons. Unlike the Athabascans farther north, they were not seminomadic, but made fairly short jaunts to accustomed places for seasonal fishing and hunting. Dwellings varied among the Athabascans. The usual winter home of the Kutchin was a large domed skin lodge occupied by two families. The Ingalik and the Tanaina, on the other hand, built spacious semisubterranean wood and sod dwellings called *barabaras* by the early Russian settlers. Several families lived in each. The floors and walls were dirt but the walls were covered with grass mats. The houses contained benches and shelves. The Ingalik made several kinds of summer huts—of spruce or birch bark, split cottonwood logs and grass mats—which were sometimes built on the beach just below the permanent village. A winter village contained up to a dozen houses.

The subdivisions of Athabascan groups given here have been traditionally referred to as bands, each with its hunting chief, its own dialect and its own territory. Some of the bands were restricted in size by the scarcity of food, and some were no larger than an extended family. Because of the comparative isolation of family groups, especially in the northern sectors, and because of the difficult, roving life, individual achievement—rather than rank and status in a structured social order—was important. Yet some Athabascans, like the Tanaina, who lived in comparative affluence, emphasized social class and wealth to a large degree. Most Athabascan groups were divided into moieties (a moiety, in its simplest definition, is one of two groups a tribe is divided into), which were subdivided into matrilineal clans (sibs). Festivals (sometimes misleadingly called potlatches) were given as death ceremonies and as a means of gaining prestige.

According to folk tales there was great hatred between Indians and Eskimos who shared a common boundary. They fought to avenge a past slight or trespassing on tribal hunting grounds. Lonely hunters were ambushed and whole villages annihilated. In the Eskimo tales, the Indians were the losers; in the Indian stories the Eskimos lost. Despite the bloodshed, these same Eskimos and Indians engaged in active trading and social interaction. This was especially noticeable on the Yukon River, where the Ingalik inhabitants kept in close touch with various coastal Eskimo hamlets like Unalakleet by means of established routes. The Indians on the lower Yukon had borrowed many Eskimo traits: clothing styles, embroidery designs, various implements

English artist and adventurer Frederick Whymper came north in 1865 with the Western Union Telegraph Expedition and traveled the Yukon the following year. In mid-July he wrote, "We passed several small encampments of Indians [Athabascans] and were accompanied by a fleet of canoes, their owners all bound for the annual trading meetings at Newicargut." This village is no longer on the map and the settlement of Kokrines, established there later, is also abandoned.

It was well peopled in Whymper's time, however, and although trading was mainly between Natives, the Athabascans he met here were well aware of the outside world.

"We are not savages, we are Yukon Indians!" a representative of the tribe informed Whymper. (FROM WHYMPER'S "TRAVELS IN ALASKA, 1869")

Although Frederick Whymper captioned this picture "A Co-Yukon Deer Corral," he actually illustrated a roundup of wild caribou, for reindeer weren't introduced into the country until many years later. Co-Yukon was the old spelling for Koyukuk, the name of both a river and an Athabascan village still very much on contemporary maps.

According to the Whymper's written description, "they [the Indians] have an ingenious mode of catching reindeer in mountain valleys. A kind of corral or enclosure, elliptical in form and open at one end, is made in a deer trail, generally near the outlet of a wood. The further end of the enclosed space is barricaded; the sides built of stakes, with slip-nooses of loops between them. Herds of deer are driven in from the woods and, trying to break from the traps, generally run their heads into the nooses, tighten them, and so get caught or are shot, whilst still bewildered and running from side to side. Near the opening it is common to errect piles of snow with 'port-holes' through which Natives, hidden, shoot at the passing deer." (FROM WHYMPER'S "TRAVELS IN ALASKA, 1869")

like the *ulu* (a semicircular "woman's knife"), masks and finger masks, and the ceremonial men's house, the *kazgi*, which was a distinctive feature of every northern Eskimo village. Furthermore, the Ingalik "potlatch" was not really an Indian festival but was more like the Eskimo messenger feast or feast to the dead, the goal being reinforcement of alliances rather than of social position. The Tanaina also borrowed from the Eskimos, especially the gutskin parka and the skin boats called kayak and *umiak*.

The Athabascans made tailored clothing of tanned caribou and moose hides: shirts, mittens, moccasins and moccasin trousers. Except for the Ingalik, who had adopted Eskimo wood carving and painting, the Athabascan tribes were generally noted for a lack of interest in art. In many cases, only simple marks were used on Athabascan utensils and clothing. The southern Athabascans, however, skillfully decorated their clothes with quills, pieces of fur and, later on, trade beads, which signified wealth.

In aboriginal times the birch bark canoe and the raft were used by the majority of Athabascans for travel on water. The Tanaina and Ingalik also made moose skin riverboats and small wooden dugouts. On land, snowshoes were important because backpacking was the most common method of transporting burdens during the winter. Occasionally dogs were used as pack animals, but sleds were pulled by hand. Containers were made of bark, twined basketry, pottery and, especially, wood. The Ingalik made wooden dishes and platters specifically to sell to the Eskimos. Fish and meat were broiled over an open fire or boiled when hot rocks were dropped in water in woven spruce root baskets.

THE TLINGITS AND THE HAIDAS

The northern boundary of Tlingit territory was at Yakutat Bay, and the southern boundary coincided with what is now the southern boundary of Alaska, at Portland Canal. The Tlingit territory included all of Prince of Wales Island except the southern tip, which was occupied by the Haidas, whose principal territory was in Canada. It is thought that the Haidas had driven out the Tlingit from the tip of the island more than 200 years ago; yet, about the same time the Tlingits were expanding their northern boundary at Yakutat Bay; had dispossessed the Chugach Eskimos from Kayak Island; and had settled among the Eyak Indians of the Copper River delta.

The Tlingits and the Haidas were famous as the makers of totem poles and givers of potlatches. Unlike the Eskimos and Indians farther north they had a rigid class system and a consuming emphasis on the amassing of wealth—an emphasis that touched every aspect of their lives and reinforced a social stratification of chiefs, nobles, commoners and slaves. Their painted carvings in wood—totem poles, storage boxes and masks—were often made for shows of wealth, skilled artists being specially hired to do this work. The acquisition of

This picture, commissioned by the Reverend Sheldon Jackson at Wrangell in the late 1870's, shows a part of the Tlingit culture that the missionaries set out to destroy. Jackson's exposure came during a celebration given for him by Chief Toy-a-att, who welcomed the preacher-educator by hoisting the Stars and Stripes and staging a lavish entertainment.

The show closed with a representation of a shaman healing the sick and Jackson wrote that it was a "strange, wierd scene. The sick man lay upon the floor in a blanket. Soon an Indian entered bearing upon his shoulder a long box, which was placed by the sick man. The box contained paraphernalia of a sorcerer. . . . The shaman shook his rattles over the sick man and threw himself into every kind of hideous attitude with horrible contortions of features. He rushed wildly around the fire, striking savagely at attendants with a dagger, flew at the sick man, ran his tongue out at him, hissed, sometimes falling on the floor as if in a swoon." There were also many changes of masks to represent different spirits. "If one spirit does not have sufficient power he tries another," Jackson reported without comment, but the stout Presbyterian made it clear he placed his faith in a Christian god and modern medicine. (FROM JACKSON'S "ALASKA AND MISSIONS OF THE NORTH PACIFIC COAST, 1880")

wealth was made possible by the great abundance of both river and ocean fish (salmon, halibut and herring), which was the Tlingits' and Haidas' primary food source.

These Indians made at least seven types of bark and wood canoes for fishing, traveling and warfare. The Haida dugout of red cedar was often 70 feet long and was made very wide by the builders' softening and stretching the sides with hot water. The building of these huge canoes, and of the big, well-built houses (sometimes 30 by 40 feet) of notched and mortised planks, were also indications of wealth. As many as 12 families lived in one house, and each family's apartment was set apart from the others by mats, storage boxes and bedding. A central fire pit was used by each wife to cook her family's meals. A village contained up to a dozen of these houses built in a row on high beach land and, unlike the villages in the Far North, was rarely completely deserted when residents went fishing or camping.

Slaves, who were usually war captives, also lived in the house with their owners. The Northwest Coast Indian tribes were probably the only nonagricultural peoples to have a well-established institution of slavery. The slaves were owned as property—wealth—and could be disposed of as the owner saw fit. During the Russian colonization, many of the slaves were handed over in serfdom to the fur-trading companies.

Both the Tlingits and the Haidas were divided into moieties. The Tlingit moieties were the Raven, which existed among the Tlingits in all their areas, and, in the south, the Wolf. The Wolf moiety became the Eagle in the northern sections of the Tlingits. The Haida moieties, which did not vary by region, were the Raven and Eagle. All Tlingits and Haidas belonged to one of these divisions and were prohibited from marrying within their own moiety. Each moiety was made up of several clans, and each clan represented a number of

lineages. One lineage might live in only one of the huge plank houses, but often several houses were necessary to contain a lineage.

Preoccupation with rank and status almost equaled the emphasis on wealth. Every person had a specific and unduplicated place in the social scale, and everyone knew another's place. Protocol was strictly observed at potlatches, and the most valuable gifts were given to the highest-ranking persons. Potlatches were given for a number of reasons, and although a potlatch might belong directly to only one person who was validating and strengthening his status, all members of a local group helped support him, and consequently themselves, by reinforcing the solidarity of the group. Incredible quantities of food and gifts were collected for a potlatch, often over a period of several years.

Although there was no currency in this near-capitalistic society, the blanket—both the aboriginal one of fibers and hair and, later on, the wool trade blanket—was a basic unit of exchange at a potlatch, and sometimes blankets by the hundreds changed hands. Originally, however, the blanket was very much a utilitarian object because it was an important piece of clothing along with a buckskin skirt for the woman and a breechcloth for the man. The Tlingits had no tailored garments and, in keeping with their comparatively mild climate, sometimes went nude and barefoot.

A northern Tlingit group, the Chilkats (as well as other groups before them) wove the famed Chilkat blankets on looms, using a weft of mountain goat wool—blue, black or yellow—and a warp of goat wool spun around a core of cedar bark. The designs were hereditary lineage crests, which were also important items of design used on totem poles, boxes and other art forms as a privilege of rank. Baskets of cedar root were one of the artistic achievements of the Tlingit women, and a well-made basket was recognized as an object of great beauty.

Frederic Liitke's Partie Histerique Atlas, *published after his voyage around the world in 1826-27, depicts Tlingits at Sitka as possessing a surprising number of manufactured items, including an ax, a cooking pot and cloth.*

"As for the dwelling depictured here, it is constructed from wooden planks which are in turn covered with earth except for a small square space of planking which serves as a foyer," wrote A. Postels who reported the voyage. "It is there, under this roof that the family gathers, spending almost all its time idling away the hours.

"At this moment dinner preparations are being made, a meal composed principally of shellfish and fish, which can be seen spread out on the floor. Other fish is suspended from the rafters to dry. Before eating the fish, one merely cuts off a piece and boils it in a small cooking pot over a fire built on the earthen floor.

"In a corner of the room one can see the family gods [idols] which are meant to represent various animals; scattered about the sides of the hut are several toys and a mask which has been artistically crafted and painted with numerous colors."

These, then, were the Alaskans when the Europeans arrived. However, the Natives long had been aware of foreign peoples living to the west because Asiatic traders had been bringing Russian goods across the Bering Strait from Siberian markets for many years. By 1867, when the United States purchased Alaska, the Russians claimed all of the land now included in the state even though their northernmost trading posts were Nulato on the Yukon River and Unalakleet on Norton Sound. Following the purchase, the status of Natives' land differed from "Indian land" in the rest of the United States because there were no treaty reservations; although most of the territory was held by the federal government, title to the land continued to be vested in the Native tribes as sovereign nations because title had not been extinguished by treaty, purchase or conquest.

Alaska's so-called reservations are more appropriately called "reserved lands," which were set aside by congressional action, presidential executive orders or by the secretary of the interior. Probably the most famous reservation is the one on Annette Island, established by an act of Congress in 1891 for a group of Tsimshian Indians who immigrated to Alaska from Canada with their religious leader, William Duncan.

Executive orders have set aside lands for various purposes such as reindeer stations or "use of the Bureau of Education and native people." Executive orders established Cape Denbigh reservation and Unalaklik River reservation for reindeer in 1901, and Norton Bay reservation for school purposes in 1917. Thirteen reserves came into being in Alaska between 1914 and 1933, through executive order. When the Indian Reorganization Act of 1934 was extended to Alaska in 1936, the secretary of the interior established six Alaskan Native reservations; these differed from the others in Alaska by having some form of self-government.

When it was time for Alaska to choose lands from the public domain under the Statehood Act of 1958, it became apparent that Native title to the land had to be resolved. In December 1971, the Congress of the United States passed the Alaska Native Claims Settlement Act, and 12 regional Native corporations were organized to administer the lands and money accruing from the act. Although aboriginal title was extinguished, and a few of the corporations have entered the world of big business, the occupation of lands generally is not much different from the time of discovery, and most of the people are still living where their ancestors lived.

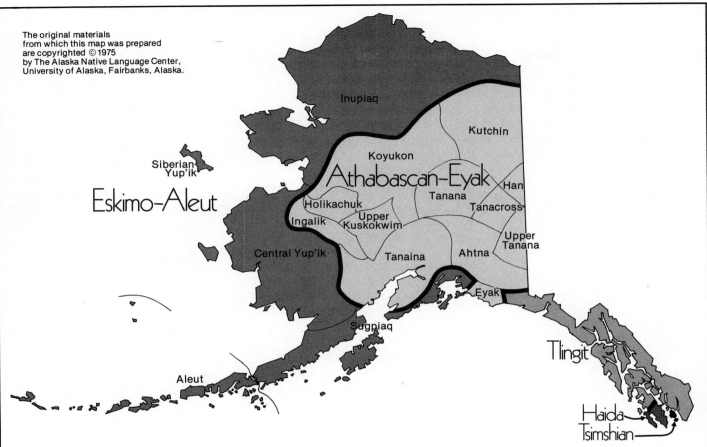

In June 1972, the Alaska legislature passed a law requiring at least one bilingual teacher if 15 or more children spoke a language other than English, and creating the Alaska Native Language Center at the University of Alaska. The center provides statewide leadership and coordination in Native language programs. Many Native groups, schools and local governments have been preparing programs for preserving and teaching virtually all of the Native languages. The work of fostering bilingual education in the state is directed by Michael E. Krauss and Irene Reed of the Alaska Native Language Center. Krauss has made the nurturing of Native languages the work of his life for the past 20 years. This map is based on his "Map of the Native Peoples and Languages of Alaska." A color legend and language map appear on the large pull-out map, "Alaska's Native People, Their Villages and Languages," included with this issue.

The Coming of the White Man and the Cultural Clash

By Lael Morgan

Beware of the term "Alaskan Natives." It is correctly used to refer to the state's aboriginal people but it is folly to think of them as one. They are alike as much as all Alaskans—white, red, black, brown and yellow—are alike; set apart from the rest of the United States by virtue of vast distance, rough terrain, harsh climate and the problems of being citizens of a young, rich, developing state. But Alaskan Natives are many races, creeds and philosophies. They are many nations.

"But aren't they Eskimos?" people far from Alaska will ask. "Aren't they the people who live in snow houses, rub noses, eat raw meat and swap their wives?" (Even today people will ask that.) No, they are not and for the most part they never were.

Alaskan Natives include the Inupiat Eskimos of the north and the Yup'ik Eskimos to the south—all Eskimos, but groups whose languages are so different they cannot talk with one another in their mother tongues. The Athabascan Indians of the Interior and of

Tlingit carvers work on totemic designs at Alaska Indian Arts, Inc., in the Southeastern Alaska town of Haines. Alaska Indian Arts and the adjoining Chilkat Center for the Arts have helped restore interest in traditional arts, crafts, dances and clothing. (RICK KIEFER)

Cook Inlet have 11 different languages among them as well as varying lifestyles. The Tlingit Indians of Southeastern, once the fierce conquerors of many tribes with whom they had little in common, are linked now by a hyphen with their Haida neighbors, becoming Tlingit-Haida for legal and business reasons, but the two groups are not the same and their languages are not the same.

The Aleuts of the Aleutian Chain have several different vocabularies, depending on where their forebears settled. Although Aleuts are technically classified by anthropologists as Eskimos, they have traditionally disliked Eskimos. Their neighbors along the southern coast of the Alaska Peninsula and on Kodiak Island speak an Eskimo language called Sugpiaq, related to Yup'ik. So they are Eskimos, not Aleuts; but they generally consider themselves part of the Aleut culture with which they live. The Eskimos on Saint Lawrence Island are Siberian Yup'iks, whose grandfathers had a wanderlust. Similarly, the Tsimshian Indians, who arrived in Alaska in the last (1887) century, traveled to Alaska from Canada—but they came under the leadership of a white preacher. And yet another group of Alaskan Natives are the Eyaks, of the Copper River Delta, and the Gulf Coast,

This purse, designed by Siberian Eskimos at Saint Lawrence Island, was worn on the belt and is embroidered with reindeer hair and decorated with beads. Eskimos made them for trade and this one, dated 1927, is now in the University of Alaska Museum collection.

so few now that the number of Eyak speakers is fewer than the fingers of one hand. They are of the Athabascan family, with no blood ties to either the Chugach Eskimos of Prince William Sound or the Yakutat Tlingits to the east.

In 1966, all these diverse people united to claim from the United States government title to their traditional lands. They joined together despite their vast differences and past wars. They won partly because of the strength of their unity.

Under the terms of their settlement, however, they promised to divide into 12 corporations (later, another corporation was formed of Natives no longer resident in Alaska) and compete with one another as separate business entities. Many Native leaders did not wish to do this, but whites who opposed land claims feared Native unity and to appease them, the Natives promised to divide.

Native spokesmen from all regions say that, should the need arise, they will ally again. But under the law they are 13 rival nations with many factions and one must keep this in mind.

It is convenient to call them Alaskan Natives, but really that means only one thing: that they have been here since before time was recorded, and other Alaskans have not.

❧

Legends tell of the coming of Outsiders to Alaska long before Vitus Bering set his name on the record in 1741 as the official discoverer.

The Tlingit Indians of Yakutat still recall the story of a fair woman whom their forebears rescued from a ship wrecked off their coast.

"Nobody knew where she came from. The ship had gunpowder and rice, but it was way before the Russians came," recalled the late Tlingit historian Harry Bremner. "Kotskaw [a legendary chief] took her back to

Icy Bay. She never died. She got so old they had to carry her around. Had a lot of children, grandchildren, great-grandchildren, maybe two great-great-grandchildren, all with red hair.

"When the Russians came to Yakutat they asked, 'How come some of the people got red hair?' Up to today, some still are redheads."

There is a similar tale among the Haida people, and it mentions red hair, too, while stories of lost Chinese sailors and ancient Chinese trade goods turn up elsewhere along the coast.

Russian traders claimed to have visited Alaska as early as 1648. It was the accounts of their adventures that prompted Tsar Peter the Great to dispatch the explorer, Bering. Even in that day there were rumors of a lost Russian colony in the new land, and the rumors persisted after discovery. As late as 1791 Russian officials undertook an unsuccessful search for the lost colony along the Alaskan coast in the neighborhood of King Island.

But the Outsiders had little impact on Native Alaskans until the coming of Bering. It was Bering's crew, returning to Russia with a rich booty of sea otter furs, that provided the first tangible evidence of the wealth and potential of the new land, sparking a stampede that would change forever the lifestyle of Alaskan aboriginal people.

From the return of Bering's ship in 1742 to the late 1780's, hordes of Russian traders, *promyshlenniki*, plundered Aleut territory, enslaving the Natives and forcing them to pay fur tribute.

"Fortunately for the Indians of the North, it was contrary to the interests of white people to kill them in order to obtain the skins of their animals for, with a few trinkets, [the white men] could procure what otherwise would require long and severe labor to obtain," noted early historian Hubert Howe Bancroft. "The policy, therefore, of the great fur trading companies has been to

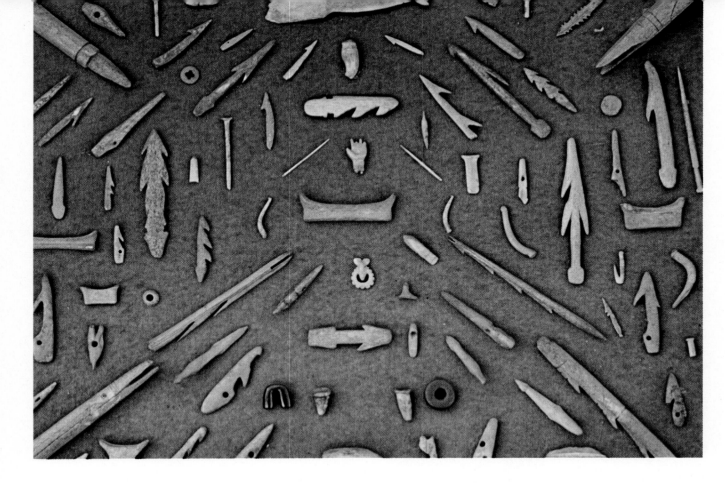

Left — *When a recent archaelogical expedition worked near Larsen Bay, Kodiak, Dora Aga, a Koniag, paid close attention and later carefully collected her own artifacts from the area. This collection, now on her living room wall, contains spear points for small birds and game, fishhooks, harpoon heads, labrets, bone needles and several items no one can figure out.*
Below — *This work of Eskimo artist Larry Ahvakana is untitled but is clearly Inupiat in style. Ahvakana attended the American Indian Arts Center in Santa Fe, New Mexico, the Cooper Union School of Art in New York City, and graduated from the Rhode Island School of Design.* (ANCHORAGE HISTORICAL AND FINE ARTS MUSEUM)

cherish the Indians as their best hunters, to live in peace with them, to heal their ancient feuds and to withhold from them intoxicating liquors."

But history also recorded that the population of the Aleutian Chain dwindled from 10,000 or 20,000 to 2,000 in the first 50 years of Russian stewardship, and that entire island populations were wiped out by the invaders, who killed to discourage Native uprisings or sometimes simply to pass the time.

Most brutal among the Russians was Feodor Solovief who is credited with lining up 12 Aleuts and firing a musket ball through them to see where it would stop (it stopped in the ninth man), but even this could be justified in the minds of the conquerors.

"A quiet citizen and friend of mankind reading of these doings will perhaps execrate the terrible Solovief and call him a barbarous destroyer of men," admits an early Russian biographer. "But he would change his opinion on learning that after this period of terrible punishment the inhabitants of the Aleutians never again dared to make another attack on the Russians. Would he not acknowledge that such methods were necessary for the safety of future voyages?"

Using the Aleutian Islands as way stations, the

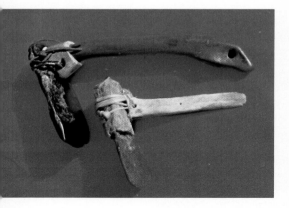

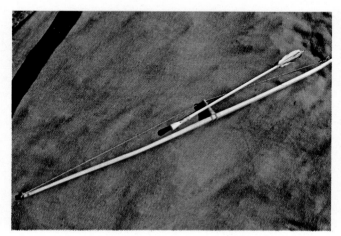

Above — *These jade axes were dug from an old midden on the Colville River in the Arctic. The handles are of bone; the leather has replaced the original rawhide which had deteriorated.* (MIKE AND JIM DALTON COLLECTION)

Upper right — *This Yup'ik mask from old Kashunak is decorated with homemade paints and varnish. Artists competed to produce imaginative masks for festival performances.*

Right — *Joe Joseph made this bow and arrow for the University of Alaska Museum in 1969 to show how his Athabascan people traditionally hunted in the Tanacross area. The arrowhead is of caribou horn.* (BOTH PHOTOS FROM UNIVERSITY OF ALASKA MUSEUM, FAIRBANKS)

Russians moved steadily toward the Alaskan mainland, taking with them Aleuts they enslaved to serve both for hunting and for defense against other tribes.

Despite fierce resistance from the Tlingit Indians, the whites successfully established bases in the Tlingit territory. They also moved into the land of the Chugach, on Cook Inlet; into the territory of the Eskimos, on Bristol Bay and along the Kuskokwim; and into the area of the Athabascans, on the Yukon.

The Natives fought back, massacring their oppressors at Yakutat, Sitka and Nulato. No treaties were ever signed, and the Natives never officially surrendered, but they eventually settled into coexistence with the Russians, growing increasingly dependent on them for trading goods.

Then, to soothe the consciences of Russian leaders, missionaries of the Russian Orthodox Church were dispatched to convert the heathens. In many areas, especially in the Aleutian Islands, the missionaries established the faith firmly and even pioneered in education, but this proved a poor swap for tribal traditions—and memories of traditions—that were almost obliterated.

"Left alone, the natives of America might have unfolded into as bright a civilization as that of Europe," historian Bancroft maintained. "They were already well advanced and still rapidly advancing towards it when they were unmercifully stricken down. But for a stranger to recreate the heart or head of a red man, it were easier to change the color of his skin."

Explorers, adventurers and traders from other nations followed in the wake of the Russians, jockeying among themselves to exploit the northern territory, and introducing alcohol and epidemics of smallpox, diphtheria, influenza, measles and syphillis to the vulnerable Native population.

Reaction to their coming varied. Lieutenant Sven Waxell, who sailed with Bering to the Aleutians,

reported that when one Native finally summoned courage to board his ship, he gave the visitor the most precious thing he had—brandy.

"The savage began to drink but immediately spat it out crying to his people that he was poisoned." And all Waxell's attempts to quiet him with trade beads, needles, an iron kettle and tobacco were in vain. The Aleut would accept nothing more.

The residents of Kodiak Island, too, were cautious. A Native named Arsenti Aminak told this tale to a researcher:

"I was a boy of 9 or 10, for I was already set to paddle a *bidarka*, when the first Russian ship with two masts appeared near Aliulik. Before that time we had never seen a ship; we had intercourse with the [Eskimos] of Aliaska Peninsula, with the Tanainas of the Kenai Peninsula and with the Koloshes; and some wise men even knew something of the Californias; but ship and white men we did not know at all. When we espied the ship at a distance we thought it was an immense whale, and were curious to have a better look at it. We went out to sea in our *bidarkas*, but soon discovered that it was no whale but another unknown monster, of which we were afraid.

"Among our people there was a brave warrior named Ishinik, who was so bold that he feared nothing in the world; he undertook to visit the ship and came back with presents in his hand: a red shirt, an Aleut hood and some glass beads. He said there was nothing to fear: 'They only wish to buy our sea otter skins and they give us glass beads and other riches for them.' We did not fully believe his statement. The old and wise people held

A portion of the fourth housepost of the Chief Shakes house at Wrangell, which features this human figure below the shark's tail area. The human figure on the pole actually is upside down, but is shown inverted here to illustrate the detail more clearly. (BARRY HEREM)

Florence. Napuk.

Saint Lawrence Eskimos, who migrated from Siberia, are Yup'ik, although they differ in many ways from other Alaskan Yup'iks. This 1927 drawing by Florence Napuk, part of a collection gathered by researcher Otto Geist, shows a couple dancing in the agra (winter house); tradition calls for the man to give the woman a gift when he chooses her as his dancing partner. (ARCHIVES, UNIVERSITY OF ALASKA, FAIRBANKS)

a council and some said, 'Who knows what sickness they may bring us?'"

In contrast, Capt. Frederick Beechey of the H.M.S. *Blossom*, the first European vessel to make contact with Natives north of the Arctic Circle (in 1826), reported that the Eskimos of Kotzebue paddled out to meet him, bringing with them goods to trade. Other Eskimos believed the white man had come to learn manners from them, and were disappointed when they found that was not the case.

"The Indians are doubtless improvident, knowing that nature has provided for them without much labor," noted Jefferson Moser, captain of a U.S. fisheries survey vessel in 1897. "Their frequent boast is that white men and Chinese must work at getting something to eat,

while the waters and forests furnish the Indians with all they want. A very small amount of money will supply them with the few necessities which money alone will buy."

But with the ever-increasing influx of newcomers, that boast soon became hollow. By the end of the 19th century, the sea otter trade had waned, but whaling was taking its place, bringing in even more ships and men. So many were there that the whaling station at Barrow could claim hundreds of shipwrecked sailors rescued off northern coasts before the turn of the century, and the Outsiders had taken much of the sea mammals and game on which the Natives depended for food.

In Southeastern Alaska and the Bristol Bay area the whites established canneries, which they manned by importing Asian laborers by the hundreds; later a succession of gold rushes carried the white man's invasion deep into the Interior.

In 1867 the Russians sold Alaska to the United States without the consent or even the knowledge of the Natives, but the sale did little to change the Natives' status. Under the Treaty of Cession they were classified as "uncivilized tribes . . . subject to such laws and regulations as the United States may, from time to time, adopt in regard to aboriginal tribes in that country."

But the U.S. government was for the most part embarrassed by its highly controversial new purchase, and did its best to ignore the territory.

Secretary of State William Seward, promoter of the $7.2 million sale, made an inspection tour of the territory and informed the residents of Sitka, once the capital of Russian America, that because Alaska had no more than 2,000 white residents and as many as 25,000 Indians, a display of military force was needed. Maj. John Tidball, one of the first commanders in the area, reported that the Indians were savages and that they possessed the same villainous traits of character found among the warring Indians of the United States.

Even after the most of the U. S. Army troops were withdrawn from Alaska to quell an uprising of the Nez Perce Indians of Idaho, white fears proved groundless; the Natives were too busy fighting for their own survival to fight whites.

In 1889 an alarmed skipper of a revenue cutter, Lt. Comm. C.H. Stockton, reported the Eskimos of Point Hope to be "in a most degraded state, physically, mentally and spiritually," as the result of contact with the white man. "Each visit of a whaling ship was followed by riot and drunkenness; the women were carried off to serve the lusts of the sailors and officers," he told the missionary division of the Episcopal Church.

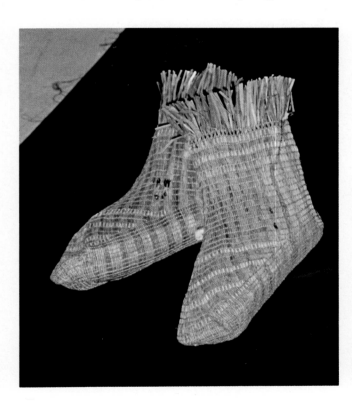

"Although [the whaling station was] under the flag of the United States, there was nothing but chaos and paganism."

And that wasn't an isolated case. Dispirited by the thundering herd of Outsiders and weakened by diseases the Outsiders had brought, increasing numbers of Natives sought solace in alcohol (then a novelty), to the complete disruption of village life.

The Natives' only salvation—in the minds of the revenue cutter commander and many others—rested in the hands of missionaries, so a new wave of clergymen flocked north, preaching Christianity and assimilation into the American way.

Strongest among them was the Presbyterian missionary Sheldon Jackson, who valued education as being second only to God and who vigorously sought schooling for Native children.

"The government has never treated them [Alaskan Natives] as Indians and it would be a national calamity at this late date to subject them to the restrictions and disabilities of our Indian system," he wrote in his annual report in 1886, after he had become the nation's first commissioner of education.

Far left — The Aleuts and their Yup'ik neighbors wove stockings from grass to serve as insoles for their sea lion and sealskin mukluks. Loose grass also was used as insulation, and proved to work well. This pair of Aleut insoles was collected by the Reverend Sheldon Jackson at the turn of the century for his Sitka museum.
Left — Little is known about the origin of this carved wood potlatch bowl. Decorated with tiny trade beads and still carrying a sheen from oil or fat from when it was used, the bowl is on display at the Alaska State Historical Museum in Juneau.

Earliest midden heaps reveal that the ulu — knife of the Eskimo woman — has been in use for many hundreds of years. The originals were of bones of this shape, carefully sharpened on the rounded edge. These are modern blades of steel set in ivory handles carved with ancient designs by Harry Shavings of Mekoryuk. Women of his area still prefer these knives to the modern kind because they save energy and are much better for skinning game.

"Among those [people] best known [to me] their highest ambition is to build American homes, possess American furniture, dress in American clothes, adopt the American style of living, and be American citizens, protected by the laws and the courts, and in common with all others furnished with schools for their children."

The U.S. government turned its back on his pleas but, undaunted, Jackson divvied up the territory among interested church groups: the Baptists getting Kodiak Island and Cook Inlet; the Episcopalians working the Yukon and the lower Arctic Coast; the Methodists moving into the Aleutian Chain; the Moravians going to the Kuskokwim region; the Quakers getting the Kotzebue area; the Congregationalists settling in the area of Cape Prince of Wales; and Presbyterians taking Southeastern Alaska and the northern Arctic Coast.

Jackson also introduced reindeer herding to many parts of the territory to counteract the depletion of game, and here he succeeded in getting government sponsorship. In addition, he eventually got small appropriations for education.

By the early 1900's Alaskan Natives were beginning to speak for themselves. In the 1890's Tlingit Chief Johnson, of the Taku tribe, sued whites who built a dock on the Juneau waterfront, which he considered his property, and when he lost the case, he journeyed to Washington, D. C., to lobby Congress.

In 1902 Tlingits petitioned for, but were refused, the right to attend white schools in Juneau and Ketchikan. In 1912 they organized the Alaska Native Brotherhood to win citizenship; they began to educate themselves and to abandon aboriginal customs seen by whites as uncivilized. In 1915, 14 Athabascans, including 6 Tanana chiefs, met at their own expense with former U.S. District Judge James Wickersham, Alaska's Delegate to Congress, and flatly turned down the reservation system.

That same year the territorial legislature enfranchised all Natives "on proof of the general qualifications of a voter, total abandonment of tribal customs and adoption of the culture of civilization." The move was ahead of its time and also ahead of the U.S. Congress, which didn't give Indians the vote until 1924. However, for the bulk of the Native people—who couldn't or didn't want to get into the white man's lifestyle anyway—the law made no difference. They retained the status of "uncivilized tribes" awarded them under the 1867 treaty with Russia, which provided them no rights.

Although missionaries enjoyed some degree of success as educators, their financial means were too limited to be of much assistance in an area where they were desperately needed: medicine. A flu epidemic in 1918 devastated entire villages, and orphanages had to be established at Eklutna, Kanakanak and White Mountain (in addition to the Jesse Lee Home, which had already been founded at Unalaska) to handle surviving children. Then tuberculosis ran rampant, leaving scarcely a family untouched.

The government made feeble attempts to cope with the Natives' medical problems, providing a small hospital for Natives in Southeastern Alaska and later a floating clinic on the lower Yukon, but funds were low and the situation was clearly out of control.

For the most part, the Native population was ignored until the outbreak of World War II, which placed Alaska in a strategic defense position. In the press to build military bases in the territory and stem the Japanese invasion of the Aleutians, great expanses of Alaska's vast coastal area were left unguarded. As a means of defense, the Native people of these remote areas were mustered and organized as the Eskimo Scouts of the Alaska Territorial Guard under the command of Col. Marvin "Muktuk" Marston, a white Alaskan. Although many of these Native defenders spoke no English, they proved exemplary soldiers and

This Athabascan virgin's necklace comes from the Stony River area near Sleetmute and marks an old tradition of adorning marriageable young maidens to catch the eye of a good husband. The necklace now belongs to Nixi Mellich, Sleetmute bush pilot and mine owner.

served—without pay—throughout World War II. Other Natives joined regular military units and returned from the war with records of distinction.

The military zeal and patriotism of the Native people was stimulated by the fact that they lost more at the hands of the enemy, on their own land, than any other group of U.S. citizens. The village of Attu on the Aleutian Chain was actually invaded by the Japanese and its population interned in Japanese concentration camps, from which only 50 percent of the villagers returned alive. Other people of the Aleutians suffered hardships when the U.S. government, as a precautionary measure, required evacuation of some of the villages.

Military service, in addition to giving protection to their homeland, provided many Alaskans with expanded educational opportunities, and as a result they became more vocal at the war's end.

Only two Natives had previously served in the territorial legislature: William Paul Sr., in 1925 and 1927, and F.J. Baronovich, in 1933 and 1935, both in the House of Representatives.

Two Tlingits, Andrew Hope and Frank Peratrovich were elected to the territorial house in 1944, and it was this session of the legislature that passed Alaska's nondiscrimination act—the first under the American flag—officially removing from Alaskan eating places, hotels and bars all signs that said, *We do not cater to native trade.*

In 1946, Peratrovich became the first Native elected to the territorial senate, and another Tlingit, Frank G. Johnson of Kake, joined Andrew Hope in the house. Eskimos William Beltz of Nome and Percy Ipalook of Wales were elected to the house in 1948, both going on to the territorial senate in 1951.

The postwar period also marked a turning point in Native health care and education. Military surplus buildings in Seward and Sitka were turned into TB hospitals, and a 175-bed facility, mainly for TB patients, was built in Anchorage (there were 2,000 applicants on the waiting list when it opened).

In addition, a boarding school for Natives was opened in a surplus military installation at Mount Edgecumbe, on Japonski Island, Sitka, and an expanded educational program, also with living facilities, was set up at Wrangell Institute. Native youngsters often had to travel hundreds of miles to attend these schools, but at least it was better than the previous option—being shipped out of the territory.

The most troublesome remaining problem was Native ownership of land. In 1935 Congress enacted legislation permitting the Natives to sue the federal government in the court of claims for land taken by the United States. A year later the Tlingits and Haidas filed against the U.S. government for $80 million in lost timberland; the case was shuttled about in the courts for three decades. The idea that Natives retained rights to some of Alaska

These labrets, worn below the lip and sometimes above, came from the Arctic Coast in the 1890's. They are of stone trimmed with trade beads of considerable value in their time. (UNIVERSITY OF ALASKA MUSEUM)

was recognized in the Alaska Statehood Act of 1958. No treaty had ever been signed by the Native people, nor had the government conquered them in war. The Statehood Act carefully stated "that nothing contained in this Act shall recognize, deny, enlarge, impair or otherwise affect such claims."

The new state was given a "dowry" of more than 103 million acres of federal lands to select, but the opposition warned that selection would be difficult with the question of Native ownership hanging fire.

In 1958 the U.S. Atomic Energy Commission (AEC) developed a plan to use a nuclear device to excavate a harbor at Cape Thompson on Alaska's northwest coast. The AEC failed to take into account the Eskimos who lived in the area, and only belatedly did officials offer to move the Eskimos to city housing projects. To defend their heritage, in 1961 Eskimo leaders from local villages held a meeting and set up a new organization called Inupiat Paitot—People's Heritage. It was backed by the Association on American Indian Affairs, a private charitable organization based in New York City that had influence and would continue to be helpful.

Until this time there had been little communication among Native communities and even less between Natives and whites. Major Alaskan newspapers seldom carried news of Indians and Eskimos unless they did something bizarre, and news media showed little concern for the problems of Alaska's remote areas. Inupiat Paitot resulted in the founding in 1962 of a crusading statewide Native newspaper, the

This Yup'ik gut parka was made in the traditional manner of Saint Lawrence Island in 1927. It is of walrus intestine sewed with sinew and decorated with the beaks and feathers of crested auklets. Simpler raincoats of gut were used for hunting and were so warm they could be worn at sea in winter. A decorated coat like this was reserved for special occasions, however. (UNIVERSITY OF ALASKA MUSEUM)

Tundra Times, edited by an Eskimo, Howard Rock, who was assisted by Tom Snapp, a white reporter from Fairbanks. The paper was financed in the fledgling stage by a wealthy physician and feisty descendant of Ralph Waldo Emerson, Henry S. Forbes of Massachusetts. Forbes was chairman of the Alaska Committee for the Association on American Indian Affairs.

Partly through the efforts of the *Tundra Times*, the harbor blasting was canceled. In addition, Rock and Snapp worked to bring the problems of discrimination in Alaska along with problems regarding the Natives' standard of living, which was the poorest under the American flag, to light.

Then, in 1962, five oil companies filed leases for lands in the Athabascan villages of Minto and Nenana. The state government got wind of this activity and started making tentative land selections in the area under provision of the Alaska Statehood Act. Nobody, however, paid any attention to Native claims over the area, which had been accumulating.

Rock and Snapp went in search of a lawyer they could trust and settled on Ted Stevens (later elected to the U.S. Senate), who had just resigned as a lawyer for the Department of the Interior. Under a departmental ruling Stevens had to petition for permission to take the Natives as clients; his petition was refused, so he worked on the claims case without pay.

The publishers of the *Tundra Times* helped the Natives file the suit, going so far as to buy land maps and plot boundaries. More Native suits followed until the whole state was tied up in litigation, causing the

Only the wealthy could afford dentalium necklaces, the mark of Athabascan chiefs. Coastal Indians sank corpses to attract the shelled creatures, and a dog was often used; but Tlingits were said to use the bodies of slaves, making a necklace worth a human life. This set belongs to Sleetmute trader Nixi Mellich.

secretary of the interior to impose a land freeze that paralyzed all land transactions in the state.

In 1966, a united group of young, articulate Alaskan Natives entered politics. There had been successful Native politicians before them. Frank Peratrovich and William Beltz had both served terms as president of the state senate, but Peratrovich and Beltz had not had the benefit of a strong Native coalition behind them. Now, even remote villages had become politically aware, and the Natives—numbering nearly 50,000 and making up one-fifth of the Alaskan population—gained impact as voters.

The potential of the Native electorate was first

This contemporary Athabascan doll sports buttons and beads introduced by traders but otherwise its outfit is traditional, designed for survival in the coldest winter. (UNIVERSITY OF ALASKA COLLECTION)

recognized by Democrat Mike Gravel, then speaker of the Alaska House of Representatives, who saw that if he could garner the bush vote, he could win a statewide election, even if he lost in all three of the state's major cities. With this in mind, he backed the building of regional high schools in rural areas and cultivated Native alliances. In the race for Congress in 1966 Gravel was defeated, but only because his losses in major population centers were heavier than he had anticipated. His faith in the Native vote was sound, however, and two years later he was elected to the U.S. Senate.

Also courting the Natives in 1966 were Republican Walter Hickel, making his political debut as candidate for governor, and Howard Pollock, a veteran legislator out to win Ralph Rivers's seat in Congress. Neither man had traveled much in remote areas of the state. When campaigning, both professed shock at the conditions of poverty they saw among the Natives and pledged to seek remedies. Both men won.

Other significant winners were three young candidates who later would add momentum to the Native drive for power. John Sackett, an Athabascan and a member of the Republican majority from the Yukon area, landed a seat on the influential Finance Committee of the Alaska House of Representatives. Willie Hensley, an Eskimo and a Democrat from Kotzebue, buckled down to his newly won job in the house, from which he would later move on to a seat in the state senate. Also winning a house seat that year was Jules Wright, president of the Fairbanks Native Association.

Hensley pressed the land claims fight against the federal government. Reading from one of his college research papers, Hensley introduced the issue at a meeting of the Juneau Democratic Club in a cramped hotel basement. Before his first legislative session was done, he mustered strength to pass a bill promising a

Aleut basket weavers have long been known for the finest work in the state. This is a contemporary basket done in 1973 by Tatiana Zaochney of Atka who, although still a young woman, had mastered the craft with remarkable skill.
(ALASKA STATE MUSEUM, JUNEAU)

royalty to Indians and Eskimos from the state if the federal government would settle their claims.

On the bill's introduction Walter Hickel, then governor, loudly opposed state royalty, then did a complete reversal and put his weight behind it, a move that later helped him in seeking Native endorsement for appointment as secretary of the interior.

In the fall of 1966 a coalition of Natives formed to push a federal settlement of Native claims through Congress. Outsiders predicted the Alaska Federation of Natives (AFN) would not survive because it required close cooperation among aborigines who had warred for centuries and who had no money.

The bulk of the lobbying funds for the ensuing years of the claims fight came from the proceeds of village bingo games or out of the pockets of Native leaders and their friends, most of whom were in low-income brackets. The Office of Economic Opportunity and, sometimes, the Bureau of Indian Affairs helped with

travel expenses. When things looked bleakest, the Tyonek Indians, briefly flush from an oil lease sale, lent the AFN $100,000 and the Yakima Indian Nation of Washington State lent the federation $225,000.

But there were strong differences among members of the AFN. When Congress offered a settlement of $500 million and a scant four million acres of land, to be allotted on a per-capita basis, regions with large populations wanted to accept. But howls of protest came from the sparsely settled, oil-rich North Slope. Stubbornly the arctic Eskimos held out for a land-loss formula and higher stakes until, finally, the barriers of diverse interests, languages and cultures were overcome.

Meanwhile, the Natives had found unexpected allies in the oil companies, who had discovered that little development was possible in Alaska until Native claims were settled. It was a strange alliance but effective. In 1971, just five short years after organizing, Alaskan

This modern totem was done by Tlingit Shanon Gallant shortly after her graduation from the Rhode Island School of Design. Raised by a very traditional grandmother in the Juneau-Haines area, she went on to the Indian Arts and Crafts school in Santa Fe, New Mexico, and to the University of Alaska before getting her degree. At first, fearing she would be mistaken for the kind of commercial artist who carves seals for the tourists, she shunned all Indian designs. Once sure of her talent, however, she began to blend old and new ideas, taking the best from her culture and that of today's modern world.
(JOHN SHIVELY COLLECTION)

Natives won the monumental federal settlement of 40 million acres of land and $426.5 million, plus a $500 million royalty on state mineral rights.

This settlement was different from settlements Congress had made with Natives in the Lower 48; this time administration of the settlement was left to the Natives themselves, who would organize for the purpose as 12, later 13, regional, profit-making corporations. Village corporations were also formed under this act with the Native residents as voting stockholders.

Thus the battle was won, but success of the war lay in future management by Native leaders and in the ability of the Native electorate to direct its leaders effectively. No Native stock would be sold for a 20-year period following the act, in order to give the youngest stockholders time to grow up, but even with this protection, outcome of the settlement remains in question.

At settlement, more than 70 percent of Natives were dependent on subsistence hunting and fishing. Transition to a money-based economy is occurring, but it has been by no means immediate. Regional corporations vary widely in management capability and natural resources; some are apparently doing well and others seem destined to failure.

"It is impossible to assess the regionals at this point," cautioned newspaper editor Howard Rock in 1975. "We won't be able to judge for at least 10 years, maybe longer."

Not every Native community went with the claims settlement. Under the law, 25 villages had the option of joining in the settlement or receiving full title to their former reservation lands in exchange for giving up all other benefits under the act. Seven villages elected to go their own way, taking title to 3.7 million acres. Without the cash to develop the land, however, they face a future that is more uncertain than that of the villages that accepted settlements. (One of the seven villages, Klukwan, later changed its mind and was enabled by the amending act of January 1976 to join with its regional corporation and receive all regular benefits under the original act.)

Aside from the immersion into corporate life, Natives are feeling the effects of other—major—changes in their towns and villages, and many of these changes are the results of the Natives' own activism.

Bureau of Indian Affairs boarding schools are being phased out, and local high schools are being built. Starting in the late 1960's, an ambitious electrical cooperative began supplying power to 48 remote settlements. Educational radio and television stations are being built around the state and tape cassette machines are seen in schools where none could have been found a few years ago.

Health care has come a long way. Most villages now have Native health aides who communicate with hospitals daily by radio (often via satellite) and serve as eyes, ears and hands for distant physicians. Health clinics are being built and staffed. Sanitation systems are being installed. Although extreme cold and permafrost conditions hamper work, the Public Health Service has built about 70 village water and sewer facilities since 1961, and other villages have provided their own.

Health statistics for Native people are now nearly on a par with those for white Alaskans, and in the mid-1970's—with considerable rejoicing—the TB wing of the Anchorage Native hospital was closed for lack of patients.

Transportation is improving. The Alaska State Ferry System gives Southeastern villages easy access to the outside world, and only a few settlements in the rest of the state are without at least a small airstrip.

Surprisingly, despite these rapid moves into the 20th century, the watchword of Alaskan educators is no longer assimilation. From the heart of the Native movement, there has emerged a new pride in cultural heritage and a determination to save what is good about the old ways. At the beginning of the 1970's Native language programs sprang up around the state under the pioneering efforts of Michael Krauss and the University of Alaska Language Center. In 1973 the legislature passed a law requiring at least one bilingual teacher on the staff if 15 or more children in a school spoke a language other than English.

Today's Native Alaskans are actively preserving their old ways while energetically taking a major place in the white man's capitalistic society. Whether they have the best or worst of both worlds is yet to be seen.

"The toughest thing is to be an Alaskan Native in 1975," noted Roger Lang, retiring president of the AFN. "We're stockholders. We're corporations. We're profit and loss. We're business. We're a little different than we used to be."

And indeed, Alaska's Eskimos, Indians and Aleuts have come a long way from the status of "uncivilized tribes."

The Indians of Southeastern Alaska used shields of copper as we use money today. Sometimes they were carefully decorated, sometimes plain, but the shape was always the same. Scholars have been unable to figure out why it was adopted. To date, all coppers analyzed in museums have been manufactured of sheet metal — the same type early traders used to sheath the hulls of their boats. But, although no Native coppers have been identified, the Southeastern Indians are thought to have traded in this valuable commodity which is native to their region, long before the coming of the whites.
(BURKE MEMORIAL WASHINGTON STATE MUSEUM)

INUPIAT

The Northern Eskimos

By Howard Rock

I was born in a sod igloo on August 10, 1911, the fifth child of Weyahok, my father, and Keshorna, my mother. By the time of my birth, my father's name, which in our language means rock, had been changed by a missionary. My father became known as Sam Rock and my mother was given the name of Emma.

I came into a world that is vastly different from other parts of the globe: Point Hope, an ancient, tiny settlement in the far northwestern part of Arctic Alaska. Stories are persistently told that the original village started about eight miles out, to the north, in the Arctic Ocean. In the winter old-timers say, "See that big pile-up of ice ridges out there? It's shallow there and the old stories tell us that was the place where the first village of Tikiqaq [Point Hope] was established." There could very well be substance to this belief because there is continuous erosion of the beach north of the present village year after year. The yearly fall storms even today are washing away the village.

I think the first thing I became aware of in life was

Howard (Weyahok) Rock, born in the village of Point Hope, successfully bridged the great cultural gap between subsistence hunters and the people of the modern world. Rock completed three years of college at the University of Washington before the Depression forced him to drop out and earn his living as a painter of Eskimo life. But he was articulate enough in his native language to serve as an assistant for university linguists working with Inupiat, and fluent enough in English to make his mark as a writer, editor and Native leader. Some of the material here is from columns Rock wrote in the 1960's for the Native *Tundra Times*. The rest was intended as an introduction for Rock's biography and was written shortly before his death in 1976.

Ribs from the bowhead whale guide travelers following a trail along the flat coast of the Chukchi Sea between Point Hope and Kivalina, where there are few natural landmarks to show the way. Point Hope is an ancient village site where Eskimos have been hunting the bowhead whale — one of their most important food sources — for centuries.

that I was cold. I also think it was meant to be that way, because a child of the Arctic must know how to cope with the dangers of extreme cold. It was said that in the old days a male child of an Eskimo family at Tikiqaq was immersed in the cold water of the little lagoon a mile east of the present village. This was a ritual a mother performed to initiate her son into the rigors of the arctic climate. It was supposed to toughen him against cold for when he hunted during his manhood.

Eight children were born to Weyahok and Keshorna. Three died in childhood; five of us survived. It was a hard life. Shortages of food were periodical. Adverse hunting conditions that always seemed to last too long disrupted the food supply in the village. Father would go out hunting day after day and return without any game. Mother would endure these difficulties with silence, never voicing her despair. She checked her husband's hunting clothes carefully each night, mended them when they needed it and dried them out with extreme care for Father to wear the next day.

And then Weyahok, along with the other hunters in the village, would come home with a seal or two or a polar bear. Keshorna treated these fortunate events with her same composure, but her conversation with my father and us children would become a bit more animated than usual. We would have more to eat on those occasions, but even before we partook of the meal we also felt pangs of disappointment and something like resentment, because Keshorna would cut up a seal, take out a portion, and say to me or my brothers and sisters, "Take this over to Samaroon's," or "Take this to your aunt."

"Mother, you're not leaving enough meat for us," I said more than once. "We'll be out of meat again soon."

"You keep quiet and take that over there," she would say firmly.

And so it was. Keshorna would save scarcely a few days' supply of meat for her own family. I often

wondered why. Then, perhaps the very next day, a member of a village family would come to our sod igloo bearing a large portion of caribou, seal or polar bear. This was a reciprocal system our people at Point Hope had used for ages. They took care of one another in times of need and the giver often received more than he gave. The spirit of mutual help was there and always accomplished with cordiality.

In the fall the women and children would go out on the tundra and search for underground caches in which mice had stored roots, which provided delightful change of diet. We walked slowly, fanning out, testing the ground underfoot with each step. Soon the ground would give way and Mother or one of us children would announce happily, "Here's one right here!"

Mother would then slit an opening in the cache just long enough to put her hand and forearm through. She pulled roots out by the handful. In the process of storing, the proprietor mouse had cut each root into about inch-long, bite-size pieces. As mother dug out the food she gave us a warning, as Eskimo mothers have from generation to generation: "You must never take all the roots in a mouse cache. Take about half of them and leave the rest for the mouse to eat during the winter. If you take all of them, the mouse will starve and die and won't be around next year to gather more roots for us."

The major event at Point Hope, and the economic base of the village both then and now, was whaling season. According to the ancient whalers of Tikiqaq, Allingnuk is the Dweller of the Moon. Depending on the heart and richness of soul of the pleader, Allingnuk allots talismans of the whales—good luck for the hunt. When midwinter moons have passed, the wives of the village whaling captains chant to this "man in the moon" their pleas for a successful spring hunt for their husbands.

They wait for a new moon that leans to the right in the night sky. That is the whaler's moon.

One of Howard Rock's early paintings depicts a scene that has not changed much in years — the bowhead whale hunt. Hunters in the painting have harpooned the whale from their umiak *and are tossing a sealskin float overboard.*

(ALASKA STATE BANK, NORTHERN LIGHTS BRANCH)

On such a night long ago Nikuwanna, the wife of a fledgling whaling captain, donned her beautiful squirrel skin parka and picked up a stone vessel that she had filled with clear fresh water from a pond. The container had a handle of polished baleen, or whalebone. At each end of the baleen, where it was attached to the sides of the vessel, was fastened, vertically, a feather.

Nikuwanna padded on her mukluks across the floor of the sod igloo, lowered herself through a trap entrance at the front, and walked, stooping, through a low and narrow hallway. She climbed up a short ladder and emerged from the *pallisuk* (sky entrance) into a cold, still night. Planting her feet on the edge of the *pallisuk*, she straightened and faced the new moon. With her right hand she raised the stone vessel slowly by the baleen string, held it aloft toward the lunar crescent and chanted:

> *O Allingnuk, Dweller of the Moon, Allingnuk,*
> *great and generous giver of whales—*
> *I, Nikuwanna, whose wife I am of Killikvuk, a*
> *young and hopeful new whaler of Tikiqaq,*
> *Implore thee for thy life-giving gift.*
> *With the aid and lightness of these, the feathers,*
> *May the spirit of my being rise and*
> *take upon a flight*
> *This vessel I hold aloft and come nigh thee*
> *So thou mayest drop a talisman or two of whales*
> *into this, the clear water of the pond.*
> *Do this, O great Allingnuk,*
> *So every being of Tikiqaq may dance and feast*
> *for thee*
> *At the close of the great season of whaling—*
> *O Allingnuk, Dweller of the Moon,*
> *Allingnuk, great and generous giver of whales,*
> *I, Nikuwanna, whose wife I am of Killikvuk,*
> *A young and hopeful new whaler of Tikiqaq,*
> *Implore thee for thy life-giving gift.*

The whaling from Point Hope is done now in much the same manner as it was hundreds of years ago, from the moving ice of the Chukchi Sea, well away from the village. It is a treacherous business, yet Point Hope hunters are skillful and within memory there has been only one tragic whaling accident—that of the *umiak* belonging to my grandfather, Kakairnok. As my father remembered it and told it to me, this happened when my father was about 13. It was his first whaling season with his father—the first exciting step to manhood. But when the season was half over, Kakairnok and his crew had had no luck.

This is the story my father, Weyahok, recounted to me.

"One day, just before midday," my father Weyahok recounted, "Kakairnok said to us, 'We are not doing well here. I think we should move our camp up north away from the other crews. We might do better up there.'

"We broke camp and loaded our gear in the *umiak* and started north, paddling along the edge of a lead [open water between masses of ice]. We passed two whaling camps along the way. Beyond the last camp was shore ice that jutted out seaward. When we rounded it, we must have been over a mile away from the second of the whaling camps we passed.

"We were cruising along at a leisurely speed about 90 feet from the shore ice, looking for a suitable place to set up camp when a larger-than-average whale surfaced about 75 feet ahead of us. Father looked back to us quickly and motioned for us to paddle. The crew consisted of my father, two other adult men, one of whom was the helmsman, a woman who prepared meals and three of us boys.

"We started to paddle after the whale with all the energy we could muster so we could catch up with it and be in a good position when it surfaced to breathe. We caught up on the third surfacing and my father raised his whaling harpoon.

Point Hope, one of the most traditional Eskimo villages in Alaska, is at the tip of a point of land that juts out sharply into the Chukchi Sea. It is an ideal village site, where the bowhead whale passes close to shore during its annual migration from the Bering Sea to the Arctic Ocean. (LESLIE NAKASHIMA)

"The harpoon was a stout wooden shaft to which was fastened a bone shank that had been rounded to a dull point at the end. On the end of the bone was the ivory harpoon head, which had a blade of sharpened slate fitted into the point.

"My father plunged the harpoon deep into the kidney area of the whale. He used the momentum of the *umiak* to help him give speed to the harpoon. The helmsman had swung the *umiak* to an angle of more than 45 degrees to the whale, an angle considered by whalers to be safe.

"The whale's tail must have shifted sharply beneath us the moment of the strike. The great flukes suddenly rose out of the water, hitting our *umiak* just forward of the beam. There was a sickening feeling of being pushed upward by a great force from underneath. There were sounds of snapping wood mingled with the scream of the woman member of the crew.

The great force under us ceased and then I felt myself sailing through the air. I seemed to sail for long moments, until I felt the impact of the water when I came down. I went under for what seemed a long time. I swallowed some water.

"Finally I felt air around my head and I gasped for breath. I saw our *umiak* upside down. There was no shape to it; it looked like a deflated sealskin float. To the left of the *umiak* I saw my father. He was bleeding badly around the head. He saw me and shouted, '*Eeqneeng*—son—try to make it to the ice. Try hard, son. I cannot make it. My bones are broken. Hurry, son, try to make it to the ice!'

"I could see my father clinging to a floating paddle with his left hand. His other hand must have been badly injured.

"I could not swim but I tried to do what my father told me to do.

"'Use your arms and hands and paddle with them,' Father shouted.

"The ice was about 125 feet away. The whale had thrown us outward. My right knee was hurting me terribly. All the while I could hear Father encouraging me. I suddenly noticed the other boys, Koonook and Akniachak. They were also trying to make it to the ice. Koonook was whimpering. They were both ahead of me to my right. Akniachak was making good progress. Father kept encouraging us. I could no longer hear the woman's screams. When I was a few feet away from the ice I could no longer hear my father's voice, either.

"Akniachak had reached the ice and was scrambling up out of the water. I passed Koonook without noticing him. Akniachak began to encourage me and soon I was close enough for him to reach me and pull me out. Koonook was still about 20 feet out. He was crying, 'I can't make it. I can't make it.'

"I was crying as I encouraged him because when I looked out over the water he was the only sign of life. Remnants of the broken *umiak* were floating out to sea. I had lost my father—my good father. . . ."

Koonook was saved but the village was saddened as it had never been before. All the people in it had known intimately those who were lost. They grieved over Kakairnok. He was a fine hunter—a fine man. And his loss was a deadening blow to his family. Weyahok felt it most keenly because he had worshiped his father. Since he was the only boy in the family he felt that the responsibility of taking care of his mother and sisters would fall on his shoulders. But he was too young to be fully effective as a hunter.

Chief Attungowruk of the village almost at once invited Weyahok to join his crew. The chief had caught a whale earlier and told Weyahok that he would be given a full share of the whale as a crew member. And he instructed the other members of his crew to give Kakairnok's family a portion of their shares.

Attungowruk caught another whale that season, in fact two days after Weyahok joined the crew; so the young hunter was able to provide his family with ample food for the coming year.

"It always amazed me to think back on how we were able to save ourselves when we couldn't swim," Weyahok used to marvel. "I used to wade in the lagoon up to my waist and once in a while even up to my neck but I had never learned to swim.

"When the whale struck our *umiak* and threw us into the water our heavy clothing kept us afloat. We had our mothers to thank for making our clothes out of winter caribou skins. The skins were very buoyant in the water and if it hadn't been for that, all of us would have drowned."

Today at Point Hope there is some "modern" whaling equipment. Hunters now use whaling guns (patented in the 1800's), black-powder bombs and walkie-talkies, but they still hunt from skin boats with paddles, like the hunters of old. The whales are still occasionally unpredictable. And the modern parka makers of today have yet to find anything that will top the traditional Eskimo parka of winter caribou fur.

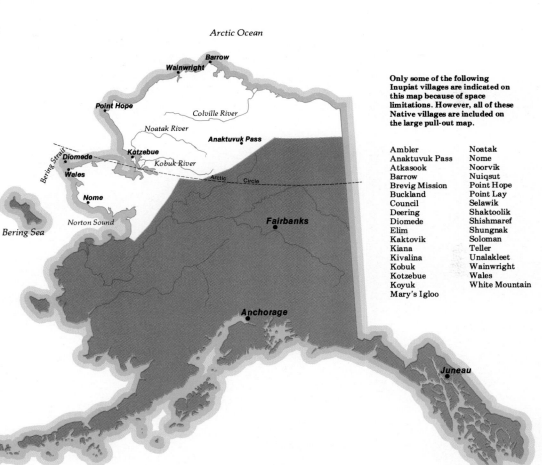

Only some of the following Inupiat villages are indicated on this map because of space limitations. However, all of these Native villages are included on the large pull-out map.

Ambler	Noatak
Anaktuvuk Pass	Nome
Atkasook	Noorvik
Barrow	Nuiqsut
Brevig Mission	Point Hope
Buckland	Point Lay
Council	Selawik
Deering	Shaktoolik
Diomede	Shishmaref
Elim	Shungnak
Kaktovik	Soloman
Kiana	Teller
Kivalina	Unalakleet
Kobuk	Wainwright
Kotzebue	Wales
Koyuk	White Mountain
Mary's Igloo	

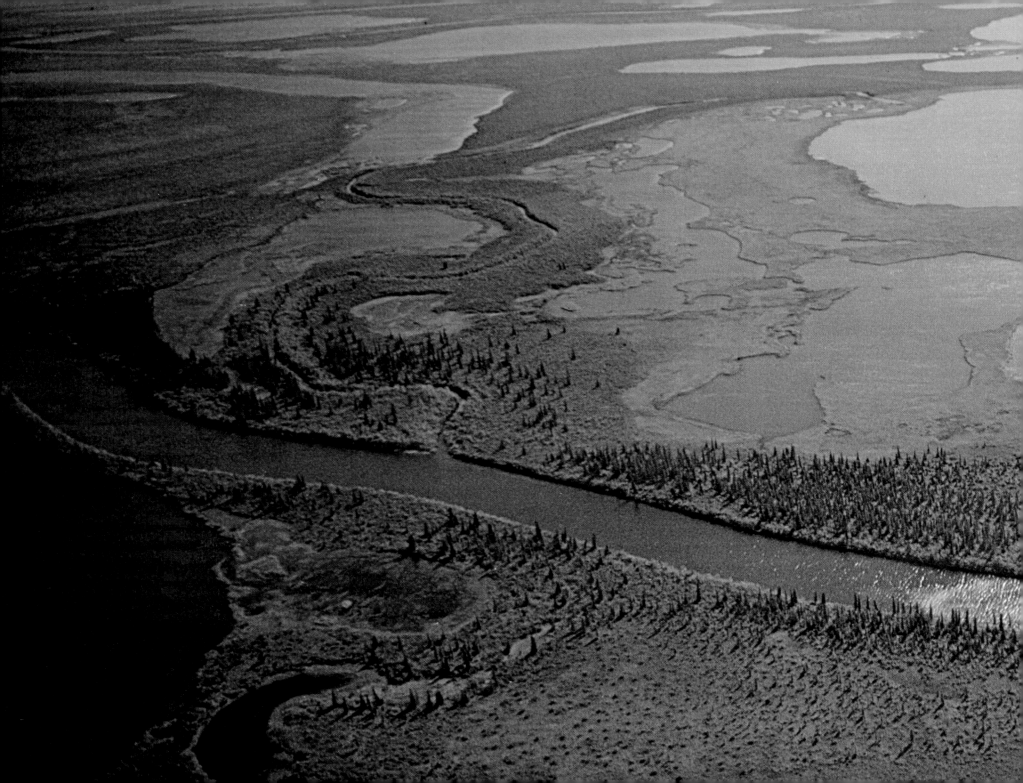

Previous page — Twisting slowly toward the waters of Kotzebue Sound, the Kobuk River works its way across the permafrost, through an endless wilderness of lakes and ponds. There are relatively few Eskimo villages in the Kobuk drainage — namely Noorvik, Kiana, Ambler, Shungnak and Kobuk.

Below — Barrow, largest Eskimo community in the United States — and also the northernmost settlement of any size — is a fast-changing village. Headquarters for the North Slope Borough, Barrow has become a focal point of Native-rights action and also is visited each year by an increasing number of tourists.

"*T*he Eskimos of the Arctic," wrote Marvin "Muktuk" Marston in Men of the Tundra, "are the most self-reliant and resourceful individuals I have ever met. The climatic conditions under which they have survived for generations would prove insurmountable to 99% of the white race. Yet Eskimos have not only survived . . . they have devised means of providing themselves with the three essentials of life — food, clothing and shelter. Could we do that alone in a barren, treeless waste, without materials or implements of any kind, when nine months of the year the earth is enveloped in snow and ice and temperatures that are below zero? . . . .*

"I would not for a moment belittle the brains and accomplishments which have given the people of the Western world so high a standard of living. But . . . are we better men than they because we have developed gadgets of comfort, while they still rely on their wits and ingenuity because they have no gadgets?"

Above — Kotzebue, north of Bering Strait at the edge of Kotzebue Sound, is the center of commerce for a 43,000-square-mile area of Northwestern Alaska. Despite modern touches, many villagers rely on subsistence hunting and fishing.

Left — The main street of Nome, photographed at midnight in May. Facing the Bering Sea on the south coast of the Seward Peninsula, Nome grew quickly after the 1898 discovery of gold on nearby creeks. Many Eskimos from outlying villages have moved to Nome — now commercial hub of Northwestern Alaska — including King Island villagers, who have abandoned their offshore settlement in recent years.

Overleaf — Nome, one of Alaska's most cosmopolitan towns during its gold rush heyday, boasted a population of 10,000 fortune hunters shortly after the turn of the century. Gold still is found near this Seward Peninsula settlement, and gold dredges have been reactivated in recent years, but most of Nome's stampeders have been replaced with tourists — many of whom seek Eskimo artwork and craft items.

Above — Shishmaref, on the north coast of the Seward Peninsula, was once a supply base for mining operations. The village, founded about 1900, is on Sarichef Island, between the Chukchi Sea and Shishmaref Inlet. Flooding, a seasonal threat, has convinced villagers they must move their entire village when a suitable site can be found.

Right — Perhaps the most remote village in the Arctic, Little Diomede clings stubbornly to the steep slopes of Little Diomede Island. In the middle of Bering Strait, only a paddle away from their cousins on Russia's Big Diomede Island, the Eskimos of Little Diomede are prevented by cold war politics from holding traditional celebrations with their relatives on the big island.

Opposite — The people of Anaktuvuk Pass were the last of Alaska's nomadic Eskimos. For centuries these people followed the trail of the migratory caribou through the Brooks Range, well north of the Arctic Circle. But the influence of the white man and pressures and promises of his culture finally penetrated their remote domain. Recognizing the importance of formal schooling for their children, the Eskimos reluctantly gave up their traditional life and in 1961 chose this broad and beautiful mountain pass — a major route for roving caribou herds — as the site of their permanent village.

Housing in the Arctic has changed rapidly; most of the sod homes are gone, and have been replaced with conventional frame-construction houses. Still, there's room for individuality.

Above — By the mid-1970's the people of Anaktuvuk Pass had given up their sod houses — the last one shown here — for modern homes. The holdout was Joe Mekiana, who had returned from school in Chicago to enjoy the subsistence lifestyle of his ancestors.

Left — When the village of Point Lay shifted from its old site to the new one, Warren Neakok made his move the easy way, placing his Quonset hut on giant runners and — with all furniture in place and his son inside — sledging it across a frozen river to its new site.

Dorcas Nukapagak (*left*) helps with housework in the tent she and her family occupied when they first resettled the village of Nuiqsut, on the North Slope east of Barrow. Although equipped with plywood floors and heated by small stoves, the tents these pioneers first lived in were none too cozy in 75-mile-per-hour winds and -50°F temperatures encountered during the winter of 1973-74. Eskimos returned to the old village site (*below*) after passage of the Alaska Native Claims Settlement Act. New houses have been built to replace the tents of the earlier days.

In the summer of 1974, Queenie Millingrook (*above*) well over 80 at the time, left her home on Little Diomede Island and traveled on the Alaska Native Service ship to enter the hospital at Nome. She recalled the old days when she and her neighbors would walk over the ice covering Bering Strait to celebrate Easter with Russian Eskimos. The first trading post she knew was in Siberia, and once her husband walked there just to buy tobacco and a sack of flour. She was one of the few Eskimo women left who wore a chin tattoo, and her early memories were those of an age that now seems centuries past.

Left — The Moses Millingrook family of Little Diomede Island — a short distance from Russia's Big Diomede Island across Bering Strait — prepares a meal inside their traditional stone house, which they prefer to the modern alternatives. Many villagers cook on pressure gasoline camp stoves, which are portable, space-saving and relatively inexpensive.

Below — Darlene Millingrook tends an old seal oil lamp in the family's stone house on Little Diomede Island. This may be one of the last homes in Alaska that continues, on a regular basis, to use seal oil as the main source of heat.

Transporting food, building materials and other supplies to Arctic villages can be frustrating and expensive, as reflected in the high cost-of-living figures.

Above — A vital lifeline for many isolated settlements is the Bureau of Indian Affairs freighter *North Star III*, here anchored off Little Diomede Island, with Russia's Big Diomede at the right. Based in Seattle, the ship makes an annual trip north during the brief ice-free season, visiting towns along the coast to as far north as Barrow.

Right — Captain Cecil "Moe" Cole, who worked his way up from crewman to captain of the *North Star II*, has long been a good friend of the Eskimos. An affable bear of a man, Moe is a soft touch for the children and often gave them candy, oranges, toys or anything else he could share during his annual visits. Here, during his 1974 voyage, Moe passes out candy at Brevig Mission, north of Teller. Anticipating the well-loved captain's much-earned retirement, Norman Manadelook, who had himself stood in the candy line as a kid, said sadly, "He gives his heart away with the candy. We will miss him."

Upper left — A Wien Air Alaska jet lands in fog at Barrow, with smaller aircraft in the foreground. In the Arctic, as in many other areas of Alaska, the airplane has become a critically important form of transportation. (TIM THOMPSON)

Above — A modern-day bush telegraph. Youngsters at White Mountain, on the Seward Peninsula east of Nome, write names and messages in the dust on an airplane that has just come from another village. The kids meet every incoming flight to find out who's around and what's happening at other villages along the line. (RICK KIEFER)

Left — The Barrow Native village corporation, Ukpeagvik Inupiat, built this large, modern store as a profit-making enterprise and also to better serve the needs of the people.

Pursued for centuries by Eskimo hunters, the bowhead whale has become a focal point in the Inupiat's battle to maintain a subsistence lifestyle — if only part-time. The whale feeds entire villages, even today, and the sharing of the whale is an important occasion.

Previous page — Whale hunters from Barrow camp at the edge of the ice to wait and watch for a bowhead whale to appear, sometimes maintaining the vigil for weeks at a time before the first whale is sighted.

Above — Junior Slwooko of Saint Lawrence Island aims his harpoon at a bowhead whale in the Bering Sea. Islanders pursue the whales during their annual migration from the Bering Sea to the Arctic Ocean. (CHLAUS LOTSHCER, REPRINTED FROM ALASKA GEOGRAPHIC®)

Right — When a successful crew brings home a whale, many people turn out to help with the butchering (which takes about 12 hours), and everyone receives a share of the meat. At 1 A.M. the villagers of Wainwright joined together to haul this whale onto the ice.

Upper right — Simeon Patkotak and his crew butcher a 30-foot bowhead whale. Though the whale was relatively small, the job took all night.

After Inupiat villagers bring home a whale — or whales — there is a whale festival to celebrate the successful hunt and to share the rewards.

Lower left — One of the delicacies served at a recent festival — boiled whale intestine. (GUY CORRY)

Below — Apples and slices of whale flippers were given to youngsters at one of the annual Point Hope whaling feasts, and no one minded when the late spring snow started falling. The flipper is eaten raw and is considered one of the choicest parts of the whale.

Right — The blanket toss, an ancient Eskimo sport, is part of most northern festivals.

At a recent Barrow whale feast, youngsters practiced their skills before the adults took over. The blanket is actually a handsewn walrus hide. Some say the toss was invented by hunters who wished to spot game at a distance on the flat tundra, but today it's just for fun.

Opposite — End of the Point Hope whaling festival. Grouped according to traditional clans, sitting in the shelter of their beached *umiaks*, the villagers and their guests are treated by successful captains to a great feast. The feature, of course, is whale meat, including the favorites — muktuk and whale flipper. There are store-bought items, too, including pop, apples, ice cream and cigars.

Fishing is important in much of the Arctic, especially in Kotzebue Sound and around the Seward Peninsula to Norton Sound. Nets dominate in summer, and fish traps and hand lines often are seen during winter months when ice covers all lakes and rivers.

Right — Henry Oyoumick of Unalakleet, who works for the Norton Sound Health Corporation when he is not fishing, returns to the village after emptying his gill nets of salmon. Oyoumick was born and reared in Unalakleet, attended college in Anchorage, served the U.S. Army in Vietnam and returned to the village, where he administers the health organization's Family Services Program. His last name means "the heat waves seen in the summer from a distance."
(SUSAN HACKLEY JOHNSON)

Right — *Ootkut* roots, called Eskimo potatoes, at Little Diomede Island.

Below — Youngsters from the school at White Mountain, east of Nome on the Seward Peninsula, are taken on a root-digging expedition. Excavating edible roots was once an important element in the subsistence lifestyle of the Inupiat — roots were a welcome variation in a diet that otherwise consisted largely of meat and fish. Mothers and children still sometimes dig roots in the spring, when the plants are young and tender. One trick from the past is to find the caches of roots gathered by mice. The rule is to take only a few of the stored roots and leave enough for the mouse to get through the winter.

Native leaders who gathered for the signing of the Alaska Native Claims Settlement Act had mixed emotions because the settlement, although larger than any in history, was nevertheless viewed as a compromise.

Joe Upicksoun, Arctic Slope leader who had protested that the settlement was too small, expressed anger and sadness.

"We Inupiat Eskimos have never wanted money as such — we wanted land, because out of the land we would make our money. We would protect our subsistence living; we would still have our heritage."

77

Above — The people of Barrow sponsored a potlatch when delegates arrived for the 1977 Inuit Circumpolar Conference. Here guests from the east sample Jell-O salad, salmon and cake with chocolate frosting.

Right — Visitors to Barrow peer down into an Inupiat ice cellar, a natural refrigerator cut deep into the permafrost to store foods year-round. (TIM THOMPSON)

Opposite — Hot dogs are roasted over a fire at a school picnic at Golovin, east of Nome on the south side of the Seward Peninsula, facing Norton Sound.

The caribou has long been an important food source in the Eskimo culture. Here, hundreds of caribou in the Arctic herd pass through the De Long Mountains near the Kuna River, on the North Slope of the Brooks Range. These animals wander over an area of about 140,000 square miles, migrating many hundreds of miles annually between their forest-edge winter range and the calving and summer ranges. In 1970 it was believed that the Arctic herd had 240,000 animals, but after a count in 1976, worried scientists concluded that the herd had "crashed." They guessed that the Arctic herd had dropped to about 50,000 members, and they urged a reduction in hunting pressure.

(GIL MULL, REPRINTED FROM ALASKA® MAGAZINE)

Left — Anaktuvuk Pass hunters return home with caribou they have killed. Modern rifles and snow machines have made hunting much easier and in some cases more controversial. (JIM REARDEN, STAFF, REPRINTED FROM ALASKA® MAGAZINE)

Below — At Noorvik, on the Kobuk River, the electric plant broke down and, with refrigerators and freezers out of action, villagers went back to the old ways — storing caribou reserves in nature's icebox.

Right — Dempsey Bodfish of Wainwright, descendant of a famous 19th-century Yankee whaling captain, feeds his dog team. Since the advent of the snowmobile, fewer Eskimos keep teams these days. Also, since the cost of commercial dog food is prohibitive in the Arctic, keeping a team means a constant effort at hunting and fishing to feed them.

Lower right — A bonus the NANA Corporation reaps from its Kotzebue-area reindeer herd is the sale of antlers (which grow anew each year) to Asian buyers, who grind the horns and use the powder as an aphrodisiac. At the first roundup for dehorning in 1975, NANA staff members and their families pitched in to help the four permanent herders.

Below — Summer has arrived in the Arctic when the geese and ducks return in great waves and when offshore ice breaks up, creating open leads near the shore.

Right — Successful polar bear hunters Rossman Pealook, left, and Raymond Aguvluk show off the hide of a bear they had taken near their village of Wainwright.

Lower right — An arctic ground squirrel in his summer coat on the North Slope. (JOEL ROGERS)

Left — An Eskimo woman from Saint Lawrence Island splits a walrus skin on a stretching rack. The skins have several uses, including the covering of Eskimo *umiaks.* The skin is split with an *ulu,* also called a woman's knife. (RICHARD HARRINGTON)

Above — Walrus haul out on the ice 30 miles west of Gambell, Saint Lawrence Island, in early June. (ALFRED L. DECICCO)

Change has been tumultuous in the Arctic since the discovery of oil on the North Slope in 1968, passage of the Native Claims Settlement Act in 1971 and construction of the trans-Alaska oil pipeline from 1974 to 1977. The only constant has been change itself.

Left — A North Slope oil rig is silhouetted against the arctic sky. Jobs related to the oil industry provided money for many arctic villagers, but the boom quieted down — for Natives as well as other Alaskans — with completion of the trans-Alaska pipeline (TIM THOMPSON)

Below — The modern headquarters of the North Slope Borough, whose boundaries coincide with those of the Arctic Slope Regional Corporation, reflects the vitality of the borough and its people. From their offices in Barrow, the borough mayor and council govern an enormous, though sparsely settled, land area. A strong voice in Native affairs, the borough hosted the first Inuit Circumpolar Conference of Eskimo people in 1977.

Right — Willie Hensley and Marlene Johnson relax during the annual *Tundra Times* banquet. Hensley, one of the state's best-known Eskimo leaders, has played an important role — as politician and Native corporation leader — since the battle for settlement of Native claims.

Education, especially the trend toward construction of primary and secondary schools in smaller villages, is helping the Inupiat bridge the gap between old and new cultures.

Below — Beltz High School in Nome holds graduation ceremonies for the class of 1977 — a class that boasted the highest grade-point average until then in the school's history. Originally a vocational school for Natives, Beltz now serves as a regular high school for the Nome community. Dorms accommodate students from villages that have not yet built high schools of their own.

Right — Teacher Dee Bolens presides over the rural school at Kivalina, northwest of Kotzebue on the shores of the Chukchi Sea.

Left — Youngsters play baseball at Ambler in April, using their own variation of the rules. (NANCY SIMMERMAN)

Below — The large enclosed entry at a modern Barrow supermarket offers a snowless, warm play area for children to use while their parents are shopping and also provides a convenient meeting place for villagers.

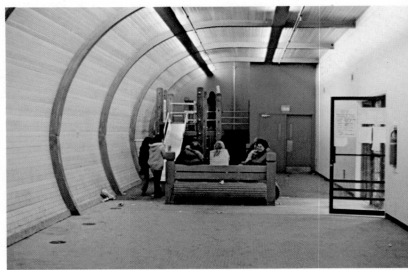

"There were 130 people living here when they put up a school in the 1930's," recalls Dorcas Neakok of Point Lay. "Then the BIA closed the school. We had to send even the little ones off. Those brave little girls — only 6, but they wanted to go to school. They had to go all the way to Southeastern Alaska."

Eskimo art has become an important source of income in many villages, and the formation of artists' cooperatives has protected artists (and potential buyers) from ripoffs in the souvenir trade.

Below — The hunters of Anaktuvuk Pass have for some time carved wooden masks representing their friends, stretching dried caribou hide over the carved wood to take its shape. Ruffed with wolf fur, the leather masks — shown hanging on Vera Ahgook's clothesline — provide cash in times when hunting is poor in the Brooks Range.

Right — Peter Shuvluk of Barrow joins fellow musicians who accompany Inupiat dancers with their skin drums, best-known musical instrument developed by the Eskimos. The drum is made of seal or walrus intestine stretched taut over a wooden hoop.

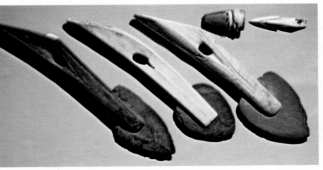

Left — Master carver Aloysius Pikonganna of Nome demonstrates ivory carving for tourists.

Top — Eskimo ivory carvings are perhaps the most valuable forms of Native art in Alaska. This caribou was carved by John Tingook of Point Hope.

Above — Artistic, if not carved as "art," these early ivory and stone harpoon heads were fashioned by Eskimo hunters to capture the giant bowhead whale and smaller marine mammals. These harpoon heads came from the ancient village of Point Hope.

(ALASKA STATE MUSEUM, JUNEAU)

"***I** am proud to be an Eskimo," Martha Aiken testified during congressional hearings on sea mammals in 1972, "and to say I can speak, read and write the dialect. [But] are we to be Eskimos in name only, though we look like Eskimos? Or will you help us to recapture our culture, customs, traditions and our dialect? Right now, Eskimos are on the edge of nowhere, balancing to keep our culture."*

Barrow youngsters enjoy an 11 P.M. sledding party in early May. Summer is near, but the temperature remains at zero. In another 30 days the snow will vanish and the tundra will blossom with delicate wild flowers — a transformation almost as sweeping as the cultural and economic changes that have hit the Inupiat world in recent decades. (ALAN R. CRANE, REPRINTED FROM ALASKA® MAGAZINE)

YUP'IK

The Western Eskimos

By John Active

Where did the Eskimos of Western Alaska come from? The most accepted explanation is that the original Natives migrated from Asia eons ago over a land bridge. It is possible this is how the first people reached our mainland and that they continued to move down the Northern Hemisphere and on into what is now South America. Other groups could have come across the bridge to settle North America: the New England and Plains Indians, the Canadian Eskimos and the Alaskan Indians and Eskimos.

Of those that stayed in what is now Alaska, several groups moved down along the coast, some settling and some moving inland. Today people from villages within a space of, let's say, 100 miles of each other can speak with and understand one another. On the outer edges of that 100 miles, villagers can communicate with other villagers in another 100-mile area. Thus the Eskimos and Indians who are neighbors have a common bond.

Ask any one of our young people who have gone to school and they will agree that a land bridge once existed. The old people, however, believe all things on

John Active was born in 1948 in Chukfaktoolik, a small western Eskimo village 80 miles west of Bethel. At an early age he was adopted by a highly traditional family who raised him to be fluent in Yup'ik and to have respect for his culture.

Active was educated in the Bethel school system and he did well enough in English to become one of the top news announcers at KYUK, the Bethel radio and television station, and to write for *Tundra Drums*, Bethel's semimonthly newspaper. He also worked occasionally for the city, for a transportation company and in the kitchen of a Bethel bar. Ironically, the writer's Yup'ik name is Akumaag, which means Person Who Likes to Sit, but he better lives up to his adoptive name of Active. At the time this photo was taken Active was also working on a book about his Eskimo culture. (*Photo by Jane Sutherland*)

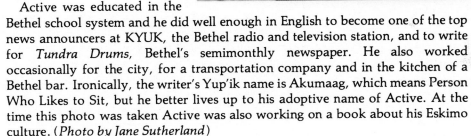

Fresh salmon dries on a rack at Stebbins, on the north edge of the Yukon-Kuskokwim Delta near the village of Saint Michael, facing Norton Sound. Subsistence fishing keeps many villages alive in the Delta, from Bristol Bay to Norton Sound.

"Once, long
ago," a
Mekoryuk old-timer
recalled, "there
was a hunter who
wandered into a
cave . . . a strange
cave. And suddenly
deep in it he saw,
floating on the air,
the feet and wings
and fins of all the
things he'd ever
killed. It frightened
him and he rushed
to get out . . . fought
his way out. But he
couldn't forget
what he'd seen, so
he made a mask to
show it. And
we still do."

the land came into existence by themselves. They know of no bridge or where they came from or how they got here, but they do feel instinctively there was a higher being who was creator of the world. Here, in part, is a legend of the people.

❧

The beginning began with a sound. A sound that was music within the silence. It was dull but sweet, a golden sound that rang and echoed through the nothingness. It was constant and went ringing over, under, sideways and through itself. It was the beginning, a start, a creation.

Then came another sound much like the first, let loose to search out something, somewhere, crying out to be heard, answered and accepted.

It was the sound of the flapping of great wings. In this manner did the great Raven fly, looking right and left, soaring through the emptiness, untiring in his movements. His features were completely black, shining with indescribable beauty. His eyes, seeing all and knowing all, did not blink. They searched into the darkness and became fixed.

The time was ripe, the moment precise; with a quick movement of his great wings this magnificent god dived down through the darkness. Still diving, he began to rotate around and around, faster and faster. In doing this he created a suction behind him which began to pull the darkness with great force. Suddenly he rose, leaving the dark mass spinning and reeling behind him, and as this happened the mass became as large as the Raven and kept on growing.

Seeing this, the god glided above and around his creation. Then he alighted upon it and stopped it. He looked at it and the great black mass became solid. He took flight and once again, this time very slowly, the mass began to rotate.

The great bird flew into the darkness and then, from

the farthest, darkest region of the black expanse, a great bright light evolved and spun through the night, burning a thousand holes into the darkness, and the stars shone forth. The huge light spun past the great black mass and stopped in the center of the darkness surrounding the mass. The darkness then began to fade away and the mass was in light.

While this was happening the great Raven was flying a short distance away. He did not approve of what he saw and immediately he dove down upon the mass and clawed it, making every mark upon the mass that his claws could create.

Once again the great bird flew away from the waste and looked upon it from a distance. And again from the farthest and darkest region a great bright light evolved and spun through the night causing the darkness to break apart and to make way for the sun.

Still the great Raven did not approve. Three times he attacked the mass; then he flew completely around it without touching its surface, and in the following moments the black mass changed from one color to a thousand. The colors were those of trees, grasses and flowers of a thousand species, yet, as he watched, the colors changed again, this time fading from green to brown.

Once more the Raven dove down and as he did a mist began to trail behind him, and this mist covered the whole of creation. When some of the mist cleared, the colors had again changed to green, and the gorges and scratches the great Raven had made upon the surface had filled up. There now were rivers and oceans on the mass.

The god flew over great oceans and miles of hills and forests, over deep valleys of flowers and thousands of plants. Yet as he flew the Raven realized that he was the only moving thing. How good it would be to see living beings roaming the earth, thought the Raven. So he alighted upon stone and with his power he caused the

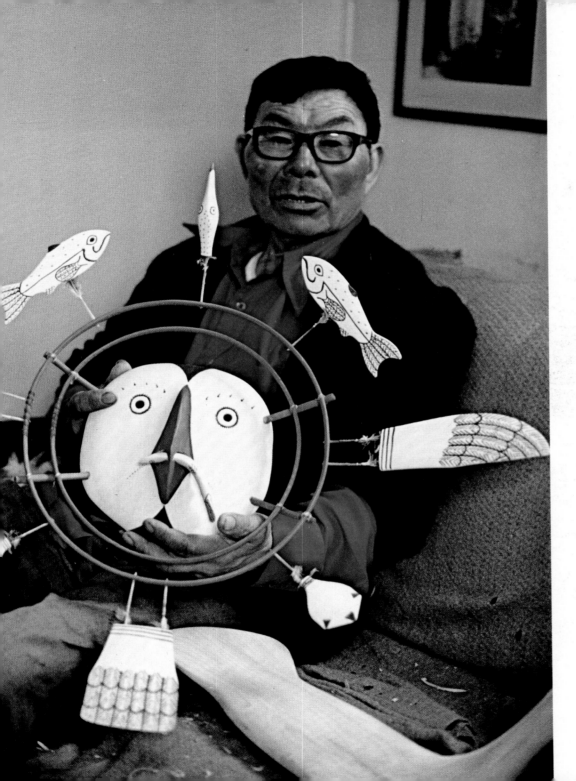

matter to move. Within a moment a spirit entered into the stone, creating a new form of life.

This new being was huge and of grayish color and, being made of stone, was very heavy. This was the first man: rugged, cold and clumsy.

The great Raven took flight and the stone man followed because he realized he and the Raven were the only moving beings. Over steep hills and deep valleys the Raven flew, the man following as best he could. Then finally, still following, the man stopped on a marshland and began to sink. The Raven, seeing this, alighted next to the helpless man, studied him for a moment and then took flight. The stone man sank from the surface of the swamp and was dead.

Now the great Raven flew high and looked at the whole terrain. Finally he saw a hill, came down upon it and began to claw the surface, making a small mound of earth. When he had finished this he took flight and circled above it, crying out and shaking the whole terrain. As the earth moved the mound began to crumble, and a figure, having the same form as the stone man, was left where the mound had been.

The Raven came close and began beating his wings, causing a great wind to enter into the nostrils of the lifeless man. The being began to breathe and a spirit entered the new creature. The man opened his eyes and stood up, looking first into the heavens at the Raven, then around him at the rest of the vast creation. Then he sat down, for he was greatly troubled and did not know where to go or what to do.

Carver Harry Shavings of Mekoryuk, on Nunivak Island in the Bering Sea, displays a traditional Nunivak "halo" mask. These masks are unique to the area and came into being — according to legend — when a hunter wandered into a cave and saw parts of all the game he'd killed floating in the air. Later he made a mask showing these disembodied parts, and the mask became a local tradition.

Again the Raven led man through all the land, testing his ability to travel. And the Raven saw that this man had no trouble at all, and he knew he would not have to create another.

But man could not be the only moving thing upon the great earth, and so it was that when the Raven came to a stream he dove into it, and when the Raven returned from the depths the man beheld in great wonderment that fish now swam in the waters. The Raven flew over the forests and cried out, and the man beheld animals. The Raven flew high into the skies and cried out again, and the skies were filled with thousands of birds.

Having seen what the great Raven had done, the man became afraid and fell upon his face and wept.

"Behold, you have walked upon this creation for but a few moments and already you begin to wonder," said the Raven.

The man said, "I am afraid, for I have seen your wondrous works and know that you are a god."

"I am a lover of life. And I have created you and all these things because I want this creation to live."

"Who am I?" asked the man.

"You are *Yup'piak* [Yup'ik], a true man. You are on my *nuna*, my earth. Your kind shall cover this land. Look and see all these things I have given you. Remember you have a spirit, and so do all these living beings upon this earth. Respect these spirits and a happy life will be yours. Go then over this *nuna* and seek a way of life, but beforehand follow the white tern, who shall lead you to your companion, a woman."

And the Raven rose into the sky and was lost in the heavens.

ᥱᥦᥩ

The Eskimos of the Yukon and the Kuskokwim river areas believe in a good spirit and an evil spirit. The good spirit is supposed to live in the higher regions where the Raven flies, and the old people would tell their children,

"Do not do anything bad, for he can look down and see you." The evil spirit had no name until the missionaries came, but the good spirit was called the Sky's Child.

Today it is acceptable to think that the western Eskimos came up the rivers from the seacoast in search of food because of population increases or because the coast was unproductive. Being from Bethel, however, I'm biased toward a legend we have here that could be as true as the more popular theory. Among the older people of the community it is said that during the time of great famine a young couple left their starving village in the north country in search of food and eventually found the Kuskokwim River, after traveling some time down the Yukon.

Every night while traveling down the Kuskokwim the couple sank their tiny fish trap into the water and one morning caught two small fish at a place across the river from where Bethel is today. It is possible that starving villages at that time heard about fish being caught in the Kuskokwim River and moved down here, starting new communities. In any case, the original settlement at Bethel was called Mumtrelegamut, the Village of the People with Many Fish Houses.

Perhaps the only true record of the lifestyle and habits of the original western Eskimo is the early missionaries' reports regarding their first encounters with the Natives. In 1883 Sheldon Jackson, a veteran Presbyterian missionary, schoolteacher and explorer, spoke before an association of Protestants in Bethlehem, Pennsylvania, and told of the pitiful condition of the Eskimos in the Kuskokwim Valley. The Moravian Church responded and in 1884 sent two men, Rev. Henry Hartmann and William Weinland, to pick a site for a mission station. That June the men found themselves at Mumtrelegamut, an important trading station. The missionaries' Bible text for that day was: "God said unto Jacob, Arise, and go up to Bethel, and dwell there; and make there an altar unto God, that appeared unto thee." (Gen. 35:1.) That explains the change in the name of the village.

The Eskimos advised the missionaries not to build a church on the ground they had selected, but the churchmen insisted on locating on the riverbank opposite the village. An old shaman got mad at this stubbornness and warned the Moravians, "The riverbank will eat away the ground, right out from under your church."

And it did. The church fell into the Kuskokwim River along with the mission house and vegetable gardens, but that didn't stop the Moravians, who simply rebuilt farther back and stayed.

However, an account by a missionary who visited the area in 1915 indicates that the Natives, in spite of the presence of the Moravians, retained their traditional ways. Ferdinand Drebert observed: "I praised the Lord for having . . . brought me a step closer to the fulfillment of my dreams: to be a missionary to primitive people. For although some of them had been baptised, they were quite primitive in their ways and some were still heathen. Their heathen customs and superstitions were in evidence everywhere. They still kept their heathen festivals and dances."

Today we still have some of those "heathen festivals and dances" and are working hard to keep them in a world where we cannot avoid being part of another culture.

Whatever the missionaries might say about us now, Bethel is the hub of a sizable area. As for the Yup'ik, the western Eskimo who lives in that sizable area, we seem to be doing all right, whatever the young people and old people may tell us about our origins.

Only some of the following Yup'ik villages are indicated on this map because of space limitations. However, all of these Native villages are included on the large pull-out map.

Akiachak	Manokotak
Akiak	Marshall
Alakanuk	Mekoryuk
Aleknagik	Mountain Village
Andreafsky	Naknek
Aniak	Napaimiut
Atmauthluak	Napaiskak
Bethel	Napakiak
Bill Moore Slough	Newhalen
Chefornak	New Stuyahok
Chevak	Newtok
Chuathbaluk	Nightmute
Chuloonawick	Nunapitchuk
Clarks Point	Ohogamiut
Crooked Creek	Oscarville
Dillingham	Paimiut
Eek	Pilot Station
Ekuk	Pitkas Point
Ekwok	Platinum
Emmonak	Portage Creek
Gambell	Quinhagak
Georgetown	Red Devil
Golovin	Russian Mission
Goodnews Bay	Saint Marys
Hamilton	Saint Michael
Hooper Bay	Savoonga
Igiugig	Scammon Bay
Kalskag	Sheldons Point
Kasigluk	Sleetmute
Kipnuk	South Naknek
Kokhanok	Stebbins
Koliganek	Togiak
Kongiganak	Toksook Bay
Kotlik	Tuluksak
Kwethluk	Tuntutuliak
Kwigillingok	Tununak
Levelock	Twin Hills
Lower Kalskag	Umkumiut

Previous page — Ice begins to form on the Yukon River and myriad side channels, lakes and ponds in October. This view of the flat, nearly treeless Delta is near Pilot Station, not far from the mouth of the Yukon.
(JOHN MCDONALD)

Below — Hagemeister Island, 24 miles long and largest in Bristol Bay, is southwest of the fishing village of Togiak. The economic lifeblood of Bristol Bay Yup'iks is the salmon, especially the sockeye that in a good year fill the bay and rivers that flow into it.

Right — Mrs. Simeon Bartman of Manokotak, a village on the Igushik River southwest of Dillingham, cleans salmon and sheefish, setting aside skeins of salmon roe.

"This has been awfully easy country to get along in until just lately," reminisced Paul Romie, long-time fisherman now retired to serve as postmaster at Ekwok. "Where else could you work just one month and live a whole year?"

Far left — Visitors to Saint Lawrence Island overlook the village of Gambell, with the Bering Sea and Siberia in the background. Most Saint Lawrence Islanders are Siberian Yup'iks, geographically (if not politically) close to Eskimos on Russia's Chukchi Peninsula. (YVONNE MOZEE)

Above — A musher and his team compete in the Bethel Winter Carnival race, held in January. Snowmobiles have largely replaced dog sleds for daily use, but the popularity of sled dog races has not waned. (JERRY HOUT)

Left — Center of commerce in the sprawling Yukon-Kuskokwim Delta is Bethel, near the mouth of the Kuskokwim River. Many supplies arrive at Bethel by barge — direct from the Lower 48 — or by jet from Anchorage, to be distributed to several dozen smaller villages in the region. Fishing, government employment and transportation-related jobs are important here. (JAMES BARKER)

Overleaf — The community of Clarks Point is strung out along the east shore of Nushagak Bay, 14 miles south of Dillingham. Like many other Yup'ik villages, Clarks Point relies heavily on commercial and subsistence fishing — especially the abundant sockeye salmon of Bristol Bay.

The Yup'ik world is resource rich and one of the last areas of Alaska to be exploited commercially.

Far left — Sockeye salmon enter Alexai Creek, part of the Newhalen River system, during a peak run in the fall of 1965. Runs in Bristol Bay fell off sharply after this photo was taken, bottoming out in 1973 and 1974, when the region was declared a disaster area. A strong recovery was made in 1977 and 1978, and the future looked considerably brighter for fishermen. (OLE MATHISEN, UNIVERSITY OF WASHINGTON FISHERIES RESEARCH INSTITUTE, REPRINTED FROM ALASKA GEOGRAPHIC®)

Left — A herd of musk ox head across the tundra on 40-mile-long Nelson Island between Baird Inlet and Etolin Strait, about 90 miles west of Bethel. (MYRON WRIGHT, REPRINTED FROM ALASKA GEOGRAPHIC®)

Below — Waterfowl and other birds return by the millions each spring, some nesting in the Bristol Bay and Yukon-Kuskokwim Delta areas, others continuing farther north to the High Arctic. These emperor geese were photographed at Nelson Lagoon, on the lower north side of the Alaska Peninsula. (ROBERT GILL JR., REPRINTED FROM ALASKA GEOGRAPHIC®)

The people along the Bering Sea coast live as traditionally as any Natives in modern-day Alaska. Nowhere else in the state, for example, do more villagers speak their original dialects than in the Yukon-Kuskokwim Delta.

Left — Henry Wuya, outside his fish house at Eek, 41 miles southwest of Bethel on the Eek River.

Below — Florence and Justin Ignatius and youngsters pose for a family portrait at Sheldon Point,

on the Bering Sea coast near the mouth of the Yukon River. Ignatius has a part-time job as janitor at the local health clinic, and he supplements his work with hunting and fishing. He is proud of the fact that he can support his family with his job and hunting, so he doesn't need to rely on food stamps.

Lower right — Martha Simon and her aunt, Emma Fallmoon, model walrus-gut raincoats at Quinhagak, on the Bering Sea coast south of Bethel.

Far left — The late Homer Apatiki of Gambell was highly skilled in engraving and carving walrus tusks. Ivory carving traditionally has been considered man's work, but today a small number of women have shown that they, too, are skilled at the craft.

Left — Nina Gozeva works with her neighbors to sew a new walrus skin onto the frame of a Yup'ik skin boat at Gambell. Saint Lawrence Islanders tried using modern boats but found they were more vulnerable and did not handle as well as skin boats in pack ice. The walrus skins are tough but rarely last more than two seasons of hard use.

Above — Senka Zauker Jr., of Sleetmute, displays a moose sinew net and a spear used to catch beaver. Both the net and spear are unique to this area of the Kuskokwim River.

Left — Susie Shavings of Mekoryuk, Nunivak Island, knits a scarf of soft and warm musk ox wool. The wool, or *qiviut*, comes from a herd established on the island in 1930 by the U.S. government and strengthened with animals from Canada.

"**Y**ou have to understand," reminds James Leonard, a Bethel welfare-eligibility worker, "that these people are terribly, terribly poor [by white cultural standards]. Nobody in the world can live on food stamps out here. Food stamps are based on Anchorage prices, and our prices are significantly higher.

"Subsistence hunting provides the protein. Food stamps at the store balance the diet. The kids going out to school have gotten used to white man's food. Won't eat enough Native food. The food stamps help. . . ."

114

Left — A clerk marks prices on items in the Alaska Commercial Company store at Kotlik, near the mouth of the Yukon River. Modern stores have come to many small villages, and some larger settlements even boast supermarkets. (JIM REARDEN, STAFF)

Below — Vegetables are sometimes worth their weight in gold in the Kuskokwim area because winter cold makes shipping them in bush planes risky. Traditionally Eskimo people here ate only summer greens for vegetables, balancing their diets the rest of the time by eating almost every useable part of their game animals, including stomach contents. Today Bethel, trading center of the area, features modern stores with good produce sections, but salads are still not a favored dish with Natives. (BARB KNAPP, REPRINTED FROM ALASKA GEOGRAPHIC®)

Yup'ik life today is a crazy-quilt mix of cultures and traditions where the tug of war still goes on between subsistence lifestyles and cash (or lack-of-cash) economy.

Upper left — Mr. and Mrs. Isaac Nick and their son "Monkey" prefer their old sod house to some of the newer, more expensive models in Akiachak. The thick sod makes excellent insulation — better than most modern homes — and the sod house is not too hard to keep warm in winter.

Left — New and old technologies: A truck collects honey buckets (raw sewage) from otherwise modern homes in Bethel.

Left — Tools of the subsistence hunter have become more sophisticated in recent decades. Powerful steel traps have replaced ancient snares, the outboard-powered skiff has largely displaced the kayak and *umiak*, and snow machines carry travelers across the winter land faster (if less economically) than snowshoes. And the fishing net on the roof of this cache is made of nylon that may never rot, unlike the old nets that were knitted with sinew. This scene is at Kotlik. (JIM REARDEN, STAFF)

Lower left — Cindy Olsen, 5, with a cabbage that shows the productivity of the rich soil and warm growing season at Ekwok, on the Nushagak River, about 70 miles inland from Bristol Bay.

Below — Anuska Nanalook of Manokotak with a pot full of *agutuk*, Eskimo ice cream made with berries, fat and sugar.

Right — Norma Silook of Gambell cuts slices of walrus skin and fat with an *ulu*, or Eskimo woman's knife. Norma, cook at the village school, also prepares standard American dishes required by the state for its subsidized school lunch programs.

"We had absolutely nothing," recalls Joe Friday of Chevak. "We took care of ourselves with what nature had to offer. We made use of everything and did not want. . . ."

Below — Women haul in nets along the shore of the Newhalen River, near the spot where it empties into Iliamna Lake, less than three miles from the village of Iliamna.

Right — Mrs. Tony Wassili braids flatfish to dry at Chefornak, using grass she has picked in the area to weave together the string of fish.

Left — Skiffs with "kickers" (outboards) line up along the riverbank at Bethel, largest Yup'ik community in the Yukon-Kuskokwim Delta. The photograph was taken at high tide in Brown Slough, Bethel's unofficial small-boat harbor. (GRACE MOORE)

Right — Quinhagak skiff fishermen line up to sell fish to a small tender near their village, on Kuskokwim Bay south of Bethel. (JAN AXELL)

Below — Bristol Bay gill-netters crowd the shoreline at dawn, awaiting the next commercial fishing opening. Bristol Bay is one of the world's largest spawning areas for sockeye salmon, and the brief commercial fishing season — from mid-June through July — brings a rush of employment for local villagers and Outside fishermen and cannery workers. (J. SCOTT CARTER, REPRINTED FROM ALASKA GEOGRAPHIC®)

Above — Dillingham is the largest settlement in the Bristol Bay region and the fastest growing. The population tripled (to almost 1,300) between 1970 and 1978.

Right — Quinhagak is at the mouth of the Kanektok River, facing Kuskokwim Bay and the Bering Sea.

Left — Clothes hang to dry at Igiugig, on the Kvichak River one mile from the west end of Iliamna Lake. The Kvichak flows from Iliamna Lake into Bristol Bay.

Below — The village of Mekoryuk, on Nunivak Island, is the only permanent settlement on the 1,600-square-mile island. Originally there were small villages all around the coastline but with the introduction of government schooling and reindeer herding — an important source of food and cash today — most families moved to the larger village of Mekoryuk. The island also is known for its herd of musk ox, transferred to the island in 1930.

123

*P*eople who elected to live in Bethel Heights, the low-income housing development, longed to return to their tar paper shacks after the Bethel Heights houses sagged, cracked and came apart at the seams during the first winter.

Left — Hooper Bay, a moderately large (population 600) Yup'ik community along the Bering Sea coast, faces a common dilemma: As the settlement has grown, game — necessary for a healthy subsistence economy — has become scarce. Jobs have not been easy to come by, and the result has been a rush of welfare payments. The cycle is too familiar, but nevertheless villagers at Hooper Bay are proud of their community and are determined to hold onto old traditions as much as possible.

Above — Kwethluk, above Bethel on the Kuskokwim River, has a modern housing development and electricity, if not plumbing. There also is a large village store, although subsistence hunting and fishing still are important.

Right — The old houses made of logs with sod roofs were once common at Koliganek and many are still in use, either as permanent homes or downgraded to fishing camps.

Pp Qq Rr RR Ss Tt Uu UU Vv Ww WH
1 ataasiq
2 maalghuk
3 pingayut
4 estamat
5 tallimat
6 aghvinlek
7 maaghraghvinlek
8 pingayuneng inglulek
9 estamaneng inglulek
10 qula
1 2 3 4 5 6 7 8 9 10
11 12 13 14 15 16 17 18 19 20
21 22 23 24 25 26 27 28 29 30
31 32 33 34 35 36 37 38 39 40
41 42 43 44 45 46 47 48 49 50
51 52 53 54 55 56 57 58 59 60
61 62 63 64 65 66 67 68 69 70
71 72 73 74 75 76 77 78 79 80
81 82 83 84 85 86 87 88 89 90
91 92 93 94 95 96 97 98 99
books

Schools, curriculums and teaching methods have been changing fast in Eskimo villages. There are more local schools, and bilingual education is becoming the rule, rather than the exception.

Left — Youngsters enter this school at Savoonga, on Saint Lawrence Island, speaking Siberian Yup'ik and they usually have little or no background in English. Teacher George Noonawock conducts a bilingual-education class.

Lower left — Lena Bell, 4, proudly displays a painting she made in her Head Start class at Hooper Bay. Lena is the daughter of Joseph and Margaret Bell. (VALERIE JENNINGS)

Below — A community college class tackles a project in the Bethel library. Interest in education has boomed in Bethel, largely due to a college program in which teaching takes place in Yup'ik and TV classes are offered for those who can't get to town.

"The roots are still alive," says Josh Weiser, discussing the gap between older and younger Eskimos, "but it's painful not to see young people pick up on the culture. They go to high school and learn to like white sugar. . . . How does it feel to be stuck in the middle?"

*T*eacher Don Kinsey reports the older Eskimos at Aleknagik are concerned about the younger generation.

"Samuel Wassilie came in one day," Kinsey says, "worried about the young kids going off on snowmobiles because the machines often break down. So he took the whole class out in the woods, cut down a tree and showed them how to make snowshoes for an emergency."

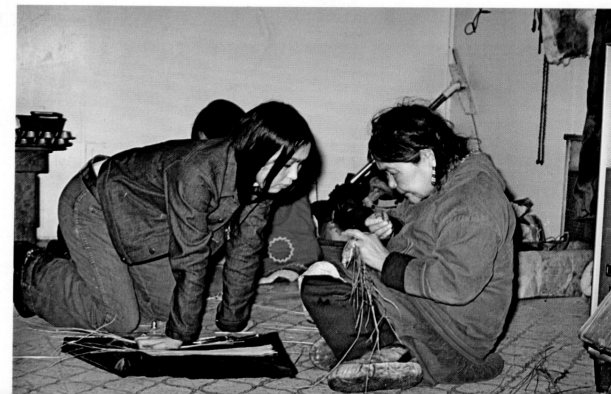

Left — Trapping is one of the few sources of cash income for the people of Koliganek. Pete Petla Jr. was excused from school and given class credit for a trapping assignment when he went trapping with his father, who holds a stretched beaver skin.

Lower left — Francis Usugan, a skilled basket maker from Toksook Bay, teaches a young student how to weave dried grass. The lesson is part of a cultural heritage program designed to teach urban youngsters skills they can normally absorb only in remote areas.

Below — Gambell and Savoonga, on Saint Lawrence Island, kept their 1.2-million-acre reservation rather than take part in the Alaska Native Claims Settlement Act. This left the two Bering Sea villages without working capital, but the local council members have been progressing without government funds.

Lower right — Philip Guy of Emmonak, at the time of this photo a member of the powerful "bush block" that has effectively represented rural Alaska since the early 1970's, at his desk in the state legislature.

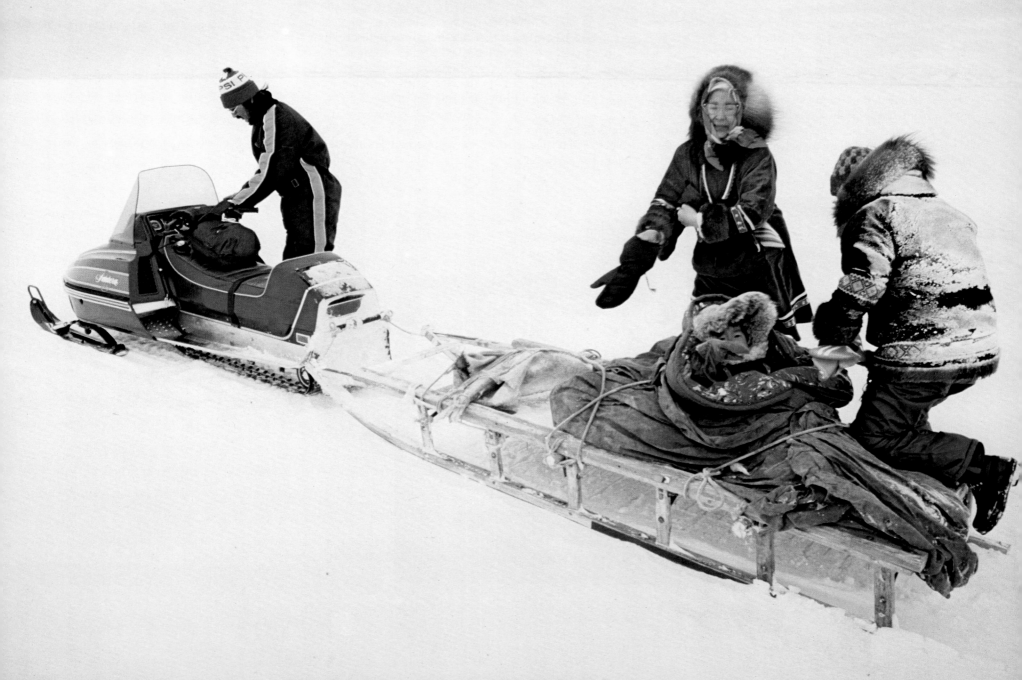

Left — Winter limousine service in the bush. Just one of six snow machines sent to transport Kotlick villagers to Stebbins-hosted potlatch, driver Ted Katcheak stops to give his passengers a rest near Point Romanof, halfway between Kotlick and Stebbins on Norton Sound. (JAMES SIMMEN)

Above — Tom Chythlook of Aleknagik uses this traditional skin boat when he is duck hunting, because it is quiet; but when he is in a hurry, or when he is out fishing, he uses a skiff with a 50-horsepower engine.

Right — In wintertime some Alaskan distances can be shortened. In this case a "road" has been plowed along the frozen Kuskokwim River from Bethel to the neighboring village of Kwethluk, where cab driver John Lieb is taking a fare.

Overleaf — Shallow-draft river workboats and barges line the Bethel waterfront, a busy place in summer when shipments come from Outside and the fishing season is under way.

Above — Pius Akaran, left, postmaster at Kotlik, accepts a planeload of mail — mostly food shipped by parcel post. (JIM REARDEN, STAFF)

Right — Herbie Jacobs, bilingual disc jockey for the Bethel radio and television station KYUK, sits at the controls. There are more than 50 villages in this region and many of the Eskimos speak only Yup'ik. For several years KYUK has broadcast programs in both Yup'ik and English — a vital service during the Alaska Native land claims struggle, when it was important to bring news and announcements to all of the region's people quickly.

Far right — This dish antenna at Kotlik is just another communications improvement. Aimed at a satellite, which is part of an earth-station telephone system, long-distance calls from Kotlik are beamed to the satellite and bounced down to the rest of the world. (JIM REARDEN, STAFF)

"W̶e old people," said Dan Joe Sr., of Nightmute, "may not understand a word of English, but our children understand. We old people will not be here long, but our children are just beginning to live and they learn from radio and TV."

Left — During the years when Russia owned Alaska, missionaries of the Russian Orthodox Church were energetic and influential travelers. This church at Igiugig, on the Kvichak River, shows that their influence remains. Similar scenes are found throughout the region.

Below — Quinhagak villagers attend an evening service at the Moravian Church — an important religious group in the Yukon-Kuskokwim Delta region.

Traditional Saint Lawrence Island houses were so warm that both men and women went topless indoors.

"The missionaries talked us out of that," laments old-timer Phillip Campbell. "Now they tell me everybody's doing it in the States."

Left — One of the modern touches at Nightmute, on Nelson Island, is the passion for bingo, a game familiar to villagers throughout the Yup'ik region. Esther Dull tries her luck, playing several cards at a time.

Below — Men and women perform a ceremonial dance during a potlatch at Mountain Village, on the lower Yukon River, as dozens of villagers look on. (**HARRY M. WALKER**)

137

"We're poor, all right, but we've got more than most people. Our most important asset is our land and our culture, and we want to protect it come hell or high water."

—— Harold Napoleon
Yupiktak Bista

Carvers work in the *qasgiq* (fire bathhouse) at Tanunak on Nelson Island in the Yukon-Kuskokwim Delta.

ALEUT

People of the Aleutian Chain

By Lillie McGarvey

Whenever I come across a map of Alaska I feel outraged. The maps are out of perspective because they cut the Aleutian Islands in half, put them in a box, and place them in the Gulf of Alaska. The islands are not only situated in the wrong location but, in order that they take up less space, sometimes they are placed at the wrong angle.

The home of our Aleut people stretches about 1,200 miles in an arc where the Pacific Ocean meets the Bering Sea. This Aleut territory is generally referred to as the Aleutian Chain, which includes, in addition to the Aleutian Islands themselves, the Pribilof and Shumagin Islands and the western part of the Alaska Peninsula to just east of Port Moller. The eastern edge of the Aleut territory is *west* of Hawaii.

It is told that before the coming of the first Europeans, the Aleut people numbered over 20,000 strong. The population lived on all the habitable islands of the chain (some of which had several villages) and on the Alaska Peninsula. In about 1830 Father Veniaminov of the Russian Orthodox Church questioned whether the Aleut population had once been so high, implying

Lillie McGarvey was born and reared in the Aleutian Islands in the village of Unalaska at a time when many herring salteries were operating and the community was a going concern. Her mother was an Aleut who passed on to her children a deep respect for Aleut tradition and an understanding of their heritage. Her father came from another island—England.

McGarvey lived outside of Alaska and traveled widely in the 1940's during her wartime marriage, but after the war she returned to Alaska and became one of the early organizers of the Aleut League, an organization that helped pioneer for Native rights and was the forerunner of today's Aleut Corporation. Her major field of concern is health care, something sadly lacking in the Aleutian Islands at the time of her return, and she has served with distinction on both state and national boards for Native health as well as with local agencies.

This writing comes, in part, from a book that McGarvey was preparing on Aleut history.

Danny Boy Snigaroff, of Atka, fills a basket with halibut and other fish from the harbor near his home. The small village, on 55-mile-long Atka Island, is near the midpoint of the Aleutian Islands chain, about 120 miles northeast of Adak.

exaggeration by the Aleuts. This humane and compassionate priest, who eventually became the bishop of Russian America, probably could not bring himself to believe that the many atrocities of his fellow countrymen had reduced a formerly flourishing population to such an incredible extent in just half a century of "civilization."

Aleut history is filled with tragic family and community disruptions beginning from the day the first Russian discoverer set foot on this land. The Russians, in their greed for the rich fur treasures found on our remote and ruggedly beautiful islands, rapidly obliterated the way of life that had sustained the Aleut people.

The disruptions that began with the Russians have not ended. In my own lifetime, I have seen the end of four villages—and just on Unalaska, the island where I was born and where I grew up. The villages, abandoned by their last survivors, were Chernofski, Biorka, Kashega and Makushin. Although the village of Unalaska still survives, the present settlement is a far cry from the Aleut villages of the past. In addition, I have seen the loss of many Aleut community leaders and loved ones due to diseases and illnesses brought by outside contacts.

Anthropologist friends tell us that inhabitants of our islands have always been Aleut and that Aleuts have been here at least 8,000 years. The Aleutian environment contained everything our early people needed for their way of life—clothing, shelter and warmth, lots of food—so they had no reason to move. And the weather, although it can be quite stormy during any season of the year, played a major role in the richness of the Aleut lifestyle. The climate is quite mild in comparison with the rest of Alaska.

It is very difficult to learn everything about a people—the language, customs and culture—just by reading written reports. What makes all those things meaningful to us of Aleut descent is the *remembering*. Remembering stories of the past that we heard in childhood from the elderly of our villages. Remembering the clothing, boats, skis, traps, toys, weapons, tools and baskets that we have seen or used and know are authentic remnants of the past. Remembering some of the practices or customs that were used on special occasions and were carryovers from ancient tradition. Remembering how the soft, beautiful language was spoken; how it sounded in a roomful of people with everyone talking at once; how it sounded in the open when a hunting trip was concluding and the village people were gathering to receive their

Remembering how the soft, beautiful language was spoken; how it sounded in a roomful of people with everyone talking at once; how it sounded in the open when a hunting trip was concluding and the village people were gathering to receive their shares of the bounty.

Xenia and Gabe Stepetin talk about life in their village of Saint Paul, in the Pribilof Islands. Stepetin was one of the early Aleut leaders in the drive for organization of villages.
(SUSAN HACKLEY JOHNSON)

shares of the bounty. Remembering the smell of various concoctions used by our people for medicine—and the taste of a few of them!

Even though this remembering by one individual may seem insignificant, it is important, because it adds to the complete picture of the Aleut heritage.

When I was very young my family lived on Dutch Harbor, which is an island in Unalaska Bay, but when I reached school age, in about 1930, we moved across the bay to Unalaska. The first house we lived in there we shared with Vassily, an elderly Aleut-Russian man of the Shaishnikof family. Vassily, who spoke mostly Russian along with a little English, still used some of the old Aleut and old Russian ways in his day-to-day activities.

I remember seeing him in the *bidarka* he owned and kept in the warehouse. I think it was the last skin boat in Unalaska. He used it when he went to his summer camp in English Bay, where he often dressed in his *kamleika* [gut raincoat] and skin boots. He must have been in his late 70's, but he was still strong. He would stay at that camp for weeks at a time, and at summer's end he would bring back potatoes and other vegetables from a garden he always kept at the camp along with salmon that he dried and smoked there.

In winter Vassily used Aleut-type skis that he made by tightly stretching and drying hair-seal skins over wooden forms. These skis were wider, and worked better, than regular skis because the sealskins were attached so the hairs would dig into the snow and serve as a brake when Vassily was going uphill; when he went downhill they helped him slide—no ski wax necessary! Vassily trapped in the winter, using these skis and using traps and snares that he had made himself.

I remember the old ivory snuffbox that Vassily carried in his pocket and kept dipping into. And I remember the heavy glass tumbler that held his tea. He would put a sugar cube between his front teeth and sip his tea through the sugar, first pouring the steaming liquid into a saucer and blowing on it. It amazed me that he never seemed to wet his big mustache when he did this.

Our close neighbors at that time were Katie and John Goldof. They were a childless couple and they wanted to adopt me, but my parents would not hear of it. I was permitted to spend considerable time with them, though, often staying overnight or even two nights if the weather got terribly stormy. John had attended the old Russian school in Unalaska until it closed and he apparently got the equivalent of a high school education. He used to tell me many things about the little village where he first lived, an hour's boat trip from Unalaska. Sometimes when I was at his house John's friends would come to sit and talk about old times, and John would explain to me things I did not understand.

I remember hearing them talk of *barabaras* and the kind of life that people lived in them. The structure and design of the *barabaras* naturally fostered a close relationship among Aleut families. Each family unit occupied a niche within the *barabara*: the elders occupied one spot; parents and their married offspring occupied other sections; and in addition there were special niches for small children, for storage and for trash. According to John's friends, these dwellings were uniformly wide—about 20 feet— but they varied in length from 20 to 50 feet. A family could lengthen a *barabara* according to need.

Such an Aleut home was constructed by first excavating a rectangular base for the floor, deep enough so that the floor and the bottom half of the walls were largely below ground level. The portion of the walls above ground level and the roof were made of thick sod supported by driftwood or whalebone frames and rafters. Sometimes windows were made of translucent sealskin. The entrances to Aleut homes found at archaeological sites required ladders, but in the later *barabaras* that John Goldof talked about the entrance to a house would be at the end of a long corridor that served to break the wind. The door of a house consisted of grass matting or skin flaps over an opening. Such a house was ideal for the setting, keeping occupants dry from the frequent rains, warm at all times, and snugly sheltered from the high winds peculiar to the area. The ground in the region does not freeze, so the mud floors were warm enough so that residents could go barefoot. These sturdy houses also withstood the numerous earthquakes that occur year-round in that locality.

There were no *barabaras* left in my village when I was growing up, but there were some abandoned ones not far away. The chief of Attu, Mike Hodiakof, who used to visit my mother, talked about the *barabaras* still in use in his village. I used to play with his daughter and son and I still have a picture of the family in front of a *barabara* at Attu. It was modern, though, built of sod and half underground, but with a glass window!

Although Unalaska looked up-to-date in those days, most of us still lived by subsistence hunting because we didn't have much money for store-bought food and we had no refrigeration for what food we did have. The men hunted every week, and fishing was important. One of the mainstays of our diet was seal meat and seal oil; others were salmon—fresh, dried or smoked—and codfish. I remember particularly one dish we used to eat: codfish stomachs stuffed with liver. And, of course, one of the favorite food items of most Aleuts is *lusta*—salted fur-seal flippers.

We still used wild plants for food and for medicine. Once my brother got so sick he had trouble breathing and grew too weak to cough. The Bureau of Indian Affairs doctor gave him up; said he was dying. But the chief's wife mixed some goose grease with herbs and fed it to my brother and within two hours he was breathing normally again and eating soup. Another time ulcerated sores that my father got from varicose veins in his legs were cured when the chief's wife wrapped the sores in a poultice of stewed herbs. I remember my grandmother using one particular plant for drawing out boils, for infections and for curing fish poisoning, and using another plant for controlling bleeding. I remember the taste of a laxative made from one plant and the concoction used for diarrhea made from still another.

I remember the great chief of Unalaska, Alexei Maronovich Yatchmenef, who died when I was away from the village to begin high school in 1937. There were chiefs in other villages on the island, too, and on all the other islands. But Alexei was the main chief and everyone went to him for counsel. His home always seemed to be filled with people, and we children were allowed to sit and listen. He always acknowledged each one of us and we felt special whenever he directed questions or conversation to us.

Unalaska, on an island of the same name, developed into the commercial center of the Aleutians in the 19th century, during the days of the Russian-American Company. The Russian Orthodox Church still exerts a strong influence here, as elsewhere throughout old Russian America.

Alexei's oldest son married a woman from another village and moved there because of better employment conditions. The two remaining sons died before Alexei did, and the men chosen as chiefs to succeed him were not strong leaders. So with Alexei Yatchmenef passed the organization that was so strong in our Aleut community. And then all organized Aleut governments collapsed under the disruption of World War II.

After the bombing of Unalaska and Dutch Harbor, military authorities evacuated all Aleut people from the villages west of Unimak Island and from the Pribilofs and sent them to various remote locations in Southeastern Alaska for the duration of the war. When, at war's end, the evacuated people returned to the Aleutian Chain, most of their homes were in shambles from looting and destruction by navy and army personnel who had been hard-pressed to find something constructive to do with their spare time. However, many of our people did not return to their villages. Some had died and some stayed in Southeastern Alaska for employment opportunities, school, marriage or hospitalization for tuberculosis. My grandmother and an aunt were among those who perished many miles away from their island homes.

The governments of the villages east of Unimak had been disrupted early in the century by the establishment of salmon canneries and the fishing industry. Many Nordic seamen were attracted by fishing opportunities in this relatively newly discovered territory and decided to stay. They married local women and became part of the communities. By the time World War II came along, many of these men had prospered and owned their own fishing boats, which they were now able to contract to the army and navy for patrol duty and cargo hauling. The people in those eastern Aleut villages were not evacuated but instead were permitted to remain. With fishing as an economic foundation, these communities underwent many rapid changes and became less and less

Aleut. Instead of speaking Aleut, the people there began to speak English, some with a Norwegian accent. In all of the schools, teachers, frustrated with a language they could not fathom, forbade their pupils to speak Aleut. And in some of our villages now the Aleut language is not used by the younger generation; they do not even understand it.

❧

Father Veniaminov believed that it was easy for the Aleuts to accept the religion that the early Russian conquerors forced upon them because the Aleuts already had a similar religion. And it is easy to understand why he thought that. In pre-Russian days our people, surrounded by many wonders of nature, worshiped, in their way, a deity who had the power to make mountains steam or erupt; the earth shake and sometimes crack; the wind blow so strong that a man could not stand up against it. This deity caused the sun to shine and give warmth and light, the moon and stars to light the darkness and aid navigation, the ocean to rise in angry waves or lie smooth as glass, the grass and flowers to grow lush and profuse, and plants and berries to provide food. And the deity provided a bounty so that Aleuts never starved. Some of the early Russians reported they found the Aleuts starving, but they probably thought that because the Aleuts ate concoctions the Russians were not familiar with and would not even try.

With the passing of time our old way of life has gone and many of our old customs have been forgotten. There is no one left of those who knew the old songs and dances and ceremonies that were used before the coming of the Russians.

Within very recent times the Alaska Native Claims Settlement Act has given the Aleut people a means of coming together in a common effort. We hope that now it will be possible to change the outlook of our

population from a dying race's despair to an outlook of
hope. Now that we have an economic base we can
develop our region, which is rich in natural resources.
We have the opportunity to build a business through
which we can prosper; we can enter and participate in
the mainstream of modern American society. We will
benefit individually and collectively.

Many Aleut people believe this opportunity can also
bring us closer together as a distinctive cultural and
ethnic group. And in coming together we
can remember and maintain the good
things from our past and build and
perpetuate a future that will not
only sustain us economically
but culturally as well. Then
we will always be able to be
proud that we are Aleuts.

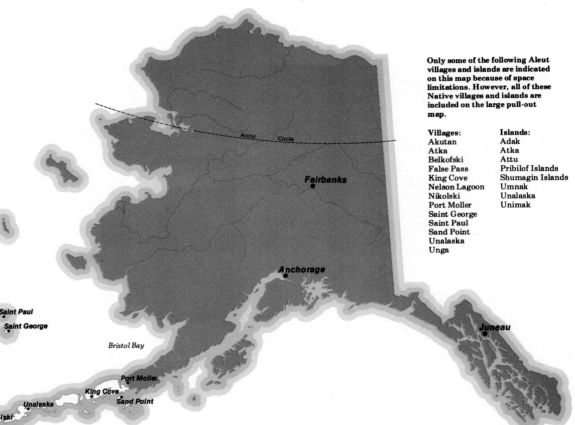

Only some of the following Aleut
villages and islands are indicated
on this map because of space
limitations. However, all of these
Native villages and islands are
included on the large pull-out
map.

Villages:	Islands:
Akutan	Adak
Atka	Atka
Belkofski	Attu
False Pass	Pribilof Islands
King Cove	Shumagin Islands
Nelson Lagoon	Umnak
Nikolski	Unalaska
Port Moller	Unimak
Saint George	
Saint Paul	
Sand Point	
Unalaska	
Unga	

The Aleutians breed some of the least inviting weather in the world. Although winter temperatures rarely fall below zero, the summer is short. Blinding snow and rain squalls are common, and unpredictable winds are a fact of life. Hundred-knot williwaws may suddenly roar out of the mountain passes onto the bays without warning, and thick clouds and fog — here seen blowing through Unalaska Bay — are taken for granted by residents. But the weather isn't always bad; the sun can shine brightly, and a surprisingly warm and clear day can bring cheer to the islands, making the rugged landscape inviting and beautiful. (SALLY BISHOP)

Villages of the Aleutians are small and far-flung, from each other and from the main body of Alaska.

Opposite — Sand Point is one of the more prosperous of the Aleut villages, with a large cannery that packs crab and salmon. The village is on Popof Island, in the Shumagin Islands group, off the south coast of the Alaska Peninsula . . . and for that reason not always considered part of the Aleutian Chain.

Upper left — West of Unalaska Island lies the island of Umnak, with the village of Nikolski set at the edge of a fine bay on the Bering Sea coast. Near the village is a sheep ranch that originally belonged to Outside interests, but title to the land passed to the villagers with the Native Claims Settlement Act. Like other villages, Nikolski faces the problem of a lack of jobs. Most men must work away from the island to support their families. Some go to the Pribilofs to help with the annual seal harvest, but most work in crab canneries at Unalaska.

Lower left — Young berry pickers head back to Atka village, just ahead of an approaching storm. Destroyed by the U.S. Navy in 1942 to deny facilities to the enemy, Atka was rebuilt after the war by Atkans and villagers from Attu. (The government refused to let the Attus resettle their farthest-west settlement in the Aleutian Chain, arguing that the distance would make it difficult for government agencies to take care of them there.)

Overleaf — The village of Saint Paul, in the Pribilof Islands — north into the Bering Sea from the main body of the Aleutians — perches on a bluff beside a wide, black sand beach. Saint Paul is the largest settlement in the isolated Pribilofs and the people now maintain a relatively high standard of living based on employment with the government-run fur seal industry. In earlier days the Aleuts were paid only a miserly ration of food and given poor housing for their labor. Now they receive a good wage and civil service benefits. The Native population here is descended from Aleuts transported to the Pribilofs by Russians to collect furs. (SUSAN HACKLEY JOHNSON)

Left — It was the valuable fur of the sea otter that first attracted white men to the Aleutians and Alaska, and led to formation of the Russian-American Company. The sea otter population was seriously depleted under Russian rule and the slaughter continued unabated after Alaska became a United States territory. Finally, just after the turn of the century when the sea otter was close to extinction, all hunting was stopped. Today the sea otter has come back strongly, but it remains a protected species. (ROBERT STENSTROM)

Below — Fur seals on Saint George Island in the Pribilofs. All killing of fur seals on Saint George was stopped in 1973 to allow a 10-year study of the animals. The Pribilofs' fur seal herd is the largest in the world, with more than a million animals in residence during the mating season.

Right — Aleuts herd together bachelor bulls, dispatching them with single blows from lengthy clubs. The clubbers are followed immediately by "stickers," who minimize suffering by thrusting a knife through the heart. The workers are sensitive to criticisms that are often voiced against the seal harvest, pointing out that no baby seals are killed, and that experts have found their method is probably the best and most humane.

(JOHN AND MARGARET IBBOTSON)

Left — Bells peal as a funeral procession leaves the church at Saint George and winds up the hill toward the cemetery. Aleut parents of children who have left the islands always hope their sons and daughters will come home, but too often they come this way — to be buried. Constantine Gromoff died in Chicago attempting to rescue an elderly woman he did not know from an apartment fire. The Russian Orthodox priest who led the service was Elory Gromoff, father by adoption of the brave young man.

Below — Andronik Kasevarof, Father Elory Gromoff and Christopher Malorausky officiate in the Russian Orthodox church at Saint George. When the Russians occupied the Aleutians they had a devastating impact — the Natives were forced to learn the Russian language, and many cultural traditions, including their music and dances, were lost. To a surprising degree, the Russian Orthodox Church filled the void and became a substitute for their disappearing culture. Today the church remains an important part of everyday life for the Aleuts.

Right — Aleuts attend a service in the Russian Orthodox church at Atka, a replica of the one destroyed in World War II.

"The Czarist Russian conquest of the proud, independent sea hunters was so devastatingly thorough," wrote linguist Richard Geoghegan, "that tribal traditions, even tribal memories, were almost obliterated. The slaughter of the majority of an adult generation was sufficient to destroy the continuity of tribal knowledge which was dependent upon oral transmission."

Left — Atka people fish year-round for halibut and cod and enjoy rich salmon runs in the fall. Their climate is rainy, however, and rare is the weather here that allows for the successful drying of fish. Here Vera Nevzeroff and Millie Prokopeuff take advantage of a clear evening to cut salmon for drying after losing an earlier batch to rain.

Below — In 1912 a Washington State-based firm built a cannery at King Cove and hired Natives from nearby villages to pack for them. Eventually a number of Aleuts settled at the site, intermarrying with Scandinavian fishermen and founding a strong community. Today the cannery, now owned by the Bristol Bay Native Corporation, is one of the most modern in the United States and the fleet of local fishermen does well indeed.

*I*slanders have occasional run-ins with conservation-minded tourists.

"We aren't going to come to the Pribilofs any more," one visitor warned Dorothy Shabolin, Saint Paul hotel housekeeper, "because we hear you Natives eat the birds."

"Well," responded the incredulous Mrs. Shabolin, "what the hell do you have on your table at Thanksgiving?"

Left — Horned puffins perch on a ledge hanging over the Bering Sea — one of many bird species found in the Pribilofs. (TIM THOMPSON)

Above — A sheep ranch near the village of Nikolski, on Umnak Island. In the background, behind the shearing shed and other outbuildings, is a snow-covered volcano, Mount Vsevidof, which rises to nearly 7,000 feet.

159

Above — Air transportation is crucial in the Aleutians, where often, if the plane doesn't arrive, you don't go! The major commercial air carrier in the Aleutians is Reeve Aleutian Airways, founded by Bob Reeve, a pioneer bush pilot who started the airline (there was little competition for the route) at the end of World War II.

Right — Atka, one of the most remote settlements in the United States, has been without regularly scheduled air service for years. Early in 1979, after three months wthout mail, the U.S. Public Health Service chartered a plane to fly in supplies for construction of sewer and water systems . . . and arranged to bring in some long-awaited mail, as well.

Left — Larry Dirks and his wife Cathy sort mail at the Atka post office. The village lacks a post office and scheduled transport is still a problem.

Below — High school students at Saint Paul in the Pribilofs produce their own TV news show, learning current media techniques. The village has a school radio, single public telephone, Public Service Health radio (with a direct link to Anchorage), communications satellite link and regular TV reception; local residents communicate with CB radios. (SUSAN HACKLEY JOHNSON)

Next to the coming of the Russians in the 18th and 19th centuries, World War II was the greatest upheaval experienced by the Aleut people. In June 1942, Japanese carrier planes bombed the military base at Dutch Harbor, then seized Attu, the westernmost island in the Aleutian Chain, and Kiska, halfway between Adak and Attu. Aleuts on Attu were interned in Japan for the duration of the war and only about half survived. The remaining Natives of the Aleutians were evacuated, most of them to Southeastern Alaska. At that time the United States believed that the Japanese might use the Aleutians as stepping stones to launch an invasion of North America's mainland, and there was a massive military build-up on the islands. The U.S. Navy built substantial bases at Kodiak, Dutch Harbor and Adak. Small airstrips were hastily constructed on many islands and lonely squadrons of Army Air Force P-38 fighters were distributed about to face what were probably the worst flying conditions of any theater of war. Submarines operated out of Dutch Harbor, and battleships, heavy cruisers and an occasional carrier played hide-and-seek through fog and snow squalls with the Japanese navy.

As it turned out, the Japanese move into the Aleutians was mainly a ploy to split the American forces. In 1943, U.S. troops made a landing at Massacre Bay on Attu and, after a bitter and bloody battle, ended the Japanese occupation. On Kiska, the Japanese forces secretly withdrew by transport in the fog, avoiding a confrontation.

Even now, many years after the event, the remains of war are strewn about the islands — grounded, rusting ships, wood barracks, collapsing Quonset huts, abandoned airstrips, rotting piers, lonely dugouts and observation posts with no one to look out on the deserted sea. The war in the Aleutians may have been a false alarm — except for a few traumatic months — but for the Aleuts it was devastating. Many died in Southeastern Alaska and others, having lost nearly everything, decided not to return to their ruined villages. But many others did go back, and have courageously rebuilt their disrupted lives.

Left — The cliffs and mountain slopes surrounding Dutch Harbor are pockmarked with small dugouts, observation posts and shelters. Many seem almost inaccessible, and serve to remind visitors how desperate those early days of World War II were.

Above — A Coast Guard turbine-powered cruiser visits Adak Island during a patrol in the Aleutian Islands. The high-speed ships have been used to discourage foreign fishing fleets in United States waters. (CHARLES CRAIGHEAD)

Opposite — Lupines grow up around an old Quonset hut, one of several remnants of a submarine base built during World War II at Finger Bay, Adak Island. (FLOYD CUMMINGS)

Above — Workers rebuild an older house in Atka. This home was built following World War II, and has survived batterings from incessant Aleutian storms.

Right — Caribou antlers decorate a modern home at Sand Point. This home, as up-to-date as most homes found in big-city suburbs, is in sharp contrast to houses found in most other Aleut villages.

Opposite — Fred Drukoff gives his corrugated-iron roof a fresh coat of paint while his wife, Anna, hangs the laundry on a rare cloudless and sunny day at Nikolski. The only thing normal is the wind — note the blowing clean clothes.

Left — Maggie Smith of Belkofski, on the southwest coast of the Alaska Peninsula, braids a rug at the home of a friend in King Cove while waiting for a boat to take her back to her own village. It was a long wait — everyone was too busy fishing to make the 12-mile run in a hurry.

Below — Luke Shelikoff displays the rusted head of an old harpoon gun, found at the site of a long-closed whaling station at Akutan, one of the easternmost islands in the Aleutian Chain.

Right — Elizabeth Leftenkof, an Aleut youngster from Saint George, borrows the photographer's notebook.

Opposite — Augusta Dushkin, left, and Agnes Sovoroff get together for a cup of coffee inside the comfortable Dushkin *barabara*, or sod house, at Sandy Beach, near Nikolski. These houses, half above and half below ground, are warm and sturdy and will weather any Aleutian gale.

166

Fast-food chains have not yet invaded the Aleutians — many people still rely on a subsistence lifestyle and traditional recipes are the rule in most villages.

Left — Meat from caribou and seal hunts dries in an open shed at Sandy Beach, a summer camp near Nikolski. Although Nikolski is a modern village with a good store, Aleuts still must hunt and fish during the summer months.

Below — Lydia Dirks, of Atka, demonstrates the preparation of an Aleut favorite, fried bread. A staple originally introduced by the Russians, fried bread takes the place of toast, and also is sometimes served with sugar or jam as a dessert.

Right — Nikolski youngsters prowl a local stream for Dolly Varden.

Lower right — Despite having a cash economy — first resulting from a nearby whaling station, and since World War II from commercial fishing — the Aleuts of Akutan still gather a significant portion of their food from the sea. Mike Shelikoff does his share by collecting prickly sea urchins (called sea eggs by the Aleuts) at low tide. Their thin shells are cracked open and the rich, yellow meat is scooped out for eating. The flavor? Somewhat like raw oysters.

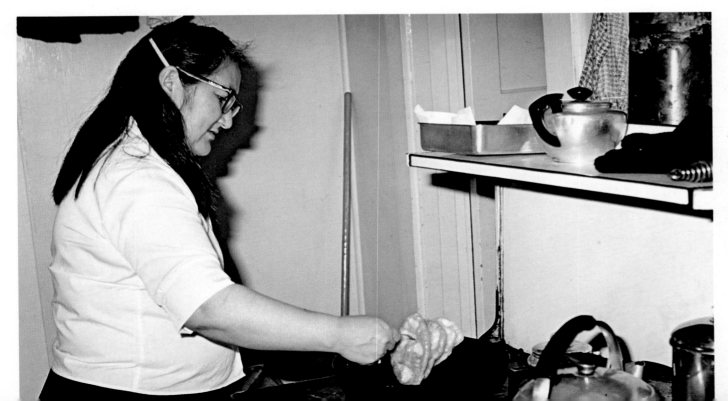

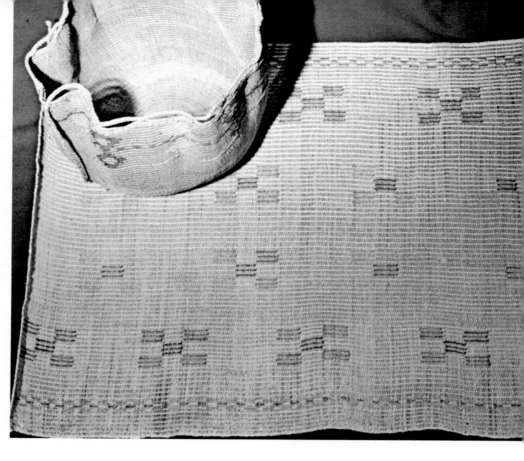

Above — Aleut Terenty Merculief of Saint George builds models of the boats once used by his ancestors. He uses seal throat to represent the skin that covered the framework of the prototypes.

Below — Vasha Golidorff, an Atka basket maker, works on a small and tightly woven model.

Right — Aleuts have long been known for their finely crafted weavings — baskets, mats and even clothes woven from the grass that grows so prolifically on the islands. (ALASKA STATE MUSEUM, JUNEAU)

Lower right — Aleut basket work is a fine art and the women of Atka are particularly skilled.

Below — Kathy Isacsen's small school at Squaw Harbor, Unga Island in the Shumagins, runs summer through early winter, as does the shrimp-processing plant around which this settlement is built. Originally settled by Aleuts, this country is now headquarters for Filipino cannery workers, with Aleuts still in residence but in the minority.

Right — Mike Dirks, an Atka artist, shows some of the woodcuts he has carved . . . after only two high school art courses at Adak, 120 miles away.

"When I came back to Atka after World War II, my buddy said, 'Why are you going back to the Aleutians? They say even the sea gulls are leaving there.' I told him I was going because it's peaceful and quiet here."

——————— Dan Prokopeuff
Atka

Sandy Beach, not far from Atka village, is a great place to fish for Dolly Varden, to beachcomb or just to be at one with nature. Not far from this shore Aleut women gather basket grass and on the horizon a myriad of islands offer shelter for little fishing boats.

KONIAG, CHUGACH, EYAK

People of the Gulf Coast

According to the linguist's map, the Gulf of Alaska, much of the Alaska Peninsula and Kodiak Island are all peopled by a group called the Suqpigaq, who are of Eskimo stock.

While this is a handy label for scientists, it is most confusing for the people, who have long thought of themselves as Aleut, traditionally warred against the Eskimo and held them in low esteem.

True, the language of these people is not the soft Aleut of the Aleutian Chain and varies from village to village around the gulf, but Aleut is more easily understood by these people than the harsh guttural language of their Eskimo neighbors and culturally the Suqpigaq have far more in common with the Aleuts, sharing not only lifestyle and tradition but a mutual devotion to the Russian Orthodox Church.

The Eyaks, of Athabascan stock, were assimilated by their coastal neighbors as their numbers decreased due to exploitation by whites who moved into their area at the turn of the century. These people have the distinction of being the last Indians discovered in North America (de Laguna, 1930) and the first to be decimated. Pure Eyaks number less than half a dozen today; the rest have been absorbed by the Suqpigaq.

Thus, despite original differences, the history of the gulf people is in the main quite similar. To write it we chose a Koniag, Karl Armstrong. — Lael Morgan

Kodiak, a large island rich in timber, fish and game, has served as headquarters for the Koniag people for centuries. Russians settled among the Koniag early, intermarried and converted them to the Russian Orthodox Church. Because of their acculturation to Russian ways, the Kodiak people had trouble qualifying under the Alaska Native Claims Settlement but eventually won their fight to be included.

THE KONIAGMIUT

By Karl Armstrong

"When the tide goes out the table is set." So goes an old Koniag saying which aptly reflects the unique ties of the Koniag people with the sea. It is unlikely that anywhere else a people has existed whose culture and lifestyle, especially before the arrival of Western white men, were so interwoven with the sea. It was the one environmental factor which completely dominated their culture and dictated their lifestyle.

Few people are aware that the Koniags, as a tribal entity, were numerically the largest Native ethnic group among the aboriginals of North America. While wholly reliable figures are unavailable, some sources estimate that at the time of the coming of the Russians the Koniag nation numbered more than 65,000 on their home islands of the Kodiak archipelago. More than 700 ancient village sites have been identified in the islands. Undoubtedly at least an additional several dozens were on the shores of Shelikof Strait, on the Alaska Peninsula, and along the Cook Inlet shorelines of the Kenai Peninsula, encompassing the English Bay and Port Graham settlements of today. Invariably these villages faced the sea—two known exceptions were villages along the shorelines of two large Kodiak Island lakes, Afognak and Karluk.

Virtually the entire coastline of their region—highly varied and longer than that of the lower 48 states—was used by the Koniag people as a source of food and clothing. Except when they gathered berries and a few other items used for food, medicines, weapons, fabrics or dyes, the Koniag people lived along the edge of the sea and rarely went more than a mile inland. They had little need to do so.

As with all people, the Koniags had legends about their origin and place in the order of things. The legends invariably related that all things, themselves included, were spawned by the sea. Tribal beliefs told them that they were the first and the special people, and while they tended toward a religious fatalism in which all things were considered equal, they reflected racial chauvinism by their tendency to regard themselves as more equal than other people with whom they came in contact.

Their outlook reflected a distinctive freedom of personal behavior, even in their handling of religious and governmental affairs. Undoubtedly their experience, in which survival was dependent more on individual action than group activities—and which was fostered by a generous and abundant sea where individuals could easily survive without much assistance from others—gave the Koniag people a noteworthy sense of personal freedom.

This sense of personal freedom was manifested by a unique lack of tribal government. There simply was no central government or authority. The Koniag nation, though mysteriously capable of maintaining communication among its many parts and able to present a unified response to outside threats, was really an extremely loose confederation of tribes, clans and bands—each with an apparent lack of leadership. However, this lack of centralized leadership did not create a lack of direction. The Koniags had learned to be responsive to leadership based on need, experience and activity rather than on a happenstance leadership based on meritless birth or mere unreasoning tradition. Thus, there was within any Koniag group a leader or chief for hunting seals, a leader for warlike activity, another for building a dwelling or a large boat and still others for other specific activities which might better be accomplished through a communal or group action.

Ridicule was a major tribal and personal instrument for discipline. Woe to the chief whose arrogance, vanity or ambition caused him to overstep and attempt to lead in any activity where another's superiority of performance was already recognized and established. In their essentially matriarchal society, the jeers and sneers of the women—who dominated tribal decisions, especially those involved with recognition of leadership roles—could result in ostracism and banishment, one of Koniag society's most feared and effective ultimate punishments for a miscreant individual.

Antisocial behavior considered dangerous to others was dealt with swiftly after careful deliberations by all adults. There rarely were crimes of greed or profit or even passion since most all good things in life usually were shared. Murder and other forms of physically dangerous behavior were perceived as insanity and inevitably resulted in execution by drowning. Thus, it was the sea which reclaimed life.

Shamanism was the usual form of religion. It recognized a Great Spirit which lived in all things, and other Good and Evil forces. The basic elements—earth, fire, water and air—were deified, and religious recognition was granted to animals and birds, especially sea birds. Aberrant behavior not considered dangerous to others would often result in the individual being recognized and treated as a shaman (witch doctor).

An honorary secret society with strong religious involvements by shamans was the Whale Killers Society, restricted to Koniag males who participated in the dangerous activity of hunting and killing whales. Only these members knew the secret of making the poison which was used on the tips of the harpoons used in the hunt.

Leading a mostly nomadic lifestyle, the Koniags traveled by one-man kayak or larger *umiaks*, using the sea as a highway. Despite a belief that one could only use, not own, land, water or air, the Koniags developed a powerful sense of identity and a dedicated feeling of community which applied to home villages, lands and

Karl Armstrong was born and reared in Kodiak. Son of the local marshal and a Woody Island woman of Aleut-Russian descent, he became a Merchant Marine seaman at 16, then enlisted in the U.S. Army Signal Corps during World War II. He was mustered out of the Army in 1948 and found work as a reporter for the *Anchorage Daily News*, where he eventually became city editor.

In 1957 he went home to work on the *Kodiak Daily Mirror*, saw it go down with the earthquake of 1964, started his own paper, and eventually returned to the *Mirror* as editor. He left the newspaper business in 1971 to serve as executive vice-president of Koniag, his regional Native corporation. Armstrong has long been an avid student of Aleut history.

waters. A "village" was more than a geographic location—it was first and foremost *people*.

The Koniags had close-knit families in which the very old and very young had niches and were given special love and esteem. In such extended families each individual had certain tasks. Sharing of all available resources was the practice of these families, clans, bands, groups and villages. In a society which had learned how to utilize all of the bounty of the sea, sharing and communal use was standard procedure and tended to provide a healthy mental climate in which tranquility was easy to achieve.

Because the Koniags were close-knit in their family and clan relationships, the elderly were honored and provided for with respect. The souls of ancestors were believed to return in children and so the young were loved and cared for by all adults. Children always accompanied their parents. The outstanding love of children was a commendable characteristic which, however, made the Koniags vulnerable to Russian invaders who made hostages of children in order to control the Koniags. The Russians found this effective and relatively few Russian women came to Russian America. This accelerated the taking of Koniag women as wives by the Russians—and the production of a new class of people to inherit the New World colony. This new class of people were called Creoles—or a closely related term which initially referred to the immediate offspring of unions between Russian males and Native women. The Creoles, who were said to be "half as good as a Russian and twice as good as a Native," quickly became the most numerous and successful group in the colony. It did not take long for this relatively pampered class (though without citizenship status, they were not taxed and were guaranteed education, land, farm animals and pensions) to decide that they were God's specially blessed and "twice as good as anyone." This racial arrogance persisted, and was especially pronounced among Creole youths selected by the church and sent to Russia for special education. While their ranks were decimated by diseases in Russia, those who survived became the leadership elite in Russian America upon their return as surveyors, ship captains, navigators, army officers and technicians. They were resourceful, skilled, competent and often cruel in their domination and rule. It is said that these Creole leaders, who organized and led the invasion and subjugation of the Calista people of the Kuskokwim and Yukon river valleys, were so ruthless that to this day the word Creole means "evil" to Calista descendants.

The Creoles were controlled by the government and were given numbers for identification. A Creole could move about, but was required to report his movements into or out of areas. The Creole centers were Afognak, Leisnoi, Kenai, and Ninilchik in the Gulf of Alaska region, Unalaska in the Aleutians and Sitka in Southeastern Alaska. Over the years, after they assimilated the few remaining Russians and after being themselves reabsorbed by the Natives, the Creoles no longer identified themselves as either Creoles or Natives, but called themselves Russians. Many of the early Russian influences, especially the Russian Orthodox Church, have been perpetuated and are apparent today. The Russians, few in number at the time of subjugation of the Koniags, brought with them as their vassel troops hundreds or possibly thousands of Aleut warriors from the previously conquered Aleutian Islands. The Russians did not differentiate between Aleuts and Koniags—always referring to any Native as "Aleut"—and most Koniags came to think of themselves as being Aleuts. Today some are surprised, and even sometimes annoyed, to be told that they are originally not Aleut at all, but rather Eskimo—the Koniagmiut.

The Koniag dwelling, called a *barabara*, made use of the most readily available materials: earth, rock and driftwood. Usually the home consisted of a main room in which food was prepared and consumed and a number of smaller sleeping rooms or alcoves around this main room. These *barabaras*, dug down into the earth or shale to a depth of three to six feet, were covered over with driftwood logs, which in turn were covered with layers of soil and sod. Seal oil and wick lamps provided light and heat within. Air vents—which also served as emergency escape hatches—were provided where needed for comfort and prudence.

There were always at least two other larger structures used communally. These were the *kashim* (meeting place) and the *banya* (steam bath). The *kashim* was used for community activities of a usually formal nature—usually by the Koniag males. (It should be noted, however, that the secretive Whale Killers Society had their own private meeting places, almost always natural caves where the bodies of great hunters and chiefs were kept mummified.) The *banya* was really the center of the community, less formal and more festive by nature. Used by the entire community without sex or age discrimination, it was the place where news and gossip was exchanged. No doubt here was where personal relationships were established and encouraged.

Though they had learned to live in a generally peaceful if wary relationship among their own numerous far-flung communities, the Koniags' experience in contact with Outsiders—especially the sometimes fierce and predatory Southeastern Alaska Tlingits—caused them to maintain a vigilant watch. When the Tlingits' great seagoing canoes hove into view, the Koniags would leave offerings of bags of down and feathers and ensconce themselves on their Refuge Rocks. Each Koniag community maintained places of sanctuary—usually small islets, little more than high rocks with steep over-hanging cliff shorelines, which were easily defended from enemies. These Refuge Rocks, always amply provisioned with food, water, and weapons, served the Koniags well from all their enemies

until the arrival of the Russians, whose shrapnel bombardment seiges decimated the closely massed Koniags trapped on their now vulnerable Refuge Rocks. The Koniags had perfected the use of wooden personal armor and wooden assault barricades and catapult weapons, but against the metal weaponry and gunpowder of the Russians, wood was useless. The Koniags were enslaved, and their proud culture soon withered under Russian rule.

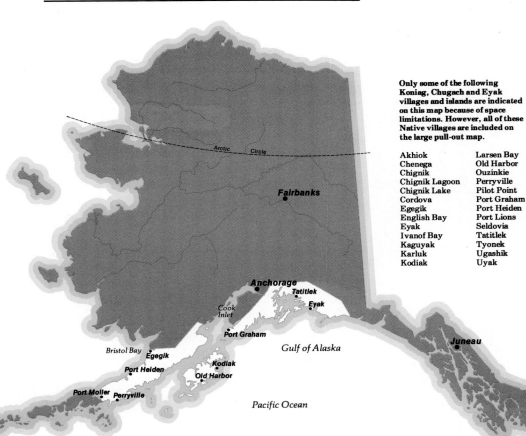

Only some of the following Koniag, Chugach and Eyak villages and islands are indicated on this map because of space limitations. However, all of these Native villages are included on the large pull-out map.

Akhiok	Larsen Bay
Chenega	Old Harbor
Chignik	Ouzinkie
Chignik Lagoon	Perryville
Chignik Lake	Pilot Point
Cordova	Port Graham
Egegik	Port Heiden
English Bay	Port Lions
Eyak	Seldovia
Ivanof Bay	Tatitlek
Kaguyak	Tyonek
Karluk	Ugashik
Kodiak	Uyak

The world of the Koniag, Chugach, and Eyak Natives, which generally faces the broad sweep of the Gulf of Alaska, begins on the north side of the Alaska Peninsula, where several villages are oriented to Bristol Bay. This is an ethnically confusing region — on the northern edge of the Koniag region and wedged between Aleuts to the southwest and Yup'ik-speaking people to the North. The influence of Russians and white fishermen, trappers and traders (many Natives here have Scandinavian last names) has further confused the picture.

Left — Egegik is one of a dozen Bristol Bay villages oriented to the red salmon fishery — a brief, often-furious midsummer season which draws hundreds of fishermen and cannery workers to the region. Egegik is near the mouth of the Egegik River, 38 miles southwest of Naknek.

Below — Philip Aletuk salts salmon for use later in the year. Subsistence is still important at Egegik — and other villages in the region — despite the cash that comes from commercial fishing.

Upper right — Silver salmon are neatly stacked in the fish buyer's cooler at Port Heiden, awaiting the next stage of processing.

Right — Mr. and Mrs. Paul Matsuno and their son David spend summers fishing at Ugashik on the Bristol Bay side of the Alaska Peninsula. In winter they live in Homer on the Kenai Peninsula, where their children can attend a modern school, but they consider Ugashik their true home.

The people of Kodiak Island have lived with disruptions — physical and cultural — for 200 years. First the Koniags were enslaved by Russians, their numbers reduced dramatically by violence and disease. Next came the 1912 eruption of Mount Katmai, on the nearby Alaska Peninsula, which covered the island with a black cloud of ash. When the cloud finally dissipated, Kodiak Island was buried under 18 inches of drifting pumice. Roofs collapsed, homes were destroyed and wildlife suffered greatly. Bottom fish, a staple food of the Natives, became nonexistent for some time. Finally, the 1964 Alaska earthquake and tidal wave wiped out the central area of the town of Kodiak, which has since been rebuilt — much of it with money from the Koniags.

Left — Dennis Murray, left, director of the Kodiak Senior Citizens' Center, chats with Moses Ewan Naumoff, one of the few citizens of Kodiak Island who claims to be 100% Aleut. (The ancestry of many Natives is "Creole," a mix of Russian, Koniag and, in some cases, Aleut.)

Below — Alex Zhoroff feeds the crows outside Kodiak's Russian Orthodox Church, the oldest parish in Alaska. Inside the church are hand-made brass metal works, beautiful paintings and icons dating back more than 150 years.

Above — Sven Haakonson, mayor of Old Harbor, in his office with Tina Pestrekoff. When the 1964 earthquake struck, he joined his people in an orderly evacuation and watched as his village was wiped out by a tidal wave.

Overleaf — Few Old Harbor villagers cared to return after seeing their homes erased by the 1964 earthquake-caused tidal wave, but their Russian Orthodox church and new school had been spared, and there was some pressure from government agencies to return and rebuild. Replacement homes were hastily built in tight rows with little regard for privacy, aesthetics or safety in the event of another tidal wave, but the Old Harbor spirit has proved strong — villagers have pulled together and have high hopes for future economic growth.

A laska Natives of mixed Russian and Native parentage were called Creoles and Karl Armstrong, vice-president of Koniag, Inc., researched their history when the Department of the Interior issued a definition of the word purely on a racial, rather than political, interpretation . . . assuming that all Russians married by Natives were white.

Not so, argues Armstrong. "The fact is that the Russians listed as 'Colonist' anyone who they sent to Russian America, and most of the persons sent here were Natives — Eskimos from Siberia and Aleuts from the Kamchatka Peninsula and the Komandorski Islands.

"In Kodiak you were never a Native. The Russians told us that a Creole was twice as good as a Native and only half as good as a Russian.

"In the beginning of the land claims we thought Creoles would not be permitted to be classed as Natives. They were almost a race unto themselves. At first I didn't think I'd qualify myself."

Right — A shrimp-processing line at the Alaska Pacific Seafoods plant at Kodiak, the second-busiest fishing port (in terms of dollar-volume of catch) in the United States. (WILLIAM B. MCCLOSKEY JR.)

Below — A modern cannery at Seldovia, a Native settlement where the Alaska Commercial Company established a fur trading station in 1894 and which became a transportation center as a result of the Cook Inlet gold rush the following year. (WILLIAM B. MCCLOSKEY JR.)

Opposite — A fishing boat moves along with the outgoing tide, entering 14-mile-wide Chiniak Bay after leaving sheltered Kodiak Harbor at the northeast corner of Kodiak Island. (GARY DOBOS, REPRINTED FROM ALASKA GEOGRAPHIC®)

Left — Until recently Ouzinkie teen-agers had to travel to Kodiak to attend high school. Now a special program provides for classes in the village. (Space was shared with elementary grades during the early stages — shown here — but better facilities are planned.)

Lower left — Victor Melovedoff was saved by a friend when the 1964 tidal wave struck his village of Kaguyak and overturned the skiff he was in with two others. Half-drowned and in shock, Melovedoff was dashed ashore by the wave and trapped among small ice floes near the bank. A friend, Max Shelikoff, came to his rescue, volunteering his own boots and socks, which Melovedoff wore during a dazed retreat to safety. Shelikoff followed him barefoot almost a mile.

Below — The size of the Ouzinkie "airport," like landing and takeoff facilities at most villages in the area, is affected by the state of the tide. Amphibians and floatplanes provide the bulk of the transportation between communities in the region. Ouzinkie is on the west coast of tiny Spruce Island, northeast of Kodiak Island.

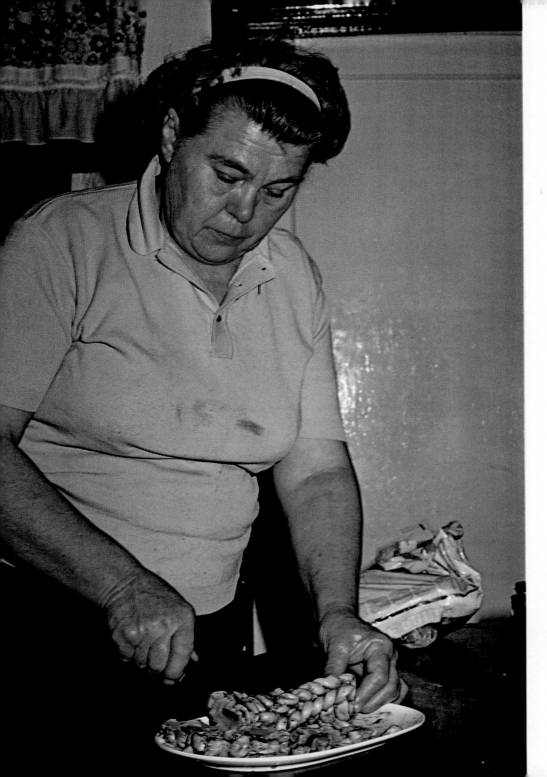

Despite educational programs devised to explain the fine print, the Alaska Native Claims Settlement Act of 1971 is still confusing to many Natives, for the law is lengthy and detailed.

Catherine "Caba" Chichenoff, 78, one of the oldest Natives born on Kodiak Island, was educated in a Russian school and helped Koniag, Inc., translate old Russian records that enabled many Aleuts to qualify for enrollment. She also testified in favor of Native claims at congressional hearings in 1968, but admitted in 1975: "I still don't really understand it. We are going to take maybe 25 to 50 years to get that sorted out. Let the young people decide. . . ."

Dora Aga of Larsen Bay on Kodiak Island, prepares braided seal gut (seal gut stuffed with fat) once a great favorite among the island Natives. The delicacy takes a long time to prepare and few make it these days, but Dora was taught by her mother, and her family won't let her forget the recipe.

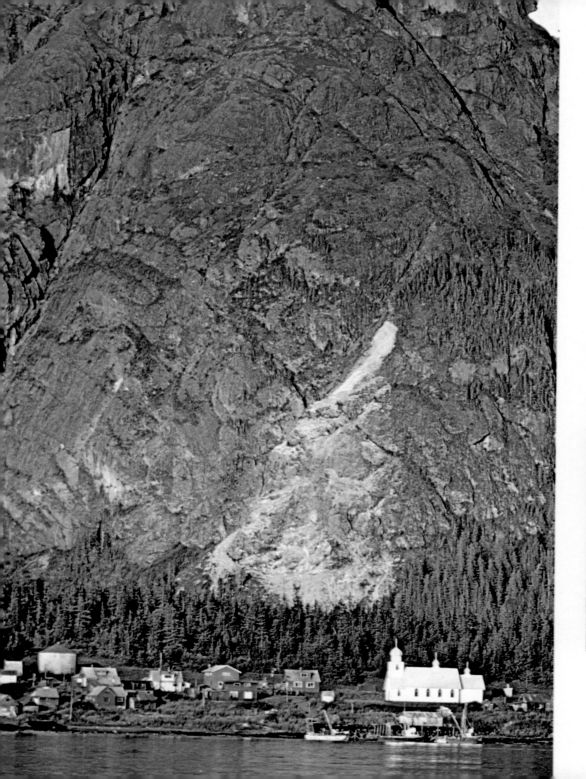

The coastal Chugach culture extends northeast from Kodiak Island to the outer coast of the Kenai Peninsula and along that coast to Prince William Sound.

Left — Tatitlek, deep in Prince William Sound near Valdez, the terminal for the trans-Alaska pipeline, boomed, languished after copper mining operations in the first decade of the 20th century. After the 1964 earthquake, survivors from Chenega, a village in western Prince William Sound that was destroyed by tidal waves, were moved here, but the refugees were not comfortable and eventually most of the Chenega Natives moved farther southeast to Cordova. Today Tatitlek residents do fairly well fishing and live considerably off the land. (NANCY SIMMERMAN)

Right — Larry Meganack, like many whose traditions come from the Aleuts, is fond of his old steam bath, in the low building behind him. Even though his village of Port Graham on the Kenai Peninsula has plumbing and bath tubs, the steam bath is still often preferred.

Below — Salmon eggs are processed in a cannery near Seldovia before shipment to markets in the Far East. Seldovia, near the lower tip of Kenai Peninsula, also is near the historic dividing line between cultures — coastal Eskimo and Tanaina Indian. (RICK FURNISS, REPRINTED FROM ALASKA GEOGRAPHIC®)

Sandwiched between the Chugach culture and the northernmost Tlingits are the Eyaks, who moved to the coast from the Interior long ago and claimed the strip of land along the Gulf of Alaska coast.

Encroachment by Tlingits from the south and the introduction of diseases and liquor by whites ravaged the Eyaks, and by 1905 there were only about 50 left; there may be none surviving today who can claim to be pure Eyak.

The Eyak branch of the Athabascan language survives because a linguist recorded it when there were still about half a dozen Eyak speakers alive.

Above — The Eyaks are few in number now, but the Glen Lankards family of Cordova is keeping their heritage alive. Mrs. Lankards is from old Eyak Village.

Left — First Street in Cordova, a town of about 3,000 on the eastern shore of Prince William Sound, 85 nautical miles southeast of Valdez. Just across the water from Cordova, on Hawkins Island, is the ancient village site of Palugvik, marking the southernmost movement of Eskimos along the Northwest Pacific coast. The Chugaches, as these Eskimos were called, migrated there some 4,000 years ago. (SUSAN HACKLEY JOHNSON)

"Our corporations, both village and regional, are required by law to make a profit from lands and monies the United States government has pledged to us. This we will do, and do well. But law or no law, the land and the sea will always mean more to us than dollars and cents. We shall continue to treat them with respect, and we ask all those with whom we do business to do likewise."
—————————— Stockholders report
Koniag, Inc.

The timber industry is not as important to Gulf of Alaska communities as it is in Southeastern Alaska, but many coastal villagers harvest drift logs for firewood . . . as in this high-tide scene at Larsen Bay, Kodiak Island.

ATHABASCAN

People of the Great Interior

By Mary Jane Fate and Hugh Fate

The ability to survive that is possessed by the Athabascans of Interior Alaska may someday be as legendary as that of their cousins, the Apaches and Navajos of the Southwest. The intimate story of the Athabascan way of life and capacity for survival, however, remains largely untold outside the circle of the people themselves.

∾

The Quest—The woman was young, almost a girl. The heavy load she carried was nearly as large as she was, for according to the tradition of her people, the woman was the beast of burden. Furs covered her entire body but could not hide her late pregnancy; her occasional inaudible gasps gave testimony to the nearness of her time. She plodded along on snowshoes, letting the small band of men, women and children, all fur-clad like herself, break and pack the snowy trail ahead of her. It was late winter; the day was crisp and cold. Finally, as the band passed a large spruce tree with low overhanging branches, she left the packed trail and

The rolling hills of Interior Alaska — typical of the Athabascan country. This colorful terrain is not far from Fairbanks in the heart of the Interior. (ROBERT LANGLOTZ)

Mary Jane and Hugh Fate. Mary Jane was born at Rampart on the Yukon River and missed much of her grade school education because her Athabascan parents moved with the seasons, trapping and hunting. When she reached high school age, however, she was able to attend Mount Edgecumbe, a boarding school for Natives at Sitka, where she did well. Now, although rearing a family of her own, she is active in public life. She has concerned herself both with Native land claims issues and with social problems of her people, and has served as national president of the North American Indian Women's Association.

Mary Jane does not claim to be a writer, and shares the byline of this story with her husband. In gathering material for "The Quest," she drew not only on her own experience but also on the help of those whose memories extended farther into the Athabascan past. She asks that credit be given those who supplied various parts of the story: her mother, Sally Hudson, whose hard work in compiling the cultural history of her people is meeting with success; Archie Moses, now deceased; and especially to Jenny Pitka, who, with her clarity of mind at four score years plus ten, and with her complete willingness to share her knowledge of the past, has enriched the Athabascan future. (*Photo by Margaret Bauman*)

sought a delivery place in the privacy of the wide boughs.

In actions as old as her people, the woman removed the furs that would encumber her movements, laid out a soft tanned rabbit-skin robe and thongs of caribou skin, and grasped a low branch and sat back on her heels in a squatting position. Then, as the pains of delivery quickened, she grunted and strained until an infant emerged. The new mother deftly tied the umbilical cord with the caribou thongs, and cut it with her thumbnail, repeating an act handed down by the old ones. She noticed the newborn was a boy. Tenderly she wrapped the baby's feet in part of the soft fur of the rabbit-skin robe before bundling him in the warm folds. The woman then made herself comfortable, and rested.

The shadows were beginning to lengthen when the young mother crawled away from the protective branches and replaced the snowshoes on her caribou-skin boots. Then, with effort, she shouldered the heavy pack, now made slightly heavier with the new infant, and hurried to catch the small band before total darkness descended. Finally she entered a small stand of spruce and found her people camping.

The band numbered six men, four women and five children. Three of the older children were gathering firewood when the young mother unshouldered her pack and immediately set to work making a fire. She worked alone, preparing food and then laying out caribou sleeping robes on spruce boughs and preparing her small family—her husband and now two sons—for the night. No one offered aid, and she ate only after the men had eaten. Her husband's sole show of emotion after her return was to pick up the rabbit-robed bundle and unceremoniously dump it into the snow. One tiny pink foot protruded into the cold, but no sound came from the bundle. The father muttered satisfaction, then turned his back. Thus the infant boy met and passed his first test of survival.

A fine example of Athabascan handiwork, these snowshoes were made 20 years ago by Birch Creek John. He used birch for the frame and caribou rawhide for the intricate lacing.

Mary Jane Fate was hesitant to submit the final draft of her people's story after researching her Athabascan ancestors with family and friends.

"It's so sad. So really sad," she said.

"Do you really want it if it's that sad?"

There was almost no food at all for the small group of Indians that winter. Fur-bearing animals were scarce. Moose, always scarce, had all but disappeared. Rabbits, perhaps the most important link in the food chain, had reached a low point in their cycle the year before and were now almost nonexistent. The summer and fall runs of salmon had been poor; the drying racks had been far from full and in July of the past summer, a great fire had forced the people to the very banks of the big river and burned the land for many days' march in all directions. A terrible pall of smoke had hung over the land and the last of the animals had disappeared. When the fall snows began, the men were gone for days following the trails of single animals. The snow grew deeper and the temperature plunged. The winter developed into one so severe that legends would one day be told about it.

And then the people began to starve. Death was constant. First the women died, sacrificing themselves for the men who must provide and for the children who must become the future, if one existed. Finally the men died, too.

This story would persist in the oral history of the people—never in song, only in hushed tones—and it may be that the remains of the dead sustained the living. But somehow, as they had before, the people of the North survived.

A new year brought many changes to the land and its people. The infant born in the winter was given away to a distant cousin of the young mother. The baby's father had perished while on an extended hunt, and the mother alone could not feed the boy. He was now her only child; the older son had died. The cousin, who had no children, gained a son and a new family was formed.

Other summers and winters passed. Through those seasons and the ensuing years, the game gradually resumed their tenancy of the land, and the people resolutely followed. Their ability to survive was based on a continual, exhaustive quest for food and clothing, a quest often made difficult by the imbalance of nature and erratic cycles of game. The search was all-consuming, never allowing time for ceremony or expansion of the basic culture. Only the arts of song and of storytelling were developed, primarily to record the history and teach the young.

The infant of the tragic winter was now a young man, as lithe and tough as a wolf. His life had been fairly normal, taken in the context of his circumstances. Through the years, he and the other young men had gone to school, one that confronted the practical problems of survival and instructed the students in finding solutions. Only the most successful hunters and the wisest elders were selected to teach the young men, and in this way a high quality of education was maintained.

The young man's natural mother had perished years earlier, a sad epilogue to her heroic struggle for survival, in the tragic winter of legend. Now, with schooling over and the days of youthful irresponsibility behind him, the young hunter took up the food quest of his people. His life involved the constant search that forced the Athabascans to hunt over an area far larger than that of their Eskimo neighbors.

No tougher human beings existed than the nomadic hunters of Alaska's Interior. By temperament and training, they could travel for days without food and exist in temperatures of 50° below zero or colder without shelter or fire. Supreme powers of endurance enabled them to run game to the ground on foot or on snowshoes over the most difficult terrain. They were proud of their physical prowess; many of their games and stories reflected the mystique of physical strength.

The young man took a mate, a young woman from a band of people that lived some distance down the river. Their coupling had been predetermined by their parents when the two were still small children.

The people, always ready to break the tedium of their tenuous existence, came long distances for the marriage potlatch, which lasted two or three days. Games, along with much feasting, dancing and storytelling took place, old acquaintances were renewed, and long hours were spent in earnest discussion of the previous year's successes and failures in the quest for food. Gifts were exchanged throughout the throng with regularity and complete unselfishness. But the intent of the potlatch was never lost. In the revelry of the seemingly disorganized crowd, a serious ritual was enacted.

The married men, in small groups or singly, isolated the prospective groom and gave advice for a fulfilling and successful marriage. The married women conducted a similar seminar at a different location. A man acknowledged by his peers as the most successful in marriage, and his female counterpart, then took the young man and the bride to a common meeting place. In a final and solemn ceremony, the older man gave an eloquent public speech of advice to the young groom. Then the woman gave equally eloquent advice to the bride. Sleeping robes of mountain sheepskin and

Athabascan babies were sometimes strapped into cradles fashioned from the branches and thin, strong bark of Interior birch trees — an abundant resource in the Athabascan world. This cradle is displayed in the University of Alaska Museum.

caribou skin with soft, short summer hair were given ceremoniously to the couple. The wedding ended with this last gesture of giving.

Three children arrived in as many years. Two survived, but, most importantly, the mother had survived the hard labor of each childbirth to produce more children. Life was fairly normal, hunger keeping its distance but always near.

These people, who lived by the river, were known as the Middle People. On either side, north and south, were the Caribou People and the Bear People. The groups to the north and south had a longstanding rivalry that sometimes led to open conflict. The Middle People supplied a few weapons to both sides but otherwise stayed neutral.

During the summer of the birth of the third child, a group of Caribou People from far to the north came to trade. One of the group was a young man who wore the coat of a minor chief and was reported to be the son of a powerful medicine man.

The days of trading continued at a leisurely pace because the work of the fishing season was not yet upon the Middle People, and as the days passed the finely dressed foreigner began to take interest in one of the local maidens. When the courtship took a serious turn, the young man from the Caribou People was tragically drowned in a boating accident. The traders headed for their homeland without goods or the body of their companion. When they finally reached their own country, the telling of the accidental drowning was corrupted until it became a tale of sinister plotting by the relatives of the young maiden.

The medicine men of the Caribou People exhorted their followers to a war of vengeance. Rumor of this impending conflict drifted to the Middle People but they were unable to believe such a confrontation would take place. But discovery of a slain fisherman lying near his fish trap and the sighting of six strangers running in single file on a distant skyline finally gave proof to the rumor.

The Middle People prepared for battle. Weapons were put in good order and shields of heavy moose skin were propped against trees so that the skin could dry and become hard. Medicine men constantly sought supernatural omens as portents of success or failure in the impending battle. The women worked with the men in preparation for war and the grief to follow.

Then, suddenly, a torrent of bloodshed enveloped the people by the river. En masse, the avenging Caribou People raided and destroyed, for in this far northern area war meant obliterating the enemy. Families were wiped out, even to their pack dogs. It was later told how the river ran red along the banks. The defenders ceased making fires at night and only the lonely howl of an occasional dog or the faint death wail of the women broke the melancholy along the river. Occasionally during the nightly dirge a basket might be seen floating, ghostlike, with the current, its fragile cargo—a human infant—thrown into the river by the invaders to drift toward its fate.

In final desperation, every person of the Middle People who was able to use weapons and to fight went to gathering points along a stretch of their beloved river, then marched to a bare hill high above to wait in the dawn for the invaders on their way to their ravages. Then on the high hill, there ensued a battle such as would mark the heights of warfare for posterity, the defenders fighting out of desperation to survive, the invading strangers determined to destroy their enemies forever. All day and into the twilight of a late summer night the fighting continued, but with darkness it ceased. The invaders, exhausted and finally defeated, withdrew silently, claiming their vengeance had been carried out.

The following winter was a mournful one. But there was sufficient food; hunting was good and although fishing had been delayed, there was enough fish because there were fewer mouths to feed. Once again the people by the river had survived. The infant of the terrible winter more than two decades before had also survived, but not without scars. He had lost most of the family that had adopted him, as well as his wife and one child. Eventually there would be another wife, other children. Life would somehow return to normal and the quest would again resume its supreme place in the lives of the Middle People by the river.

∽

Epilogue—The man had been very old. The pallor of his weathered face accentuated the deep lines of age. He was dressed from head to foot in furs newly sewn and never worn before. Branches of a large birch tree supported the pallet upon which his body rested. The sadness and agony of the old man's quest were over.

A great potlatch was held to honor the old man's life and his departure from it. Again his people came from afar for a rare gathering, for death was the time for sharing and for comradeship. Respect was given the person who had gone, but those who survived did not dwell on their grief for that would make the road tougher for the departed.

The potlatch was to promote love and happiness with the spirit of giving.

The name of the old man, already renowned, they enshrined with story and dance. The songs they composed about his long and eventful life would be sung by the people of many tribes for many generations to come.

Only some of the following Athabascan villages are indicated on this map because of space limitations. However, all of these Native villages are included on the large pull-out map.

Alatna	Kaltag
Allakaket	Kenai
Anvik	Knik
Arctic Village	Koyukuk
Beaver	Lime Village
Bettles Field/Evansville	McGrath
Birch Creek	Manley Hot Springs
Cantwell	Mentasta Lake
Chalkyitsik	Minto
Chickaloon	Nenana
Chistochina	Nikolai
Chitina	Ninilchik
Circle	Nondalton
Copper Center	Northway
Dot Lake	Nulato
Eagle	Pedro Bay
Eklutna	Rampart
Fort Yukon	Ruby
Gakona	Shageluk
Galena	Stevens Village
Glennallen	Stony River
Grayling	Takotna
Gulkana	Tanacross
Healy Lake	Tanana
Holy Cross	Tazlina
Hughes	Telida
Huslia	Tetlin
Iliamna	Venetie

199

The Athabascans were, and are, people of the rivers, living along the banks of the Interior's many waterways and traveling over river highways in summer and winter to fish, hunt and trap. Main artery of travel, long before white men crowded in to chase their cherished gold, was the Yukon River.

Previous page — Alaska's largest river and one of the great rivers of the world. The Yukon courses over 1,400 miles from the border with Yukon Territory to the Bering Sea. With its tributaries, it drains over more than 150,000 square miles of the Alaska Interior — virtually all Athabascan country.

Left — Fish wheels, anchored in many Interior rivers, scoop up passing salmon which slide into a box to await pickup by Athabascan fishermen. A huge king salmon has just been caught at this trap in the Tanana River. (LEN SHERWIN)

Below — Tlingit Sam Kito, left, and Athabascan John Sackett, long recognized as among the top leaders of Alaskan Natives, team up to fish in the Yukon River, near Galena. Although educated in Western school systems, Kito and Sackett were reared in the traditional Indian manner and were taught the skills of a subsistence lifestyle . . . and both like to get away from their busy schedules to renew their acquaintance with the land. Sackett was the youngest man ever elected to the Alaska House of Representatives, and was an early leader in the Alaska land claims battle. After passage of the act he was chosen as the first president of Doyon, Inc., the Athabascan regional corporation.

Left — Charlie Evans of Galena, whose father was a riverboat man, keeps an eye on the Yukon River from his old riverside bench. Rivers are crucially important in the Interior and much time is spent watching . . . and talking about . . . the rivers.

Below — Galena, once an Athabascan village called Natulaten, became a supply point for nearby galena (lead ore) prospects in 1919. The village is 275 miles west of Fairbanks, near the confluence of the Yukon and Koyukuk rivers.

A message posted over Hobo's Bar in the Athabascan village of Galena:

"When the white men discovered this country the Indians were running it. There were no taxes, no debts, women did all the work — and the white man thought he could improve on a system like that!"

Left — The Interior at its best — the Nenana River, rolling hills, fall colors and early snow on the peaks in the background. The Nenana flows 140 miles out of the Alaska Range to meet the Tanana River at the village of Nenana. The Tanana then picks up several other Interior rivers before joining the Yukon River at the village of Tanana. (JOHN JOHNSON)

Below — Nenana, 64 miles southwest of Fairbanks along the George Parks Highway, is at the confluence of the Nenana and Tanana rivers, and is one of the main river-freighting centers in Alaska. Life in the town (population about 500) was dramatically changed by completion of the Alaska Railroad, commemorated in 1923 when President Warren G. Harding drove a golden spike at Nenana. Chiefs of the village knew they could not prevent construction of the line, so they made the best of it by demanding railroad jobs for local people. The railroad agreed, and today townspeople continue to hold railroad jobs.

Right — Mita Lord, owner of Mom & Babe's Cafe in Nenana, is active in Athabascan politics. She is also a shrewd businesswoman and an excellent cook. (Her specialty is a cheese omelet which some local connoisseurs believe is the world's finest.)

Below — At the confluence of the Yukon and Tanana rivers is the village of Tanana, one of the largest on the Yukon. The village depends mainly on hunting and fishing, with occasional injections of money when villagers are hired to help battle fires that often blaze through Interior forests.

Right — A winter food cache and fish-drying racks at Koyukuk, a small Athabascan village on the Yukon River. The salmon drying on racks will be used in winter for dog food. Dry grass, cut for bedding in doghouses, is stored beneath the cache. When hard and dry, the fish will be baled — 20 whole fish to a bale — and stored inside the cache. Many families in the Interior have more than one of these small, handy, elevated buildings — especially useful during flood season, when the Yukon overflows its banks and sweeps into cabins. (BETSY HART)

Claude Demientieff Jr., who was reared on the Yukon River and spent a year at Harvard, has no question in his mind as to who has the better policy of land management:

"The Native people have been here thousands and thousands of years, but take a look at the land and you cannot find a trace of where they've been. Western civilization has been here maybe 200 or 300 years and you can see everywhere it's been."

Left — Athabascan fire fighter Herbie Vent is from Galena, a Yukon River village supported largely by fishing and hunting.

Above — Amelia DeWilde and her children beside one of the family's cabins at Huslia. The DeWildes have 12 children . . . and each learns the elements of subsistence living. (Their bush lifestyle was chronicled in a three-part series Amelia wrote for *The Alaska Sportsman*®, August-October, 1969.)

Overleaf — Spread among the birch and spruce trees along the Koyukuk River, Huslia exists contentedly on what is basically a subsistence economy, supplemented by money from fire fighting.

Left — Captain Art Peterson's powerful riverboat *Yukon* is a familiar sight on the river for which she is named. Yukon riverboats have long been a primary means of transportation for goods and people through Interior country. It takes expert piloting and considerable experience to navigate the river because of its many false channels and constantly shifting bars.

Above — The *Ramona II* is one of the few riverboats still running and trading on the Yukon, and unlike others this one is owned and operated by an Athabascan, Claude Demientieff Sr. Demientieff previously owned a prosperous store in Galena, but he sold it because he prefers the roving life of a riverboat captain. Family members often serve as crew members, including the skipper's son, Claude Jr., pictured on page 11.

Upper right — Winter transportation stands guard over summer transportation . . . awaiting their turn. Sled dogs have been making a comeback along the Yukon River.
(HARVEY BOWERS)

Right — Air transportation also is important in the Interior, where the only roads are the river highways. A chartered floatplane brings a teacher and a handful of supplies to Lime Village. Until recently there was no school in this isolated village on the Stony River, 85 miles northwest of Lake Clark, and the children had to be sent away to boarding school.

Although the Athabascan culture is associated with Alaska's Interior country, there are several coastal Indian villages in Southcentral Alaska — most in the Tanaina Indian country surrounding Cook Inlet.

Right — Tyonek, a Tanaina Indian village on the west shore of Cook Inlet, southwest of Anchorage, has had several ups and downs. The Tyoneks were considered well-heeled before the coming of white men, but by the 1960's they were regarded as the poorest people on Cook Inlet. Then, in 1963, they received a windfall — $11.6 million in oil-lease revenues. Oil was never discovered on the leased Tyonek land, but the tribe was able to rebuild their village with the funds.

Below — Esther Kaloa, sister of a bright young chief who led the village of Tyonek through their oil boom, is in training to become a lawyer. Her brother died in a hotel fire and the tragedy was followed by a streak of bad luck for the Tyoneks, who speculated with and lost part of their oil investment.

Ninilchik (*below*) established in the 1800's by the Russian-American Company for "colonial citizens" and Creoles (part Russian, part Native), faces Cook Inlet on the lower Kenai Peninsula. Descendants of those first residents are included under the Alaska Native Claims Settlement Act, and many of the community's early dwellings — such as the one at right — are still standing. These museum pieces are being preserved, and those that are relocated are carefully numbered log by log, then disassembled, moved and rebuilt exactly as they originally stood.

"**W**e use an area of 1,648 square miles for hunting, fishing and for running our traplines. This is the way in which our fathers and forefathers made their living, and we of this generation follow in the same plan." —————— Stevens Village Council, 1963

Athabascans rely heavily on wildlife for food, clothing and — in some cases — income.

Above — A snowshoe hare — brown in summer, white in winter. (JOHN JOHNSON)

Upper right — The Interior of Alaska is one of the state's prime nesting areas for birds and waterfowl, also sought by Athabascan hunters. These migrating Canada geese were photographed in May near Anchorage, perhaps on their way to the Interior. (JOHN JOHNSON)

Right — One of the important mammals hunted by Athabascans is the moose whose meat has carried many a family through long winter months and whose hide has provided protection from the cold. In earlier times, Athabascans would also use heavy, dried moose skins as shields in battles with enemies. (JOHN JOHNSON)

Jonathan and Hannah Solomon of Beaver Creek, north into the bush from Fairbanks, live a subsistence lifestyle that includes "ratting," the shooting and trapping of muskrats.

Left — Hannah Solomon's meat cache includes dried muskrat (in the rafters) and black bear meat. The cache was fashioned quickly using plastic sheeting over a wood frame. Rotten wood is burned as a smudge to keep flies away. (JIM REARDEN, STAFF)

Below — Jonathan Solomon skins a muskrat during the late spring "rat" season. The skins will be sold and the meat consumed during the winter months. (JIM REARDEN, STAFF, REPRINTED FROM ALASKA® MAGAZINE)

Athabascan arts and crafts may not rival Tlingit totemic art or Eskimo ivory carvings when it comes to commercial success, but the work is beautiful, and often has a purpose.

Above — Maggie Isaac, wife of Chief Andrew Isaac of Tanacross, is highly skilled at beadwork. Although her upbringing and her husband's position place her in the traditional role of Athabascan women, Mrs. Isaac is also comfortable in today's modern society.

Right — A masterpiece of Kutchin Athabascan beadwork — closeup of a portion of the altar at Chalkyitsik's Episcopal Church. The backing is bleached moose hide. (RICHARD NELSON)

216

Left — A rarity in the modern world — fish skin boots, made by a woman in Nondalton, near the southwestern edge of Athabascan country on the shore of Lake Clark. The boots are waterproof and surprisingly warm.

Below — The Athabascans are expert at knitting fishnets and Jessie Edwin of Koyukuk made this big one, which helps keep the drying rack full. For Jessie, an old-timer on the Yukon, the musical flow of Athabascan is still the first language.

Mrs. Jessie David of Tetlin proudly models the chief's necklace — dentalium and trading beads — which has come down through her family. The shells for such necklaces came from the coast, sometimes costing the life of a slave who was killed and sunk in the sea to attract the ocean creatures that produced them, and by the time they got to Interior Indians their price was exorbitant. Often they served Athabascans as a form of money and usually only a chief could afford a necklace, so Mrs. David is justifiably proud of her heirloom.

Below — Formed under the Alaska Native Claims Settlement Act, Toghetthele Corporation, Nenana's village corporation, invested in this small sawmill which produces good lumber for construction and jobs for some of the residents.

Right — Fishing is important to most Athabascans for subsistence, and to stretch the food budget for those with paying jobs. Some Athabascans are also engaged in commercial fishing along rivers of the Interior. Edmund Lord owned this small commercial fish-processing operation in Nenana and employed a few of his neighbors during the busy season.

Octber 1975 Fortune magazine classed Doyon's assets as about equal to those of Norton Simon, and placed the Native corporation 123rd on its list of the nation's top 500. Doyon did have some features that were distinctly its own, the magazine noted.

"Because Doyon operates with as small a staff as possible (14), its executives might review a multi-million-dollar gold-mining deal in the morning and tend the furnace in the afternoon."

Something is always going on in the Interior — a fire, a flood, a heavy fish run, a poor trapping season. The best and worst seem to follow naturally, each taken in stride.

Left — Like many Athabascans of the Interior, Huslia villager George Wholecheese earns money fighting forest fires for the Bureau of Land Management. For many years fire fighting was about the only paying job available to Athabascans, and in some remote villages this is still the case. A common plague in the Interior, the fires are usually started by summer thunder storms.

Below — The villagers of Chalkyitsik, a community near Fort Yukon, northeast of Fairbanks, matter-of-factly accept regular flooding of the Black River. In the spring their log cabins sit like little islands amid the floodwaters. (JUNE MACKIE)

Overleaf — An awesome cloud of smoke rises over the Interior as a forest fire threatens hundreds of thousands of acres near Huslia. A cache of supplies airdropped for firefighters lies waiting in an open field.

Education has come to many remote villages in recent years, gradually replacing a system which forced youngsters to leave their homes for an education in larger villages or towns.

At the Nulato school (*right*) Josephine Mountain teaches the craft of Athabascan beadwork to a class of girls.

Lower right — In 1974 the Natives of Lime Village hired their first teacher, a young Californian. When Max Mitchell flew in to take up his post, he found a few things lacking — school building, desks, books, even paper. Undaunted, he immediately began organizing. He first obtained the use of a partially finished house that had been built under a government housing program (refused by the intended occupant, reportedly because the construction was so poor). Then he bought several gas lanterns to provide light during the long winter months, borrowed a handful of books from other villages in the area and set to work giving the children of Lime Village an education.

Right — Lucy Frank of Minto, whose father, husband and sons all worked for Native rights, sits with a prized photo of the Tanana chiefs who met in 1915 with U.S. District Judge James Wickersham, Alaska's Delegate to Congress. The Athabascans firmly rejected Wickersham's proposal that reservations be established in the Interior.

Below — John Sackett, right, an early leader in the land claims movement, sits with Governor Jay Hammond at the annual *Tundra Times* banquet. Sackett was the first president of Doyon, the Athabascan regional corporation, and was the youngest person ever elected to the Alaska House of Representatives; he has since gone on to become one of the more powerful members of the state Senate.

I n 1915 United States District Judge James Wickersham presided at a meeting of Athabascans to consider the possibility of their settling on reservations, and Chief Alexander of Tolovana clearly outlined the Native view:

"You told me that you were our people's friend, and you did not like to see us get into any kind of mischief. You stated to me that anything we want, we talk to you about now. Therefore . . . I tell you that we are people that are always on the go, and I believe if we are put in one place we shall die off like rabbits. . .

"I ask you not to let the white people come near us. Let us live our own lives in the customs we know. If we were on government ground we could not keep the white people away."

The chief prevailed — there would be no reservations.

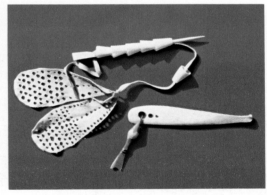

Athabascans have historically been strong competitors in physical contests, which today include marathon sled dog races and the annual Alaska Eskimo-Indian-Aleut Olympics.

Left — Carl Huntington races to victory in the 1977 North American Sled Dog Championships, held in Fairbanks. Huntington was raised traditionally on the Yukon but his grandfather — a white prospector and riverboat man — instilled in the family a deep respect for education, and Carl received a good one. Nevertheless, he did not neglect his heritage and sled dog racing became his first love. Like other members of his family, he did well in business as a fish buyer, investing his proceeds in a crack dog team. He became a top musher in the highly competitive racing circuit and made back his investment in prize money. (TIM JONES)

Above — Roy Folger and Janice Folger kneel over a fire they are building to boil water during a tea-making contest — part of Nuchalawoyya, an annual festival of Athabascans held at Tanana. In the tea-making race, contestants have to boat to the opposite shore of the river for wood, boat back, build a fire, make tea and rush the finished product to the speaker's platform. (KEN CASH)

Above right — Two Athabascan games — a ring and pin game fashioned from antler and moose-hide, and a small dart game. Both are on display at the University of Alaska Museum, Fairbanks.

"H e owned a million acres of land, a thousand rivers and lakes, though he had no deeds, titles or taxes . . ."

——————— Henry Kaiser,
Reviewing the life
of his Athabascan uncle,
Charles Smith, who was
"born free" in
Tanana, Alaska, 1904

At the end of a successful day on the Yukon River, an Athabascan tows his fish wheel back to the village of Galena.

TLINGIT, HAIDA, TSIMSHIAN

Indians of Southeastern

Two Southeastern Indian people, the Haidas and the Tlingits, are often referred to as one, although their languages are different and so, originally, were their customs. They stood apart from other Native Alaskans, however, because their systems were strongly capitalistic while others were socialist, and, early, it became common to think of them as one.

The Tsimshians, a neighboring Indian group, are often overlooked because they moved here late — 1887 — from Canada to live unobtrusively but well on Annette Island.

Despite different roots, the lifestyles of the Tlingits, Haida and Tsimshians are much the same and they share much, too, in history and tradition. Therefore we have chosen a single historian, William Paul Sr., to represent them; one whose forebears traveled widely and dealt with them all. — Lael Morgan

William Paul Sr., born in 1885, was one of the first Tlingits to receive a college degree. As soon as he could he began to practice law, and in 1924 he became the first Native Alaskan to win a seat in the territorial legislature. Ten years later he helped bring suit against the U.S. government in behalf of Tlingits and Haidas for lands taken from them. The case dragged on for more than two decades and the settlement in 1959 (not paid until 1968) proved disappointingly small. But Paul continued to push his case until his people were further compensated with passage of the Alaska Native Claims Settlement Act. Although for years Paul's name ranked with the avant garde of Native Americans, his background was traditional, and it was not surprising that his memory of family history is inseparable from the history of his tribe. Paul died in 1977. (*Photo courtesy of Dr. Erna Gunther*)

Public interest in preserving artifacts of Alaskan Native history is at a high point today, but that does not mean there was no preservation before now. At the head of Kasaan Bay, on Prince of Wales Island, stands the Chief Sonihat tribal house, built in the 1930's by old-time Natives under the auspices of the United States Forest Service.

MY FAMILY CAME TO CLAIM THIS LAND

By William Paul Sr.

Where did my people come from? Let me begin by telling you where I came from so you will not get the impression I know it all.

❧

I was born on the edge of the change which came to the Native people when the United States bought Alaska from the Russians. I was born in 1885. My mother was born in Victoria, British Columbia, where my grandmother had gone with her family to trade, around 1863. My grandmother was married to a white man. They had two daughters, and one of them was my mother, Kaa-lee-yudt. When my grandmother learned that the children's father planned to leave and take the two girls to Scotland to educate them, she and her brother fled with the children to Wrangell, Alaska. This they did in a small canoe, traveling at night and holing up in the day deep in the woods for protection from the bands of marauding Indians who would capture other Indians for slaves.

Safe at Wrangell, my mother and her sister were "raised Indian," in the style of their class, which was high caste.

When Mother was about 12, she entered a Presbyterian school for girls at Wrangell, over the objections of her mother and stepfather; her parents had arranged her marriage to a Tsimshian chief at Old Metlakatla, British Columbia. She refused to be married, prevailed in her refusal, and entered the school.

She was such a reliable person that she became a sort of unpaid servant, to the great disgust of her parents, in whose home *she* had been waited on by *t'ow-gaats*,

slaves. (The naval officers who were then governing the territory had not bothered about slavery among the Natives.) But Mother was so hungry for learning the new ways that she did not consider such work disgraceful. She became an interpreter for the preacher, Rev. S. Hall Young, and from him she received her education. On Saturday afternoons, the minister would go over his sermon with her and explain the meaning of words.

In due course, a man came to Wrangell en route to his home in Port Tongass who so suited Kaa-lee-yudt in caste and education and character that she was willing to marry him, and she did. His name was Louis Paul. They had three children, all boys, and he became a lay-preacher of the Presbyterian church.

The Presbyterian missionary, Dr. Sheldon Jackson, requested my father and two other men to find a place where a school and church for Indians could be built. The three were to go to the place now occupied by the town of Metlakatla; at that time it was the site of a town founded by my father's uncle. That was the last time anyone saw my father; the three men never returned from their trip.

Eventually my mother remarried; her new husband was Sheesh-gow. They moved to Salmon Bay, an incomparable fish stream, when the previous occupant, a chief, left after the death of his wife. This was in keeping with the Tlingit law of occupation of land.

Sheesh-gow was the only Indian fisherman in the bay—and the Norwegian fishermen from Petersburg were crowding him out. So when four Tlingit boats came from the town of Klawock that was just too many. Sheesh-gow told my mother to prepare a banquet to which he would invite the four crews from Klawock.

Kaa-lee-yudt marshaled her help, two teen-age daughters and a son, and prepared the dinner as directed by her husband, who was about to apply the law of the Tlingit-speaking Indians.

That evening 24 guests were at Sheesh-gow's house. There was no restraint because they were all friends. The fire burned brightly as the men seated themselves in the two rooms. The son stirred a dish of the Tlingit equivalent of ice cream, made from "soap berries," so called because they foam like soap when stirred vigorously. The berries foamed with a pinkish color that deepened as the stirring continued. Sugar was added, and the foam became thicker, until it was thick enough to float a teaspoon.

Before each group was placed a large dish of the whipped berries. Each man dipped into the dish, and when he had mouthed it, he would smack his lips, as if to say "Um! um!" and smile at his neighbor. This is traditional in opening a feast among the Tlingit-speaking people.

The bustle of preparation continued till the food was served. The table was loaded with great quantities of the most luscious venison, two hindquarters, roasted to a tasty brown, the outside crisp and covered with gravy made from the rich juices.

For a side dish there was goose tongue, a vegetable finer and more tender than lettuce or spinach, with a stem like green onions. Then came a course of *uhl-xy*, a tasty chowder with just enough salmon to give it that wild taste which no restaurant can duplicate. After the soup and roast venison came the delicious dried sockeye salmon, roasted in a quick fire, with the oil still dripping hot, the skin soft and easy to tear. Long strips of the salmon were placed before the guests, who reached out and dipped each piece into the eulachon oil—*saak ix*—that comes now only from the Nass River in British Columbia.

Totems stand as reminders of the past throughout Southeastern Alaska. Many are reproductions, including this one at Sitka National Historical Park, which features a hand holding a ceremonial rattle. (SCOTT CHAMBERS)

231

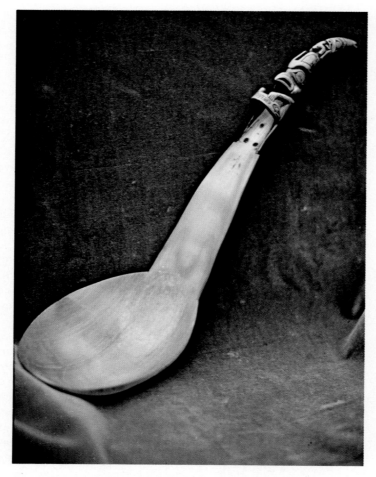

Horn spoons were made by steaming and molding the horns of a mountain sheep or goat. The spoons were made in large numbers for use at potlatches . . . large gatherings which included generous feasts and gift-giving. This particular spoon, on display at Sheldon Jackson Museum in Sitka, has a bowl and handle of near-transluscent sheep horn decorated with black, intricately carved goat horn.
(SHELDON JACKSON MUSEUM)

When all those at table were surfeited, they leaned back and awaited the speeches which Tlingit law demanded. Each man, as he was moved by the spirit, arose and thanked the host and hostess, always ending with the words, "That is the way in which I am thankful—*Yei a-weh, shtoo-gah xut ya tee*"—and always ending with a laugh.

When there were no more guests to speak, Sheesh-gow arose and addressed them.

"My good friends, how wonderful are my inner spirits because you are here. All of you are known to me. Some of you are closely related from a long time back. Some of you were students at Sheetka when my wife was a teacher there. Your presence reminds us of the many happy times that we all have had in the days that are now gone.

"My family and I came here because there was nobody else to claim this land of our grandfathers. We had heard that the white man was making full use of the land of the red salmon that were so plentiful here, and it grieved us to think that the friends and relatives of the people who are the true owners were not making as much use of this place as the white people. And so it made our innermost parts feel good when we learned that the Tlingit people of Klawock were making this long trip to our place.

"But even though we were made glad, you know how it is when the ghosts of our departed uncles and grandfathers seem to stand before us asking us what we are going to do about the lands they handed down to us. Perhaps it will be like *Gi-diksh* . . ."

Sheesh-gow paused. *Gi-diksh* is a mystical word evoking the eternal spirit. The men from Klawock were old-time Tlingit Indians trained to obey the law of respect and property—the basic law of their people. They knew they were violating their law and that they had no right to be on my stepfather's land. They would suffer the penalties of shame.

"Now the fishing season has started and soon the boats of the foreigners will come. You and I will take our share, and next winter I will be glad when I realize that you, my own relations from Klawock, are enjoying your homes because of the rich bounty that our god has given to this place that we call the place of the red salmon."

And with that the party was ended and the guests went out to their boats. That night three of the boats pulled out and departed.

The next morning the last boat made a set; then, with a certain defiance, the men took in their empty net. As soon as the seine was on board, that boat, too, left the bay, traveling at full speed, stern down close to the water, obviously for a long trip. None of them returned.

The law requiring courtesy and the law requiring respect for another man's property had both been upheld.

This story regarding violation of other Indians' land is not original with the Tlingit-speaking Indians. It comes from the time they were of a different ethnic group and language, namely, the Tsimshians, at which time the people who are now Tlingit-speakers were a part of the tribe known as "Git-sheesh" or as the Tsimshians would pronounce the word "Git-sees." That name comes from a time when, in Work Channel, in back of Prince Rupert, Tsimshian hunters would sit at the point where seals would gather to await the tide so they could swim to the upper bay. The men would hiss to get the seals to turn their heads, "s-s-s-s," and so they got the name of "Git-sees."

These Tsimshians of the Nass and Skeena river areas migrated, and I believe they were the ancestors of the Tlingit-speaking Indians. The motive for migration was, I think, food; the route of migration was northward along the mountains and on the seacoast. Some proof of this is in the names that were left behind and in the legends the Indians took with them.

This mask, probably of Tlingit origin, is part of the 1791 Malaspina Collection in the Museum of the Americas in Madrid, Spain. The helmet was fashioned from wood, copper and sea shells and was far more than just ornamentation; it was used as protection in battle by Native warriors. The mask portion of the helmet represents a humanized figure of a bear. (ERNEST MANEWAL)

Dave Ketah, Tlingit from Ketchikan, pulls abalone from the rocky shore at low tide about 15 miles from his home. Ketah, like others of his family, subsistence hunts and fishes the coastline near his home, living a literal translation of his people's name: Tlingit — those who live on the tidal area. (R. J. HOFF)

The original group splintered and the splinters divided and redivided. When they settled and mixed with other groups they had to obey the Tlingit law that requires marriage outside of one's clan.

There was one group of people who eventually settled in Tlingit territory who did not come from the Nass-Skeena area. They came down the Copper River and were known to the Tlingits as Eeyuk-kwan. After many years they settled on the Gulf of Alaska, some of them at Yakutat, others at Hoonah.

In my study of our language, I wondered about the origin of the word Tlingit. I discovered that the *git* portion meant man and was from the Tsimshian language. Then what about *tlin*? I discovered that this word refers to the ebbing tide, and when I asked our old and respected historians about it, I learned that *tlin*, or *lein*, was a portion of a descriptive phrase, the whole of which referred to a way of living: *lein eeti nuX has koodis-teeyi*—those who lived on the tidal area. I found that the principal Tlingit stories, too, were of Tshimshian origin, variations being made in the course of many generations.

One difference in stories concerns the Raven; there were really *two* Ravens. The one I call the Great Raven was the Raven Above the Nass River, *Naas-sha-kee-yeil*. Nass Raven lived in the upper firmament and guarded the great lights: the sun, the moon and the stars. The Raven who did all the tricks and who was the master in deception was Scamp Raven, the grandson of the Nass Raven; this relation is usually overlooked by white ethnologists and our young Tlingits. Scamp Raven disguised himself as a needle of hemlock and worked his way into the drinking water of the maiden daughter of Nass Raven, and thus was born in the very household of Nass Raven. From that household he was able to steal first the stars, then the moon, and at last the sun, all for the benefit of mankind. People forget that in spite of his rascality, Scamp Raven benefited himself in such a manner that all mankind benefited, too.

Fire, for instance, was one of the benefits brought to mankind because of Scamp Raven. Scamp Raven persuaded the red-billed duck to fly to the land of the setting sun, which is the repository of fire, to get some fire and carry it away. The duck had a beautiful beak and when that beak kept getting shorter and shorter from the fire, and the heat about overcame the duck, Scamp Raven would say, "Just a little way more," pointing indefinitely beyond the beyond until the duck reached the shore. That is the way mankind got fire and the duck his nice short red beak.

&

That is some of what I have to tell of the Tlingit-speaking people: our traditions, our legends. As for our origins, I have only barely suggested the complexity of the numerous groups we descended from. One has to be born in it to fathom that complexity.

Tlingits are related by blood, rather than by government. It is like a father with 16 children. Upon reaching majority they establish their own dwelling places and soon produce their own progeny, households and customs.

Tlingits are their own governors, which is the purest democracy. Their link to their origins is one of respect; indeed, that is the basis of Tlingit law.

Only some of the following Tlingit, Haida and Tsimshian villages and islands are indicated on this map because of space limitations. However, all of these Native villages and islands are included on the large pull-out map.

Villages:	Islands
Angoon	Admiralty
Craig	Annette
Hoonah	Baranof
Hydaburg	Chichagof
Juneau	Kupreanof
Kake	Prince of Wales
Kasaan	Revillagigedo
Ketchikan	
Klawock	
Klukwan	
Metlakatla	
Port Chilkoot/Haines	
Saxman	
Sitka	
Yakutat	

Arctic Circle

Fairbanks

Anchorage

Yakutat

Gulf of Alaska

Hoonah

Juneau

Sitka

Pacific Ocean

Ketchikan

Metlakatla
Dixon
Entrance

Tlingits, Haidas and Tsimshians are people of the forest and the sea, drawing from both for food, clothing, protection and spiritual strength. The forests, such as shown in the photo at left, begin at the water's edge, extend to about 3,000 feet in the southern part of Southeastern and to about 1,800 feet farther north. Although western hemlock predominates in the southern forests, Sitka spruce, red cedar and Alaska yellow cedar are also present. In the north the percentage of hemlock increases; red cedar is found north only to the northern shore of Frederick Sound. (TIM THOMPSON)

Below — The wily raven appears frequently in legends, and is a symbol for many clans in Southeastern Alaska. According to William Paul Sr., there were really two ravens in Tlingit legends: Nass Raven, who guarded the great lights — the sun, the moon and the stars — and his grandson Scamp Raven, who did all the tricks and who was the master of deception. (JOHN JOHNSON)

*I*n Ketchikan they tell the story of a Haida lad who returned home from grade school greatly upset.

"The teacher said it wasn't true that we were descended from the raven, like you said," the boy told his father. "Now sit down, son," the father said firmly. "I want to have a talk with you.

"You were descended from the raven. The white man may be descended from the monkey, but you were descended from the raven!"

237

Most Native villages in Southeastern Alaska are Tlingit, but in the southern part of the Panhandle there are a few Haida settlements, and the Tsimshian town of Metlakatla, on Annette Island.

Upper right — Angoon, on Admiralty Island, was the home of what were said to be the wealthiest and fiercest of Tlingits — never defeated by the Russians. The village of about 500 is largely dependent on the sea and surrounding island wilderness for subsistence. (REVEREND GORDON OLSON, REPRINTED FROM THE MILEPOST®)

Right — Hydaburg, home of the Haidas, has revitalized a once-closed cannery and is providing jobs for local people. When the village was founded in 1911 on the southwest coast of Prince of Wales Island (a consolidation of several villages that banded together to improve educational opportunities), the people adopted many of the white man's ways. Now they are also energetically bringing back many of the old traditions.

Metlakatla, with a population of about 1,000, is the only Tsimshian settlement in Alaska. The town, on Annette Island south of Ketchikan, was founded in 1887 when the Reverend William Duncan led a religious migration of about 400 Tsimshians from their former village near Prince Rupert, British Columbia. Today the village relies heavily on commercial fisheries.

"These are the least Indian-like of all Indians," observed Tsimshian Jack Hudson, who retraced his people's migration trail to Canada and then, in 1975, returned to teach art in Metlakatla, the village where he was born.

"In this town," he said, "there's no use for our culture. People had to learn to survive in the white man's world and they do it very well."

Yet they hired Hudson to teach traditional art. A step forward — or perhaps backward?

Colorful dances tell stories in the Southeastern Indian culture.

Opposite — The Chilkat Dancers of Haines, who have demonstrated Chilkoot tribal dances throughout Southeastern Alaska — even abroad — are the "descendants" of a Boy Scout troop whose leader, Carl Heinmiller, encouraged a revival of Native dancing. The dancers are not all Native, but their movements are traditional Tlingit.

Left — Henry Denny of Saxman, the last potlatched chief of his line, can recall when white men sailed to the village and traded firearms for furs. Here Denny's great-granddaughter Sherrie Seirerup plays a Tlingit drum while Denny sings traditional songs. Saxman is just south of Ketchikan.

Lower left — Georgina Kamas models an old Tlingit hat, decorated with carved fish and a bird, at Sheldon Jackson Museum, in Sitka.

Below — Ellen Lang Hays, then superintendent of Sitka National Historical Park, tells the story of a totem that is being dedicated at the park.

Overleaf — Kasaan, which once boomed with copper mining and canning, was almost a ghost town by the mid-1950's. But a handful of people stayed and the town, on Prince of Wales Island, won recognition as a Native village under the Alaska Native Claims Settlement Act. Population in 1977 was still only 38, but the village is looking forward to a brighter future.

Wildlife abounds in the forests and seas of Southeastern Alaska.

Right — A black bear is reflected in the water near Bell Island, north of Ketchikan. Larger brown bears — notably the big *Shiras* grizzly of Admiralty Island — also are found in Southeastern Alaska. (TIM THOMPSON)

Lower right — Another neighbor of Natives in Southeastern is the whale — this one a large humpback in Glacier Bay. Unlike Eskimos and Aleuts to the north, the Indians of Southeastern did not heavily hunt whales, but included them in traditional tales and utilized beached whales whenever they were spotted. (WILLIAM BOEHM)

Below — Tlingits, after moving from the Interior to the coast hundreds of years ago, retained their superior hunting and trapping skills, continuing to use skins for clothing to a greater extent than some other coastal tribes. The occasional object of a hunt — then and now — is the Sitka blacktail deer. (JERROLD OLSON)

244

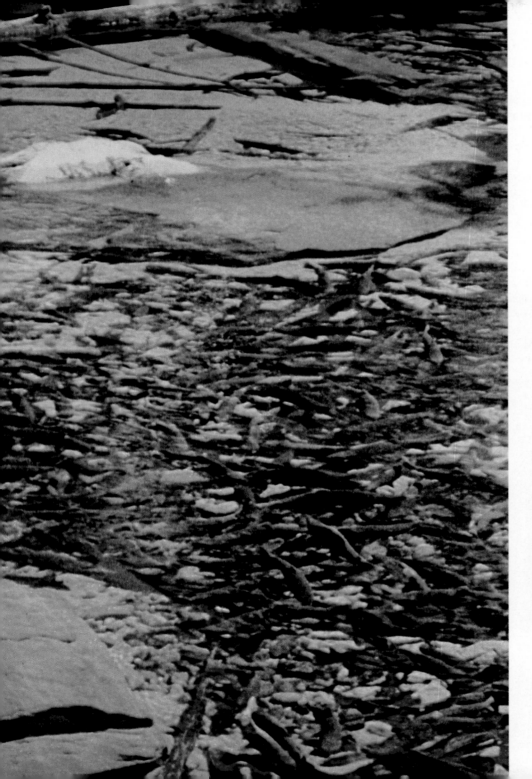

Left — The abundant salmon are a basic element of life in Southeastern Alaska. These sockeye salmon, in the "Glory Hole" of Chilkoot Lake, near Haines, are near the end of their spawning cycle. (RICK FURNISS)

Below — The Tlingits, "people of the tide," share their tidal areas with thousands of bald eagles . . . perhaps as many as 25,000 in Southeastern Alaska. This adult eagle is in a cottonwood tree near Haines. (STEVE WASTE, REPRINTED FROM ALASKA® MAGAZINE)

Seafood is abundant in the waters and on the beaches of Southeastern Alaska; it is important both to the economy and diet of Tlingits, Haidas and Tsimshians.

Below — Don Miller (*left*) and Dave Ketah, a Tlingit from Ketchikan, search the waters near Revillagigedo Island at low tide for octopus and abalone. (R. J. HOFF)

Right — Dave Ketah takes a break from clamming at Carroll Inlet near his Ketchikan home to sample one of the butter clams raw, too anxious to wait until he returns home and the clams are fried, steamed or made into fritters and chowder. (R. J. HOFF)

Lower right — Seaweed is dried in Angoon, Admiralty Island, before serving. Some fresh plants are pan-fried; others are partially dried and dipped in vinegar. Another method is to sun-dry small strips of seaweed or gather the strips in large covered baskets, allow them to rot for four or five days, then press them into drying frames which are hung outside until the pressed seaweed cakes are hard and dry.

T lingit Andy Hope, *writing for the now-defunct*
Alaska Advocate, laid it on the line to Native
corporate leaders:

*"The acculturated and sassy Native vanguard cannot
have it both ways . . . they cannot advocate development of
finite resources on Native lands — a development that
could cause irreversible environmental and cultural
changes — and at the same time use subsistence as the
motherhood issue of proving Nativeness. Offshore and
onshore development of mineral resources will have deep
impacts on Native land.*

*"In the 1976 Alaska legislative session Native lobbyists,
born-again conservationists, joined with the multi-national
oil corporations to kill legislation that would have
increased taxes for mineral developers. The revenue of
these taxes could pay for badly needed social and
educational programs and facilities. The rationale given by
the Native leadership for this action was that such
increases would discourage development and exploration
for mineral resources on Native lands. No mention was
made of the need to continue development of subsistence
resources on these lands.*

*"It's time for the Native decision-makers to carry water
for their own traditions. Time for them to acknowledge the
ancestors. Time to hold the line, time to fight for continued
existence, perpetual existence of the real people's
culture."*

Brothers Al (*left*) and David Ketah, Tlingits of the
Wolf/Eagle clan, display the results of a successful day's hunt at
Carroll Inlet: a deer, a hair seal, clams and several surf scoter
ducks. (R. J. HOFF)

Traditionally Tlingits fished with ornately carved hooks into which they hoped magic spirits had been imbued. Today hand-trollers go modern and the fishing is still good.

Above — Hand-trollers from Angoon work the waters off Danger Point. The Southeastern hand-trolling fleet, now operating under new regulations enacted by the state, operates from a wide variety of vessels — from small skiffs to fancy boats costing as much as $20,000. (ROBERT HENNING, STAFF)

Right — Tlingit Raino Hill, a lifetime resident of Hoonah, hand-trolls near his home. Hill, whose father was a halibut fisherman, began fishing on a purse seiner, and has been hand-trolling since he was 15. (ROBERT E. JOHNSON)

Opposite — Raino Hill and his son Patrick (steering the skiff) hand-troll near Hoonah. Fishing is a long-time family occupation for the Hills. Raino's wife Lori also works in the fishing industry, for Thompson Fish Company in Hoonah. (ROBERT E. JOHNSON)

Above — Dave Jensen, nephew of skipper Joe Demmert, fishes aboard a 56-foot purse seiner in Icy Strait. At the time the Native skipper was on the board of the Alaska Department of Fish & Game, and lived in Ketchikan. (DOYAL GUDGEL)

Right — The purse seiner *Jerilyn* of Angoon, skippered by Captain Peter Jack, goes after salmon in Chatham Strait, on the west side of Admiralty Island. (JOE UPTON, REPRINTED FROM ALASKA GEOGRAPHIC®)

Left — Lights reflect off the slick dock as employees of Annette Island Packing Company, processing salmon roe for shipment to Japan, work into the night during fishing season. The company is in Metlakatla, Alaska's only Tsimshian community. (TIM THOMPSON)

Below — Alaska's only legal fish traps are operated in tribal waters by Tsimshians from Metlakatla. The traps lead fish into a funnel-like series of net enclosures from which there is no easy escape. (JERROLD M. OLSON, NATIONAL MARINE FISHERIES SERVICE)

Totem parks have appeared in many towns and villages as old totems have been rescued from the forest . . . or reproduced by modern carvers.

Above — Relatively new totems and a few restored originals stand at Klawock's totem park, overlooking the village on the west coast of Prince of Wales Island. In the background is a large sawmill that helps support villagers. (DIANNE HOFBECK)

Right — U.S. Forest Service workers salvage a totem at the site of Old Kasaan, under an agreement with the descendants of Chief Sonihat, who established the village. The salvage job was begun in 1970. (PAUL BECK, REPRINTED FROM ALASKA GEOGRAPHIC®)

The village of Kake, on the west coast of Kupreanof Island, depends on logging, commercial fishing and fish processing, but also relies to some extent on subsistence fishing and hunting. Logging clearcuts are visible on hillsides behind the village. In fact, if you squint, there's a silver balloon on the horizon near the center of the photo — used to transport logs down steep hillsides that cannot be reached by logging trucks. (STEVE HILSON)

The October-December 1974 issue of People and Progress, a newsletter published for Native stockholders of the Sealaska Corporation, gets down to the capitalistic basics:

"What does stock ownership mean to you? Money!

"There is absolutely nothing wrong with that answer. And there is nothing wrong with money. . . . With money you can acquire the things you need, and gain a measure of independence and security.

"Your stock ownership in Sealaska and your village or urban corporation, if you are enrolled in one, represents a source of money — or income — over a long period of time."

Education, character and a social system based on property and class have combined to help make the Natives of Southeastern successful — perhaps more than some other Native groups — in the business world.

Above — Carol Duncan runs a waterfront gift shop in Juneau, serving as a one-woman information center for tourists who have questions about her Native ancestors.

Right — The Sealaska Building in Juneau, one of the most modern in Southeastern, was built by the Sealaska Corporation.

Upper left — Martin Strand, a talented Tlingit photographer, prefers non-traditional modes of travel. He is well known in Sitka for his work as an announcer on one of the local radio stations.

Left — Marlene Johnson of Hoonah, an early leader in the land claims movement and vice-president of the board of Southeast Skyways at the time of this photograph.

Above — Another example of Tlingit corporate endeavors is the Shee Atika Lodge, a major hotel facility in Sitka. The lodge was built by the local Native corporation in 1978. (BETTY JOHANNSEN, STAFF)

Not all Natives are building new hotels or houses, of course. For many, life has gone on more or less as it did before the Native Claims Settlement Act.

Left — An old section of Juneau, long known as Indian Village, nestles on the flat a few hundred feet below the governor's mansion. The brown house is a Tlingit tribal house. (There has been talk of tearing down these houses because of their age, but for the same reason there also have been proposals to restore them. They may not be quite old enough to go either way.)

Lower left — At the beginning of the 1970's Angoon showed one of the lowest per capita incomes in the state. Native fishermen, among the first to build their own cannery, had been wiped out by fire and the village was quite rundown. Today new housing gives the town sparkle and a modern community center helps bring the town together.

Below — Natives traditionally had summer camps, such as this one across the channel from Angoon, for planting gardens, fishing or storing gear. Although this scene might appear to a non-Native to be a picture of abandonment, that is not the case — Native buildings and lands are rarely deserted. (ROBERT A. HENNING, REPRINTED FROM ALASKA GEOGRAPHIC®)

Right — Klukwan, its houses extending in a long line along the Chilkat River, is the headquarters of the Chilkat tribe of Tlingits. The village, 22 miles from Haines, is the site of the traditional Whale House, which contains priceless paintings and carvings.

Transportation between villages and towns of South-eastern Alaska is primarily by floatplane and state ferry, although many Southeasterners — Native and white — rely heavily on their own smaller boats.

Above — The people of Hoonah, on the north coast of Chichagof Island, had cause to celebrate when the small state ferry *LeConte* was built and Hoonah was included on its route. Until then the villagers had been dependent on expensive air transportation for travel and freight.

Right — A Grumman Goose amphibian, beloved and aging workhorse of the Panhandle, idles to the dock in the Tlingit village of Angoon. When completion of the new airport near Ketchikan forced Alaska Airlines to retire the amphibians it had used to shuttle passengers from downtown to the old airport on Annette Island, the airline purchased a full-page ad in the *Ketchikan Daily News.* The only copy in the ad was a large headline over a small photo of a departing amphibian: "Good-bye, Goose . . ." (TIM THOMPSON)

Overleaf — The handiest football field at Hoonah is the gravel beach, literally at the village's front door. Hoonah has been occupied almost since prehistory. Legends describe an earlier home in Glacier Bay, before the last glacial advance. When the great ice masses threatened, small bands of people were forced to search for new homes. One group settled here, naming the village Hoonah — "place where the north wind doesn't blow." (TIM THOMPSON)

A n observation from Bill Blackstad, cannery watchman at the revitalized village of Kasaan:

"There are 10 youngsters back in the village and school is open again. After so many years it sounds so good to hear children screaming and hollering and fighting. At first I kept running out to find out what was going on. But it's a good noise . . ."

Education has long been important to Natives in Southeastern, and the interest in learning has apparently paid off. According to the late William Paul Sr., the first Native nurses, teachers, lawyers and legislators came from Southeastern.

Right — Students learn how to repair snow machines in a manual-training shop in Yakutat.

Opposite — Sheldon Jackson College, in Sitka, is one of the two largest colleges in Southeastern Alaska. The other is the University of Alaska's Southeast campus near Juneau. Founder of the Sitka school, Presbyterian missionary Sheldon Jackson, salvaged lumber from a deserted cannery to erect the first building on the present campus . . . in 1882. (ERNEST MANEWAL)

"**S**ince the early traders' commercial practices often bordered on extortion, it is not surprising that [the Tlingits'] relations with the outside world began on a bad footing. The Tlingits, however, were warlike people quite equal to the task of protecting their interests. In 1799 they wiped out a Russian trading station, and a century later did not hesitate to dispatch two war canoes to Seattle to press for return of a totem pole stolen by a group of tourists. . . . The past century and a half has seen changes in the tenor of Tlingit life, but, at the same time a remarkable continuity."

— *Harvard Magazine, 1974*

Left — Built in 1894, Saint Nicholas Russian Orthodox Church is the oldest Russian church in Southeastern Alaska. The Russian Orthodox Church has many Native members throughout the state, and Southeastern is no exception.

Above — At Tonowek Narrows, near Klawock, a wooden figure overlooks a canoe in which a Tlingit shaman was laid to rest in the traditional manner. The canoe rests on ground just to the right of the overgrown log. The dead shaman, along with some of his possessions, was placed in the canoe — probably within the past three generations — with a figure guarding each end. (BARRY HEREM)

Delegates attend the 1976 convention of the Alaska Native Brotherhood at Hoonah. The ANB, first Native organization to be formed on more than a local basis, was put together in 1912 by one Tsimshian and nine Tlingits, and has been a strong political force ever since.

"The Native vote is simply not going up for grabs any more. I don't think we're ever going to see that happen again. Whoever is going to take a statewide election is going to have to deal with the Natives. Nobody can ever take us for granted again."
—— John Borbridge
first president
of Sealaska
the Southeastern
regional Native
corporation

Arts and crafts of the Southeastern Indian world have become well known — especially totemic wood carvings and silverwork.

Above — The silver bracelets of Frank Wrenn are displayed in Sitka. Carved silver bracelets generally cost $100 to $600 apiece. (FRANK SHOEMAKER)

Upper right — Selena Peratrovich, 87, is one of the few remaining Haidas skilled in the traditional art of basketry. Tlingits and Haidas used spruce roots and dyed grass to make baskets for many household uses. The same skills and materials went into hats such as the one she is working on.

Right — Ed James, a Tlingit silversmith, at work in the Alaska Native Brotherhood Cultural Center, Sitka. (ERNEST MANEWAL)

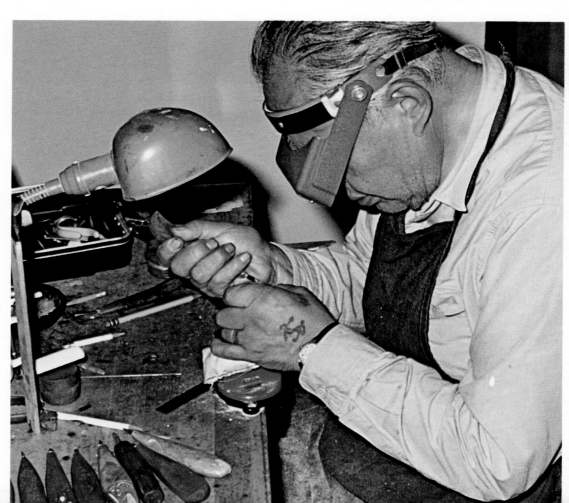

Left — Lani Strong Hotch of Klukwan, north of Haines, works on a Chilkat blanket in her grandmother's house; a portrait of her great-grandmother is on the wall.

Below — A Chilkat ceremonial blanket on display at Sitka National Historical Park. Such blankets, made by a subgroup of the Tlingits, were woven from cedar fibers and spun goat hair that had been dyed with pigments from local plants and minerals. (ERNEST MANEWAL)

Archivist Pam Transki is dwarfed by totems from old Haida and Tlingit villages at the Totem Heritage Cultural Center in Ketchikan.

Left — A 200-year-old housepost, one of four in the Chief Shakes house at Wrangell. This post, which once was painted, makes use of a frequent carver's device — representing two people by carving one face on the tongue of another. (BARRY HEREM, REPRINTED FROM ALASKA® MAGAZINE)

Below — Helmet of Katlean, famous Tlingit warrior who lead his people in their last assault against the Russians (1804). Carved out of a knot of wood and covered with bearskin — spotted with human blood some say — the relic was given to the Sheldon Jackson Museum for safekeeping by Katlean's descendants.

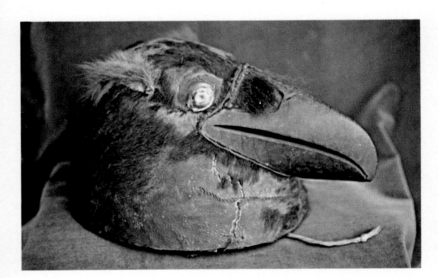

"I am proud of my tribe — two of us were the first to go to the Atlantic coast to school; we were the first to have members who were given registered-nurse status; the first to obtain judicial sanction to our claim to U.S. citizenship; the first to have a college graduate; the first to have a member qualify as an attorney; the first to have a lawyer admitted to practice before the Supreme Court of the United States and the U.S. Court of Claims; the first to initiate legislation that would give Natives the right to sue for value of their lands; the first to file claims to the Arctic Slope area, Tanacross, Copper Center and other places."

——— Letter from Willam Paul Sr.
Tlingit leader

Lillian Hammond, left, and Tommy Jimmy of the Gei San Dancers from Haines perform at an Alaska Native Brotherhood Convention in Hoonah. Jimmy, a Tlingit carver, recently carved two replacement totems for the Sitka Totem Park.

We came to the city
All dressed up and pretty
In clothes that we bought
    that cost quite a lot . . .
Yet why are they laughing?
Almost in tears?
After all, these are clothes
    mail ordered from Sears . . .
We tried to be friendly
    and be of good cheer,
Instead we are "Natives,"
    and (it's) said with a leer . . .

From "The City"
Phil Kelly 1973

URBAN NATIVES

By Lael Morgan

The history of urban Natives began in the mid-1700's when fur traders took Aleuts home to Russia to satisfy the curiosity of the royal family or to serve as hostages. It's thought that the majority of the early transplants died of diseases encountered on foreign soil or from the brutality of their captors, but a few returned to their villages as teachers, priests or interpreters, and encouraged others to make the trip.

Today, 200 years later, traffic is up considerably and cultural shocks endured — though less dramatic — are still extreme. They vary, of course, as does the sophistication of different Native villages and cultures, and because of this we have asked three historians to chart their course.

Fred Stickman, born in Nulato in 1907, entered the wage economy at 17, working first for the Alaska Railroad, then as a civilian employee for the Air Force and, most recently, on construction of the trans-Alaska pipeline. His roots, however, are traditional and he is well known throughout Alaska for his "Letters to the Editor," which expound his views of contemporary subjects.

An arctic Eskimo in the ice fog of Fairbanks. Sometimes only the cold is familiar, but an increasing number of Natives are trading village life for jobs in Anchorage or Fairbanks.

Mrs. Edna McCurdy was raised by traditional Aleut grandparents in Unalaska, lived briefly in the orphanage there, then moved to the Lower 48 where she worked her way through college and earned a teaching degree. Her expertise was heavily relied on by the Unalaska Corporation in enrolling Aleuts like herself who had been dispersed outside the state, and she keeps in close touch with her people.

Phil Kelly emerged with Native leadership in the mid-1960's to work on the land claims movement, then went with the Community Economic Development Corporation. In recent years he has returned summers to fish commercially with his family at Egegik, but he lives in the city in the off-season.

Fred Stickman

Edna McCurdy

Phil Kelly

TIM JONES, STAFF

In the early 1970's, drawn by jobs, educational opportunities, the need for better health care or perhaps just the spirit of adventure, village people began migrating in earnest to Alaska's major cities. Soon Anchorage, the state's population center, was referred to jokingly as the "biggest Native Village of them all." But now, with more than 10,000 Indians, Aleuts and Eskimos in residence, that is no longer a joke. Fairbanks, Alaska's second-largest city, has attracted more than 5,000 Natives, and Juneau, Dillingham, Bethel and other regional centers also are swelling in size.

For those who arrived early, it was generally a traumatic experience. Phil Kelly, then 15, was among the first, moving with his family from the small village of Egegik to Anchorage. Kelly's father, a successful trapper and commercial fishermen, had enough money to weather the change and Kelly's sister already had a job but there were problems, nonetheless.

"I felt uncomfortable that I wasn't dressed like everybody else," he recalls. "I wanted to be accepted. In a little community, if you help someone you don't expect an immediate return. In the city you get weird looks if you help people."

Early villages were an extended family; supportive, even to those who were not particularly well liked. If a

Upper left — *Natives who move to the city often need job training. Fannie Gemmill of Arctic Village is a case in point, learning to type at a vocational school run by the Kenai Native Association. (She saves babysitting money by taking her daughter, Faith, to class with her.)*
Left — *Annie Makalik moved to Fairbanks from Barrow hoping to find a milder climate for herself and better opportunities for her children. Instead she found rents so high that she was forced to spend the first winter in a garage, even though she earned money sewing skins and got help from Social Services.*

man was sick or broke, traditionally the village would come to his aid. If he got drunk and fell down, someone would take him home. There were no locks on doors. There were no strangers.

More important, since villagers shared the same standard of living (mainly that of subsistence hunters) and had little idea how the rest of the world lived, it was a rude awakening for urban imigrees to discover they were considered poor and that being poor was a stigma.

Still, for many the move was worth the cost; and for some it even proved fun and exciting.

"We spent two whole days just exploring Fourth Avenue," recalls Phil Kelly of his first trip to town. "A cousin and I, we took one side a day and went every place that wasn't a bar. And we ate a hamburger whenever we could. I'd never seen hamburgers."

For Native housewives — especially mothers of large families — the urban move often meant an introduction to electricity and running water; luxuries that they were soon loath to give up. And in those early days, television was also a novelty; not only to be enjoyed but providing an unexpected avenue to easy acculturation.

As the numbers of migrants increased, services were created to help them. In Anchorage the

Alaska Federation of Natives pioneered driver's training and traveler's aid for Natives during the land claims fight. Then the nonprofit arm of Cook Inlet Region Inc., backed by city-wise Natives, descendants of those who claimed the territory before Anchorage was dreamed of, landed multimillion-dollar funding for emergency aid, welfare, programs for youth and oldsters; even traditional social get-togethers — berry picking excursions out of town and potlaches — to make newcomers feel more at home.

Fairbanks Native Association, with many members second-generation city dwellers, undertook similar programs in the Interior. The University of Alaska established an orientation program for growing numbers of bush/Native students. Alcohol treatment and sleep-off centers were set up, not only in major cities but in outlying areas. Still the transition remains tough for many.

"I see more and more Natives on Fourth Avenue in Anchorage and Second Avenue in Fairbanks, in the bars," observes Fred Stickman whose heart still lies in his Athabascan village of Nulato although he left as a young man to work on the railroad and long since gave up subsistence hunting for a union job.

"They leave the villages because there is no work, no excitement; and some places is poor living. A lot of them leave for schooling or to get married to GI's. I left

Left — *Anchorage has more people, more money and more jobs than any city in Alaska. It may not be the ideal "village," but more than 10,000 Natives have settled here.*
(GEORGE HERBEN)
Right — *Fairbanks is the transportation, population and financial center of the Interior — a fairly short air trip from any village in the region. The University of Alaska has drawn many Natives to Alaska's second-largest city, and quite a number have stayed.* (ATMS, BOB GIERSDORF)

[after a recent return to the bush] because there is no recreation for old people."

But the increasing numbers of downtown drunks, of Native youngsters in the pool halls at all hours of the day and night, of Natives frequenting the bars, worry Stickmen considerably.

"I tried to keep my boys in the village and my daughter, but as soon as they reached 17 they wanted to make their own living," he says.

Still, wood for heat and cooking is getting scarce in Nulato, he considers, and few youngsters seem interested in trapping nowadays. One of his boys went off for training as a doctor, something he certainly couldn't have done at home. And, although Stickman, himself, returns ritually to the Yukon every fall to fish for salmon as his grandfather before him, there is much he enjoys about city living.

"Now I'm 71 and I started to live here. Eat in the

Opposite — Eskimo Laura Wright, who once delivered mail by dog team, is an urban success story, having developed a lucrative business making parkas. A widow, Laura has raised six children on profits from her business and sewing skills.
Below — The Cook Inlet Native Association in Anchorage holds weekly dinners where Natives can enjoy familiar foods. The association, serving Natives from all parts of the state, has among its projects trips to the country for those who need to get away from the city atmosphere.
Lower right — Charles Anderson, Anchorage Chief of Police, is an Aleut who started working for the department when it was almost unheard of for a Native to do police work. Even today, despite affirmative-action programs, there are few Natives on the Anchorage force.

277

restaurants; go to the bars [although he's a teetotaler] and meet different people from all over Alaska."

Even the simple pleasure of driving . . .

"I like to go on the highway, paved; with a nice car," Stickman admits. "I like to stop all along and meet a lot of nice people."

Under the land claims settlment, a 13th Region was established for Natives long settled outside Alaska, and Edna Pelagia McCurdy, who taught school for 22 years in California, would have qualified had not she elected to return to her village of Unalaska in 1967.

The trip was a shock because the village had been bombed by the Japanese during World War II, then turned into an enormous fort, which the U.S. government subsequently abandoned, leaving the landscape scarred by roads and ruins.

"My first thought was . . . 'Well, you see the same hills; the same sky, but I think I'll write Lady Bird Johnson and tell her about this beautification program. . . . What the military has done.'"

Only a few of the original families had returned but displaced Aleuts from other settlements, now abandoned, had taken their places and Mrs. McCurdy was delighted with her young Aleut students. She spent happy hours combing familiar beaches; was glad to be back.

What she remembers best was the day she was finally trusted to work in her family's Russian Orthodox church: she requested the humble task of cleaning candle drippings.

"My grandmother did this job," she told the church ladies when she insisted on taking the assignment.

Giving up television and telephones proved no problem. The only thing she really missed was newspapers. And she stayed for some years in the village, helping organize its Native corporation until sickness in the family and the weakening of her own health brought her back to Washington State.

Today, in a comfortable condominium at Oak Harbor, Washington, she counts her blessings.

"I like Whidbey Island. Everything is within walking distance. Medical care is handy. But I'm not satisfied. I want to go back. . . ."

And surprisingly, even as the number of city migrants continues to grow, so, too, do many village populations. For one thing, Alaska's aboriginal people are in the midst of a population explosion, and more and more the amenities — electricity, better transportation, better health care — are making village life more attractive.

Often nowadays, young Native couples leave city jobs to raise their young children in the relaxed, traditional village setting; then return to the city — to better educational and job opportunities — when their youngsters reach high school. Some opt for complete acculturation but the average urban Native will go home again, if only to visit; thereby managing to keep a foot in both worlds.

Left — *At the Sitka Pioneers' Home, Bella Hammond (wife of Jay Hammond, governor of Alaska at the time the photo was taken), serves tea to Gertrude (Mrs. George) Beck.*
Above — *Tlingits Lillian Nielsen (left) and Cynthia Williams, members of the Gajaa Heen Dancers, hurry to a totem-raising ceremony in Sitka where they are to perform.*
Opposite — *Barrow residents and conference delegates gather for an evening of entertainment during the Circumpolar Conference in that city; the June 1977 conference drew Eskimo delegates from Alaska, Canada and Greenland to discuss common political goals.*

Epilogue: And Looking to the Future

The Alaska Native Land Claims Settlement Act of 1971 was unique. Not only was it the largest settlement ever made by the United States government with an aboriginal people — approximately $1 billion and 40 million acres of land — but it was also one that allowed the beneficiaries to manage the proceeds, to determine their own future.

It made Alaska Natives the largest private landowners in the state, but, although they are free to sell this land as soon as they receive title, stock in the regional corporations endowed under the act must be held for 20 years from the date of settlement, until the youngest stockholders have reached the age of majority.

The value of this legacy will vary from region to region. Some regions have already lost great sums, while others have turned remarkable profits, providing new economic stability for their people.

But even where regional corporations do poorly (and aside from the Settlement Act) there is new opportunity open to Natives — far broader horizons than those enjoyed by their forebears, due to better health care, better education and a definite political coming of age.

Alaska's Native people have proved themselves to be hearty survivors and with their strong roots and rich cultural heritage, their future may well prove as fascinating as their past. —*Lael Morgan*

Left — Josephine Mountain teaches beadwork to children at Nulato, an Athabascan village on the Yukon about 25 miles west of Galena.

Below — Anna Capjohn, Native teacher's aide at Old Harbor, works after school with her young charges.

Right — Aleut Danny Boy Snigaroff, on the dark sands of Sandy Beach at Atka, hurles a javelin-like piece of driftwood out to sea. This is the way his Aleut ancestors hunted and like most Aleut boys Danny knows the importance of his past. Although he speaks excellent English and has lived in cosmopolitan areas, he is also fluent in Aleut and prefers his Native island and living off the land.

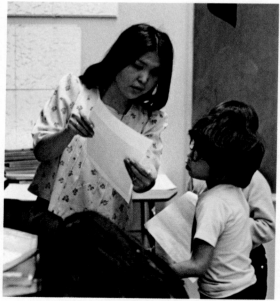

"**A**ny race of people, given a chance to educate themselves, they're just as good as anybody else. I didn't think I was going to see in my lifetime my people going to college and universities; getting professional positions. Now I see these young people getting education. Our manager has two years of college. Our council members have high school. Now I don't think I have to worry when I retire."

— Gabriel Stepetin
Council President, Saint Paul

Important Dates in Native History

1728—Vitus Bering and Alexei Chirikov sighted and named Saint Lawrence Island, the first part of what is now Alaska to be sighted by westerners. They also passed the easternmost point of Asia and concluded that it was not joined to the American continent, although they did not see the latter.

1741—Alexei Chirikov in the *Saint Paul* made a landfall in what is now Southeastern Alaska in July and sent two boat crews ashore. Both disappeared and it was thought they had been captured by Natives. Natives in canoes were sighted but no communication was established with them.

1741—Vitus Bering in the *Saint Peter* sighted the Alaska coast at Mount Saint Elias in July and sent a party ashore on Kayak Island. Georg Steller, naturalist, found a camp but did not actually see Natives. The artifacts he gathered inclined him to believe that they were much like the Siberian Natives.

1742—Alexei Chirikov, making a second voyage in the *Saint Paul*, sighted Attu Island but did not land.

1745—Mikhail Nevodchikov led a party of fur hunters in the vessel *Yevdokia* to Agattu Island where they fought with the Natives, then moved to Attu Island. There they fought again and spent the winter. This was the first Russian beachhead in Alaska.

1745—The first Aleut blood was shed by a Russian fur hunter on Agattu Island on September 26. A Native was wounded in the hand by a musket shot.

1749—A system of collecting tribute from Native residents, already in force in Siberia, was extended by the ministers of Empress Elizabeth to include the Aleutian Islands. The tribute was collected in the form of furs.

1749—Late in the year the vessel *Saint Ioann* set sail for the Aleutians and went to the Near Islands. It returned in 1752 with 700 sea otters and 700 blue foxes.

1753—A vessel owned by Alexei Serebrennikov and skippered by Petr Bashnakof was credited with discovering Tanaga Island in the Fox Islands group of the eastern Aleutians. They intimidated the Natives with musket fire and then secured furs.

1760—The merchant Andriian Tolstykh reached Adak Island in the vessel *Andriian i Natalia* and over the next three years made a detailed census of that and other nearby islands. He gave Russian citizenship to all of the Natives he encountered. Bancroft gives the date of his arrival at the island as 1761.

1763—Stepan Glottov discovered Kodiak Island on September 8. He attempted to persuade the Natives to pay tribute to the Imperial government and to furnish hostages, but they refused and attacked the Russians.

1774—Spaniard Juan Perez in the *Santiago* sighted the southern end of what is now Prince of Wales Island. He also saw an old bayonet and other pieces of iron implements in the hands of the Natives and concluded that they had come from the Chirikov voyage of 1741. This finding was instrumental in establishing the eventual 54°40′ boundary line.

1778—Captain James Cook sailed along the Alaska coast and made some contact with both Natives and Russians. The furs his sailors acquired and later sold in China aroused the interest of both English and Yankee traders and brought many of them to the Northwest Coast in subsequent years.

1781—Gregory Shelikov, who had been in the Alaska fur trade since 1776, formed a partnership with Ivan Golikov. Later other Russian merchant-traders joined the association which eventually became the Russian-American Company.

1784—The Shelikov-Golikov Company established a settlement at Three Saints Bay, Kodiak Island. This was the first permanent settlement of the Russians in Alaska. There was a continuing conflict between the Kodiak Natives and the Russians.

1785 (1786)—Gregory Shelikov established trading posts on Afognak Island and Cook Inlet, followed by one near Cape Saint Elias. Tikhmenev places these events in the year 1786.

1786—The Lebedef-Lastochkin Company established a fur trading post at the mouth of the Kasilof River on the east side of Cook Inlet and named it Saint George.

1786—Gerassim Pribylov in the *Saint George* discovered Saint George Island in what is now known as the Pribilof Islands. Saint Paul Island was sighted the following year. Residents from the Aleutian Islands were later settled on the uninhabited Pribilofs.

1786—Gregory Shelikov, in a letter to his manager at Three Saints Bay, mentioned a school he opened there for Native children and stated that he would take 40 Natives to Siberia, some of whom would be sent to the Imperial court while some of the children would be instructed in the schools at Okhotsk and Irkutsk.

1787—Grigor Kozlof-Ugrenin, commander of the province of Okhotsk, gave orders to traders and fur hunters that Aleuts were to be treated kindly and were not to be carried away from their homes without their free consent.

1788—Empress Catherine II issued an Imperial ukase on September 28 which among other things revoked all former laws for the collection of tribute from the Aleuts.

1788—Fur trader Gregory Shelikov proposed to augment the labor force of his company by buying from Alaska Natives some of the slaves they had captured in war and who were known as "kalgi."

1789—A Russian expedition commanded by Englishman Joseph Billings sailed for Alaska to make geographical and astronomical findings. The expedition reached Alaska in 1790 and returned to Siberia in 1792.

1790—Aleuts were ordered by Empress Catherine II to hunt furs for the Shelikov Company.

1790—Gregory Shelikov formed his own company, known as the Baptist Company, and employed Alexander Baranov as manager. Baranov arrived in Alaska where he was to remain for 28 years.

1791—The ship *Saint George* of the Lebedef-Lastochkin Company arrived at the mouth of the Kenai River and established a trading post named Saint Nicholas. The site is now occupied by the town of Kenai.

1792—Alexander Baranov, who had just become chief manager of the Shelikov Company, moved its headquarters from Three Saints Bay to Saint Paul Harbor, Kodiak Island. The new settlement became known as Kodiak.

1793—Baranov and a party of hunters were attacked at Prince William Sound and lost two Russians and nine Aleuts. The attacking Natives lost at least 12 killed. Bancroft gives the year as 1792 but Dall and Tikhmenev agree on 1793.

1793—On June 30, Empress Catherine II issued a ukase granting the petition of Shelikov and Golikov that clergymen be appointed for missionary work in Alaska.

1794—Two supply ships reached Kodiak with the first missionaries sent to Alaska. Bancroft says there were "18 clergymen and lay servitors in charge of Archimandrite Ioassaf." Tikhmenev says there were 10 clergymen.

1794—Members of the Billings expedition of 1789 returned to Saint Petersburg and reported some of the cruelties and injustices of the Shelikov Company to the Aleuts. Apparently the reports had some beneficial effect.

1795—In the spring most of the missionaries, at the urging of Baranov, went to the mainland along Cook Inlet to attempt to Christianize the Natives and make them less hostile to the Russians.

1795—Archimandrite Ioassaf reported to Saint Petersburg the conversion of 12,000 Alaska Natives to Christianity, but the claim was received with doubt at the Russian capital.

1795—Baranov made a trip around Kodiak Island during which he took a census. Total population was 6,206, with 3,221 males and 2,985 females.

1796—Settlement of New Russia was established at Yakutat Bay. An unsuccessful effort had been made to place a colony there the previous year.

1796—The first Russian Orthodox church in Alaska built at Three Saints Bay, Kodiak Island, in July.

1797—Natives destroyed the Russian outposts at Iliamna and Tu-i-u-rakand killed 20 Russians and nearly 100 Natives who were employed by the Russians. The year may have been 1798, as the authorities are unclear concerning it. The missionary, Father Juvenal, had been killed at Iliamna in 1795.

1798—Baranov was instructed that Russians who wished to could return to Okhotsk from Alaska and that they could be replaced by Aleuts who were to be paid with goods from the company's stores, at the rate of 50 or 60 paper rubles per year.

1798—Dall reports that a trading post was established at Nuchek, Hinchinbrook Island, at the entrance to Prince William Sound, this year. Bancroft's account seems to place the post there earlier, but his dates are vague.

1799—The Russian-American Company, organized from the old Shelikov companies, was given a 20-year charter by the Emperor, Paul II, amounting to a monopoly in Alaska. The company was required to organize settlements, promote agriculture and commerce, and to propagate the Russian Orthodox Church. Each Aleut was obliged to spend at least three years in company service and to sell all his furs to the company, while Natives of the Kenai and Chugach were required to pay an annual tribute in furs. Alexander Baranov became Chief Manager of the company.

1799—Baranov, en route to establish the first post on Sitka Sound, lost 30 men in a storm at Cape Suckling and about 26 more to an attack by Tlingits.

1799—On May 25 Baranov arrived on Sitka Sound, bartered for a piece of ground, and built a fort which was named for the Archangel Michael. Dall gives the name as Fort Archangel Gabriel. The site is now known as Old Sitka, about six miles from Sitka.

1799—In July, 115 Aleuts, engaged in hunting furs for the Russians, died after eating poisonous mussels in what is now known as Peril Strait, north of Sitka. Some accounts have placed the death toll as high as 200.

1802—A party of 90 baidarkas under Urbanov, returning to Old Sitka after a successful hunt near Dall Island, was attacked by Tlingits in or near Frederick Sound. Only Urbanov and either 13 or 22 Aleut hunters escaped.

1802—Tlingits at Sitka Sound sacked and burned the Russian settlement. According to Tikhmenev, 20 Russians and 130 Aleuts perished; three Russians, five Aleut men, 18 women and six children escaped. Other writers have given other figures.

1802—Natives in the Yakutat area complained that the Russians had taken their furs and robbed graves. There were several attacks on Russian-Aleut hunting parties in the Yakutat-Dry Bay area.

1803—Baranov furnished the American Captain Joseph O'Cain, in the vessel O'Cain, 15 (or 20) baidarkas with 34 Native hunters to hunt sea otters in California. These apparently were the first Native hunters furnished to a foreign ship, a practice that became common in subsequent years.

1804—In September a large force headed by Baranov and assisted by the cannon of the ship Neva under Captain Lisianski battled the Tlingits at Sitka Sound and routed them. The Russians then established the post of New Archangel or Sitka near the site of the battle.

1805—Tlingits at Yakutat totally destroyed the Russian fort and settlement.

1805—The condition of the school for Natives and Creoles was reported far from satisfactory with less than 20 pupils and a lack of qualified teachers.

1805—A census showed 1,652 male and 1,566 Kodiak Islanders living under control of the colonial administration. At Unalaska the number was 997 men and 1,019 women.

1805—Nikolai Rezanov, a director of the Russian-American Company, ordered the colonial clergy to learn the Native language. He began to collect Native words for a dictionary.

1808—As a result of a report by Admiral Krusenstern, the directors of the Russian-American Company ordered Baranov that "in no case are Aleuts and other islanders of either sex to be used in any work against their will and without previous agreement on payment . . . Nor are levies to be imposed on them." Also, the 166 Aleuts moved in 1807 to Sitka were to be settled there permanently if a need for them was foreseen and were to be joined by their families at first opportunity.

1808—Smallpox vaccine was sent to Alaska from Russia with orders to vaccinate the Russians and as many Natives as possible.

1811—The Russians established the settlement of Fort Ross in California and sent a number of Natives there as hunters and workmen.

1816—The French vessel Bordelais under Lieutenant Roquefeuille obtained Aleut hunters at Sitka and went to the Prince of Wales Island area where an attack by Tlingits killed 20 hunters and three women. The company gave 350 paper rubles to the family of each of those killed.

1817—The first Russian Orthodox Church was built at Sitka.

1819—A census taken January 1 showed the population of the Russian colony included 391 Russians, 244 Creoles and 8,384 Natives.

1819—A party of Russians crossed from Cook Inlet to Bristol Bay and established a trading post, Fort Alexander, at the mouth of the Nushagak River. The date of the founding of the fort has also been given as 1820.

1824—The Russian priest Ioann Veniaminov was sent from Irkutsk to Unalaska and took up his long work among the Natives. The Unalaska parish consisted of 254 Russians and Creoles and 1,497 Aleuts.

1826—Captain Frederick Beechey in the H.M.S. Blossom visited Point Hope and estimated that there were 1,000 Eskimos in residence.

1830—A Russian expedition under Ensign Vasilev explored the Kuskokwim River for a considerable distance and found the Natives hostile.

1832—Upon orders from Governor Wrangell, a Creole named Lukin (or Lukeen) built a one-man post on the Kuskokwim River. Later this was moved and in 1841 it became the Kolmakov Redoubt, an important trading station.

1833—The Russians established a trading post named Mikhailovskii, or Saint Michael, on an island in Norton Sound.

1836—A party of Russians from the fort at Saint Michael was attacked by Aiakmiuts, inhabitants of Aiak Island, while cutting wood. Seven Russians were wounded and one was killed.

1836—Smallpox appeared at Sitka where 400 Natives died. It spread to other villages and was reported to have wiped out many settlements in the Yakutat-Dry Bay area. The epidemic finally died out in 1840.

1838—An expedition under Lieutenant Kashevarov explored the Arctic Coast to a point 35 miles east of Point Barrow but turned back because of the hostility of the Natives.

1839—A Russian named Malakhov ascended the Yukon River to the site which became known as Nulato and built a blockhouse there. Bancroft gives the date as 1838. The fort was destroyed by Natives the following year and rebuilt in 1841.

1840—A diocese of the Russian Orthodox Church was formed to include all of Alaska and the precincts of Okhotsk and Kamchatka. Father Veniaminov became Bishop Innokentii and had his headquarters at Sitka. At that time there were four churches and eight chapels in Alaska.

1840—The number of schools for Native children in the Russian colony had grown to four for 100 boys and four for an undisclosed number of girls.

1840—The Russian-American Company, apparently for the first time, sent one of its vessels, the steamer *Nikolai I*, to trade with the Natives on the islands of Southeastern Alaska. The trade was reported profitable for the company.

1842—An ecclesiastical mission was sent to Nushagak by direction of Veniaminov, Bishop Innokentii. The number of Christians there rose from 200 to 600 during the next three years.

1842—Creoles were qualified for entering the Russian Orthodox Church as priests.

1843—As of Easter of this year, 102 Tlingits, including two shamans, had become Christians at Sitka.

1844—Because the Kodiak Island Native settlements had been decimated by the smallpox epidemic of the 1830's, the 65 inhabited places were consolidated by the Russian-American Company into seven settlements.

1844—Czar Nicholas I issued an Imperial ukase relating to the Russian-American Company, which stated: "Children born of a European or Siberian father and a native American mother . . . shall be regarded as creoles" and "creoles who have elected to follow an independent means of livelihood, and who desire to establish themselves in the colonies shall be regarded as colonial civilians." This was interpreted as giving them the status of subjects of the Czar.

1847—A party of Hudson's Bay Company men traveled down the Porcupine River and built a trading post near where the river joined the Yukon. It was named Fort Yukon.

1848—Natives killed a Creole named Serebrennikov and three other company employees who had been sent to explore the Copper River country.

1848—There was an epidemic of measles along much of the Alaska coast and at least 300 Natives died.

1851—The Russian post at Nulato was attacked by Indians and Lieutenant Bernard of the Royal Navy, who was visiting the fort, was among those killed.

1851—Chilkat Indians destroyed the Hudson's Bay Company post, Fort Selkirk, on the upper Yukon River in what is now Yukon Territory.

1852—Natives at Sitka killed 40 Stikine Natives who had come to Sitka for a council with the Russians.

1855—Natives attacked the Russian establishment at Sitka and used the church built especially for the Natives as a fort. Two Russians were killed and 19 wounded; about 60 Indians were killed.

1860—According to a report made this year there were 12,028 Christians in Alaska, including 784 Russians, 1,676 Creoles and 9,568 Natives. Another Russian census, quoted by the U.S. Census Bureau in 1890, shows a total population of only 9,845, including 557 Russians, 1,886 Creoles, 4,486 Aleuts, 931 Kinaitz, 1,398 Kuskokwims, 587 Chugatz and Copper River.

1862—Smallpox appeared among the Natives of Southeastern Alaska but since many of them had been vaccinated by the Russians, it did not reach epidemic proportions.

1863—Total number of Natives in Southeastern Alaska was estimated at 25,000 to 40,000, but those actually counted in various settlements totaled 7,502, including 828 slaves.

1867—Alaska was sold to the United States and the formal transfer was made at Sitka in October. Russian subjects were allowed either to return home or to become American citizens, and many chose the former.

1868—Act of Congress of July 27 extended customs, commerce and navigation laws of the United States to Alaska. It also prohibited importation and sale of distilled liquor and importation and sale of breech-loading firearms within Alaska.

1869—Congress on March 3 made the islands of Saint Paul and Saint George in the Pribilof group a special reserve for government purposes.

1869—After two white prospectors were killed by Indians, several villages of the Kake Indians were shelled and destroyed by the U.S.S. *Saginaw*.

1869—The Indian village at Fort Wrangell was bombarded by cannon fire from Fort Wrangell following some altercations between the soldiers and Natives.

1869—Vincent Colyer, Secretary of the Board of Indian Commissioners, visited Alaska. He submitted a written report on his observations and secured an appropriation of $50,000 for school purposes. In the absence of anyone to administer the funds, they were not expended.

1870—The Pribilof Islands and certain sealing rights were leased to the Alaska Commercial company. The company was required to maintain a school on each Saint Paul and Saint George Island for the children, who were predominantly Natives, for each month of each year.

1870—The Secretary of the Treasury issued an order modifying the Customs Act of July 17, 1868, to permit "inhabitants of Alaska to hunt sea otter." At that time the only sea otter hunters were Natives. See also 1879 for further modification.

1877—Philip Clah, a Tsimshian Indian, started a school at Wrangell. Later in the year a Presbyterian mission was established with Mrs. A. R. McFarland in charge. The mission included a boarding school for girls which continued until 1884, when the building burned and the home was moved to Sitka and consolidated with the Presbyterian mission there.

1877—United States troops were withdrawn from Alaska to assist in putting down an Indian uprising in Idaho. Except for some exploring expeditions, the Army did not return to Alaska until the Klondike gold rush.

1878—In April Presbyterian missionaries Miss Fannie Kellogg and Rev. John G. Brady opened a day school for Indian children at Sitka. The school closed in December.

1878—The first two salmon canneries were built in Alaska, at Klawock and at a site near Sitka.

1879—Residents of Sitka petitioned both the American government at Washington and the British Navy at Esquimault (Victoria) for protection against the local Natives. The British sent the gunboat *Osprey* in March and Washington sent the gunboat *Alaska* in April. Thereafter for nearly 20 years a Navy ship was constantly stationed in Alaska.

1879—The Secretary of the Treasury issued an executive order providing that "No fur bearing animals will be allowed to be killed by persons other than natives . . . or white men lawfully married to natives and residing within the Territory." The portion of the order pertaining to white men was rescinded in 1893.

1879—Commander L. A. Beardslee of the U.S. Navy ship *Jamestown* enlisted three Sitka Tlingits to serve as policemen.

1879—A Roman Catholic church and mission were established at Wrangell.

1880—Miss Olinda Austin, Presbyterian missionary, reopened the day school for Indians at Sitka that had closed in December, 1878. In July, through the cooperation of the Navy, the school was moved into the old Russian hospital building and became partly a boarding school.

1880—In January, Commander L. A. Beardslee, U.S. Navy, ordered a census of the Sitka Native village. It showed that about 15 slaves were being held there. In March, Commander Beardslee freed two condemned witches in the Sitka village.

1880—In February, Indian policeman "Dick" was sent from Sitka on a special mission to the Chilkat country. He persuaded the chiefs there to open the Chilkoot Trail to white prospectors.

1880—A trading post was established among the Chilkat Indians at what later became Haines. Dr. Sheldon Jackson arranged for the opening of a summer school there, taught by Mrs. Sarah Dickinson.

1880—Led by Chief Cowee of the Auks, two prospectors found gold in October on a creek flowing into Gastineau Channel. This was the first major gold discovery in Alaska and resulted in the founding of the town of Juneau.

1880—The first Alaska census under the United States counted 24,516 Natives and 145 whites in the main part of Alaska; 8,900 Natives and 1,900 whites in Southeastern Alaska.

1881—In February, Commander Henry Glass, U.S. Navy, adopted a rule at Sitka compelling the attendance of the Native children at the day school operated by the Presbyterian Church. He also ordered the Native village at Sitka cleaned up with drainage ditches around the houses and the houses whitewashed.

1881—A Presbyterian mission was established and named Haines, with Rev. and Mrs. Eugene S. Willard in charge.

1881—Commander Henry Glass, U.S.Navy, in April negotiated treaties between Stikine and Hoocheenoo tribes and between Stikine and Sitka tribes, ending feuds of long standing.

1881—In May, Commander Henry Glass, U.S. Navy, found that 17 persons were being held as slaves in the Sitka Native village. He gave each a certificate of freedom and served notice to the Native chiefs in other areas that slaves were to be released.

1881—A schoolhouse and teacher's residence were erected at the Tlingit village of Hoonah under the direction of Dr. Sheldon Jackson, and a school was opened by Mr. and Mrs. Walter B. Styles.

1882—In February the old Russian hospital at Sitka, in use as a Presbyterian mission school, burned to the ground, thus eliminating the boarding school for Native children. Day school was continued in makeshift quarters until first building erected on present Sheldon Jackson campus in 1883.

1882—The Northwest Trading Company opened a whale fishery at its trading post at Killisnoo. The explosion of a whale bomb killed two Indians and the tribe took two white men as hostages. The Navy and Revenue Cutter Service combined to shell and largely destroy the village of Kootznahoo (Angoon) and secured release of the hostages. The company changed from whales to herring as raw material for its oil and fertilizer plant.

1882—First salmon cannery on Cook Inlet was built at the mouth of the Kasilof River.

1882—The first salmon cannery on Kodiak Island was built at Karluk and operated this season.

1883—The first building of the Sitka Industrial Training School was erected under the supervision of Sheldon Jackson. This later became the Sheldon Jackson School and is now the Sheldon Jackson College.

1883—An expedition under Lieut. Frederick Schwatka, U.S. Army, using Native guides, crossed from the head of Lynn Canal to the headwaters of the Yukon River and drifted down the river to its mouth. Lieutenant Schwatka later published an extensive report on his travels.

1884—An Organic Act was passed by Congress making Alaska a civil and judicial district. It decreed that Natives were not to be disturbed in the possession of land they used, occupied or claimed. The act also provided for a special commission to "examine into and report upon the condition of the Indians residing in [Alaska] what lands, if any, should be reserved for their use, what provisions shall be made for their education."

1884—The Organic Act, May 17, 1884, provided $25,000 "for the education of the children of school age in the Territory of Alaska without reference to race."

1884—The Congressional Act of July 4, 1884, appropriated $15,000 "for the support and education of Indian children of both sexes at industrial schools in Alaska." This was in addition to the $25,000 appropriated for general education on May 17 and resulted in the establishment of the Sitka Industrial Training School which later became the Sheldon Jackson School.

1884—The first salmon cannery on Bristol Bay was built at Nushagak and made a small pack this year.

1884—A school was established by Dr. Sheldon Jackson at the Tlingit village of Tongass with Louis and Tillie Paul, Natives, as teachers.

1885—By the Organic Act of March 3, Congress appropriated an additional $20,000 for the education of Indian children in industrial schools in Alaska.

1885—In April, Dr. Sheldon Jackson was appointed General Agent for Education in Alaska. He had charge of expending the $40,000 appropriated by Congress in 1884 for Alaska education.

1885—Representatives of a number of churches interested in educational missionary work in Alaska met with Dr. Sheldon Jackson, recently appointed Agent for Education in Alaska, to divide territory so as to further the educational effort. Some of the church schools were to participate in the use of funds appropriated by Congress for educational purposes.

1885—The first public school in Juneau was opened June 1 with 62 Native children, three white children and 10 children of mixed blood in attendance.

1885—A public school was opened at Jackson (Howkan) in September with 57 Native pupils. This school was operated under contract by the Presbyterian mission there.

1885—First public school at Wrangell opened in September with 27 Native children in addition to several whites and children of mixed breed.

1885—First public school at Unalaska opened in October with Sol Ripinsky as teacher and an enrollment of 45 children, all Aleuts or Creoles.

1885—First public school for Native children opened at Sitka in November with 77 pupils. This was in addition to the Sitka Industrial Training School operated by the Presbyterian Church.

1885—The Moravian Church established a mission and school on the Kuskokwim River at the village of Mumtrekhlogamute and named it Bethel.

1885—Governor A.P. Swineford recommended to the Secretary of the Interior the continuance of the Indian police force started by naval officers. (See 1879.) The governor recommended salaries of $20 or $25 per month for Indian policemen.

1886—School was established at Saint Michael by the Missionary Society of the Protestant Episcopal Church and maintained during the winter of 1886-87. In the summer of 1887 it was moved to Anvik on the Yukon River.

1886—The Evangelical Mission Union of Sweden established a mission and school at Unalakleet.

1886—A public school was opened at Klawock in November with a total enrollment of 124 and average attendance of 40.

1886—A public day school opened at Kodiak in a cooper shop in the absence of any other suitable building.

1886—A contract was entered into between the Bureau of Education and the Moravian Church to open a school for Natives at Fort Alexander on the Nushagak River, Bristol Bay. The school was to open in 1887. The place was named Carmel.

1886—A school for Native children opened at Afognak under great difficulties because no interpreter was available.

1886—In the case "In re Sah Quah," U.S. District Judge Lafayette Dawson at Sitka held that both the Thirteenth Amendment to the Constitution and the civil rights bill of 1866 would apply in Alaska and that Sah Quah and any other person held in slavery in Alaska must be freed.

1887—The Secretary of the Interior created a Territorial Board of Education to supervise all schools in Alaska. The board consisted of the governor, the general agent for education in Alaska, and the United States district judge for Alaska.

1887—A second public school opened in Juneau, for Natives. Most of the pupils in regular attendance were from the Presbyterian mission.

1887—Father William Duncan and a large group of Tsimshian Indians moved from British Columbia to Annette Island in Alaska and established the town of Metlakatla.

1887—A man-and-wife teacher team was landed at Unga during the summer to open a school. There were 174 children in the village.

1887—In October the people of Unga "erected and paid for a neat and substantial school building measuring 20 by 24 feet. This is the first community in Alaska to erect its own public school building."

1888—Governor A.P. Swineford reported 13 public schools in operation in Alaska, primarily in Native villages. These were in addition to the many church-supported schools.

1888—A school was opened at the new community of Metlakatla early in the year with Fr. William Duncan as teacher and an enrollment of 170.

1888—The Swedish Evangelical Mission Union established a mission and school at Yakutat. The school opened in the fall of 1889.

1888—Governor A.P. Swineford, traveling on the Navy vessel *Thetis*, made the first inspection trip of Alaska villages by an American governor. The villages included Nuchek, Kodiak, Afognak, Kenai, Seldovia, Karluk, Unalaska, St. Paul, villages on the Nushagak River, Belkofski, Unga, Saint Michael, King Island, Wales, Kotzebue, Cape Lisburne and Barrow.

1889—The first salmon cannery in the vicinity of the Copper River was built on Wingham Island.

1889—At Douglas a school for Natives opened in the fall with an enrollment of 92. It was followed by a school for whites in February, 1890.

1890—Jesse Lee Memorial Home was opened at Unalaska by the Woman's Home Missionary Society of the Methodist Church. It was both a boarding and day school.

1890—A school building and teacher's residence were built at Karluk and school was opened in the fall.

1890—Miss Francis Willard graduated in June at a young ladies seminary at Elizabeth, N.J., and returned to Alaska as an assistant teacher. She is believed to be the first Native to return from school in the states as a teacher.

1890—Census taken by U.S. Bureau of Census showed a total population of 32,052 of whom 23,531 were Natives, 4,298 were whites, 1,823 were of mixed blood, and 2,400 were of other races.

1890—At Cape Prince of Wales the American Missionary Association of the Congregational Church established a mission station and a school which it operated under government contract.

1890—At Point Hope the Protestant Episcopal Church established a school which it operated under government contract.

1890—Presbyterian Board of Home Missions established a mission and school at Barrow.

1891—St. James Mission was established at Fort Adams, mouth of the Tanana River, by the Domestic and Foreign Missionary Society of the Protestant Episcopal Church.

1891—The first Siberian reindeer, purchased with private funds raised by Sheldon Jackson, were landed from the *Bear* on Unalaska Island September 21. They all starved to death because of lack of reindeer moss.

1891—The Commissioner of Indian Affairs in Washington authorized a Native police force for Alaska, with provision for up to four officers and 50 privates. By the end of the fiscal year an officer and 14 privates had been appointed.

1891—Congress created the Annette Island Indian Reservation covering the entire island where the Tsimshian Indians had moved from Canada four years earlier. The reservation was placed under the jurisdiction of the Interior Department.

1892—Members of the Indian Police Force were located at Metlakatla, Wrangell, Klawock, Howkan, Juneau, Douglas, Chilkat and Sitka.

1892—Second load of Siberian reindeer brought by the *Bear* were landed at Port Clarence where the Teller Reindeer station was established. These deer survived.

1893—Congress made its first appropriation, $6,000, for the importation and care of reindeer in Alaska.

1893—The Woman's American Baptist Home Missionary Society established an orphanage and school at Woody Island near Kodiak.

1895—A school was established at the new village of Saxman in the fall with an enrollment of 31.

1900—There was an epidemic of measles and pneumonia among the Natives of the Aleutian Islands and along the Bering Sea coast, with an estimated 2,000 deaths. The revenue cutter *Bear* distributed provisions at Bering Sea settlements to prevent starvation.

1900—The first local Native government was organized at Howkan. On November 30 a mass meeting at the village adopted a constitution providing for a city council, street commissioner, school board, village police and a village clerk.

1900—The Bureau of the Census counted 63,592 people in Alaska including 29,536 Natives and 29,365 whites.

1901—There was an outbreak of smallpox in Southeastern Alaska, and in some of the villages the schools were closed for a time. While there were some deaths among both whites and Natives, the disease did not reach epidemic proportions.

1902—President Theodore Roosevelt by proclamation on August 20 created the Alexander Archipelago Forest Reserve which encompassed most of the larger islands of Southeastern Alaska. This reserve later became the Tongass National Forest.

1902—The importation of reindeer into Alaska ceased this year. A total of 1,280 animals had been imported from Siberia since 1892 and these had increased to 4,975 deer in nine herds.

1902—School boards of the public schools at Juneau and Ketchikan refused to admit Native children on the grounds that Native schools were available to them.

1904—The U.S. District Judge at Juneau ruled that Chief John of the Taku tribe did not enjoy "squatter's rights" to a tract on the waterfront within the corporate boundary of Juneau which he had occupied only after the town was established. Appeals to the Land Office and Congress upheld the ruling.

1904—President Thedore Roosevelt appointed ethnologist George T. Emmons to investigate and report on the condition of the Natives of Alaska. The report was submitted to Congress by the President in January, 1905.

1904—Judge James Wickersham in the case "In re Naturalization of John Minook" decided that Minook, a Creole or mixed blood under Russian rule, had become a citizen of the United States either through the Treaty of Cession in 1867 or through the Organic Act in 1884 and that this rule would apply to others living in a civilized manner.

1905—A law approved on January 27 provided that "The Eskimo and Indian children of Alaska shall have the same rights to be admitted to any Indian boarding school as the Indian children in the states or territories of the United States." This enabled Alaskan children to attend such schools as Carlisle in Pennsylvania, Haskell in Kansas, and Chemawa in Oregon.

1905—Indian policemen were listed for 14 Alaska communities, mostly in Southeastern but including Iliamna, Bethel, Tanana and Circle.

1906—Congress passed the Alaska Delegate Act and the first territory-wide General Election was held. Frank H. Waskey of Nome was elected for a short term and Thomas Cale of Fairbanks for a full term in the House of Representatives at Washington.

1906—Congress enacted a Native land allotment act to grant up to 160 acres of nonmineral land to any Indian or Eskimo who was the head of a family or 21 years of age. The land was to be untaxable and required none of the activities such as cultivation required of white homesteaders. No appropriations were made for surveys, however, and few allotments were made.

1907—An act of Congress approved March 4 provided that all Indians of the Tsimshian and Haida tribes who had emigrated from Canada and settled at Metlakatla should, if otherwise qualified, be entitled to receive licenses as masters, pilots or engineers of steamboats and other craft.

1909—An Act of Congress approved February 6 made it a felony to sell intoxicating liquors to Natives of Alaska.

1910—For the first time the Bureau of Education employed physicians to treat Alaska Native patients and to give instruction in hygiene and sanitation.

1910—The Bureau of the Census reported a total Alaska population of 64,356 of whom 25,331 were Natives.

1911—The Native village of Hydaburg was established by the government to provide for one central school for residents of the villages of Howkan, Klinkwan, Sukkwan and others.

1911—The North Pacific Sealing Convention was signed by the United States, Great Britian, Russia and Japan and prohibited the taking of fur seals in the open ocean. Natives of British Columbia and Alaska, however, were permitted to hunt fur seals as in the past.

1912—The Alaska Native Brotherhood was organized in Southeastern Alaska with the announced intent of preparing Natives to exercise the rights and duties of citizenship.

1912—Residents of the village of Kake resolved to give up all Tlingit ways and adopt the white culture. To observe the event, January 8 was designated Kake Day.

1912—Congress passed the second Organic Act, making Alaska a territory with some strict limitations. First legislative election was held.

1913—Native fur seal hunters at Sitka petitioned to be allowed to use guns instead of the traditional spears for hunting seals.

1913—An official of the U.S. Public Health Bureau was detailed to Alaska to act substantially as a territorial commissioner of health.

1914—The Surveyor General of Alaska, acting under instructions from the Department of the Interior, began the survey of lands in Southeastern Alaska claimed by Indians, with the objective of making allotments to the claimants.

1915—The Second Territorial Legislature passed an act enfranchising all Alaska Natives who could show proof of general qualifications of a voter and total abandonment of tribal customs and the adoptions of a civilized culture.

1915—Tanana Chiefs and other representatives of Natives along the Tanana River met at Fairbanks with government officials to discuss land and other resources problems.

1915—Congress appropriated $25,000 and the Bureau of Education put in $20,000 for the construction of a 25-bed Native hospital at Juneau. Previously the bureau had operated a small hospital in rented quarters there.

1915—Three small hospitals were being maintained by the Bureau of Education—at Nushagak, Nulato and Kotzebue—for Native patients. In addition to the doctors and nurses at the hospitals, doctors were maintained at five other locations and nurses at six locations.

1916—The U.S. Bureau of Education reported it was operating 70 schools for Natives in Alaska with an enrollment of 4,000.

1918—Influenza epidemic swept most of Alaska this year and in 1919 and caused many deaths in Native villages.

1918—In the fall the Bureau of Education opened a tuberculosis sanitarium for Natives in the building formerly occupied by the Presbyterian mission hospital at Haines.

1920—A school census showed 930 full- or part-Native children enrolled in the territorial public schools. Enrollment was 166 in incorporated towns, 764 in unincorporated towns. This was aside from the enrollment in Bureau of Education schools maintained by the federal government.

1920—The Bureau of Education was maintaining hospitals for Natives at Juneau, Kanakanak, Akiak, Nulato and Kotzebue and was employing nine doctors and 13 nurses.

1920—The Navy training vessel *Boxer* was transferred to the Bureau of Indian Affairs for use as a supply ship in Alaska. It was converted to diesel power at Seattle and made its first supply trip to Alaska in 1923.

1920—The U.S. Bureau of the Census reported an Alaska population of 55,036 of whom 26,558, or 48.3%, were Natives.

1921—Orphanages were being maintained by the Bureau of Education at Kanakanak and Tyonek to care for children left homeless by the influenza epidemics of 1918 and 1919.

1923—Steps were being taken to convert the orphanage at Kanakanak into an industrial training school for Southwestern Alaska.

1924—Tlingit William L. Paul, Sr. was elected to the territorial House of Representatives. When he took his seat in the seventh Legislature in 1925, he was the first Alaska Native to do so.

1924—Congress passed legislation extending citizenship to all Indians in the United States who had not yet received it. This act was held to apply to Alaska.

1926—The riverboat *Martha Evangeline* was remodeled as a floating medical clinic for Native villages on the lower Yukon River. It served in this capacity until 1933.

1926—Congress enacted a law to authorize the issuance of deeds to certain Indians and Eskimos for tracts set apart to them in surveys of townsites and to provide for the survey and subdivision of such tracts and of Native towns and villages. The individual tracts were exempt from taxation, were inalienable and could be sold only with the permission of the Secretary of the Interior.

1927—Congress passed Public Law 766 of the 69th Congress to prescribe qualifications for voters in Alaska. They were required to be able to read and write but there was an exemption for those who had voted at the General Election of November 4, 1924, thus permitting many Natives to qualify.

1927—The Bureau of Education established three boarding schools for Natives: Kanakanak with an enrollment of 99; Eklutna with an enrollment of 67; and White Mountain with 56 pupils.

1929—The Tlingit village of Klawock incorporated as a first-class city.

1930—The administrative offices for Alaska of the U.S. Bureau of Education was moved from Seattle to Juneau on July 1.

1930—The Bureau of the Census reported a total Alaska population of 59,278 of whom 29,983, or 50.6%, were Natives. This was the first time since the gold rush that the population included more Natives than whites.

1931—The responsibility of the U.S. Bureau of Education for Alaska Natives was transferred to the U.S. Bureau of Indian Affairs on March 16. A special branch of the latter, known as the Alaska Native Service, was created to administer programs in Alaska.

1932—Five buildings were completed for the Wrangell Institute, a boarding and industrial school near Wrangell.

1932—An orphanage and school for the blind was opened at Tanana by the Alaska Native Service.

1932—The wooden motorship *North Star* was built in Seattle to replace the *Boxer* as supply ship for the Bureau of Indian Affairs. She was the first of a series of vessels of this name which served Alaska coastal villages.

1933—The orphanage operated by the Alaska Native Service at Tanana was closed and the school for the blind was moved from Tanana to Eklutna.

1933—In October the Bureau of Indian Affairs opened a new hospital at Unalaska.

1934—Congress designated Eskimos as "Indians" for verbal expediency in laws and documents of the U.S. government.

1934—John Collier became Commissioner of Indian Affairs and remained in that office for 11 years. During this period the bureau financed anthropologists to collect and publish legends and issued a dictionary of the Aleut language; set up an Arts and Crafts Board to assist the sale of Native handicrafts; and attempted to establish several large land reservations for Natives.

1934—Congress passed the Indian Reorganization Act, of which certain sections were made specifically applicable to Alaska. These provided that groups of Alaska Natives could organize to adopt constitutions and bylaws and to receive charters of incorporation and Federal loans.

1934—Several abandoned buildings at Fort Gibbons, Tanana, were transferred to the Bureau of Indian Affairs and remodeled for a hospital.

1935—Congress passed the Tlingit-Haida Jurisdictional Act to give Natives the right to sue the government for lands taken from them.

1936—Congress authorized the Secretary of the Interior to create Native reservations, but each reservation had to be ratified by a majority vote of not less than 30% of the Native residents of the proposed reservation. Individual land ownership on such reservations was prohibited.

1937—Congress passed a reindeer act which provided that all reindeer in Alaska must be owned by Natives.

1938—Congress granted to the Secretary of the Interior authority to withdraw and permanently reserve tracts not to exceed 640 acres each of the public domain for schools, hospitals and such other purposes as he might deem necessary in administering the affairs of the Natives of Alaska.

1939—The federal government purchased all reindeer in private ownership in Alaska and turned them over to Native groups to manage.

1939—The U.S. Census Bureau reported a total population of 72,524 of whom 32,458 were Natives.

1942—An opinion issued by Nathan R. Margold, Solicitor of the Department of the Interior, concluded that original occupancy under the Organic Act of 1884 established possessory rights in Alaskan waters and submerged lands, and that such rights had not been extinguished by any treaty, statute or administrative action.

1942—First units of Alaska Territorial Guard, known as the Eskimo Scouts, organized by Marvin R. "Muktuk" Marston. Japanese planes bombed Dutch Harbor in June and landed troops on Attu and Kiska Islands. Attu people were taken to Japan as prisoners. Aleuts evacuated from the other islands to Southeastern Alaska.

1943—Seven reservations were created in Alaska under the Indian Reorganization Act of 1934, for 1,470 Natives. The reservations were at Shishmaref, Wales, Akutan, White Mountain, Karluk, Unalakleet and Venetie.

1944—Alberta Schenk was ejected from the Dreamland Theater at Nome for failure to sit in the Eskimo section. The theater was later integrated.

1944—R. H. Hanna, representing the Secretary of the Interior, held hearings in Southeastern Alaska regarding the possessory rights of the villages of Kake, Klawock and Hydaburg. In his report, issued in March, 1945, Judge Hanna concluded that there was no basis to claims of exclusive aboriginal possession of the waters in Southeastern Alaska.

1945—The Alaska Territorial Legislature passed an anti-discrimination law which provided for equal treatment of Natives and whites in all business establishments and public places.

1946—Hoonah incorporated as a first-class city on June 8.

1946—The Indian Claims Commission was created by Congress.

1946—Surplus military buildings at Seward and Sitka were converted to tuberculosis hospitals. The Navy installation on Japonski Island at Sitka became the Mount Edgecumbe boarding high school for Natives.

1946—Tlingit Frank Peratrovich was elected to the territorial Senate, the first Native to be elected to that body.

1947—Congress passed the Tongass Timber Act which provided for the sale of timber from Tongass National Forest with proceeds to be held in a special fund until the issue of title to the land had been settled under the Tlingit-Haida Jurisdictional Act of 1935. This did not occur until 1965.

1948—Congress enacted legislation permitting the issuance of unrestricted deeds for townsite lands held by Natives, provided that the Secretary of the Interior found that the claimant was competent to manage his own affairs.

1948—Percy Ipalook of Wales and William E. Beltz of Nome were elected to the territorial House of Representatives, the first Eskimos to be elected to the Alaska Legislature.

1949—On November 30 the Secretary of the Interior created large reservations at Barrow, Shungnak and Hydaburg. Subsequently, the Natives of Barrow turned down the reservation by a vote of 231 to 29, and the residents of Shungnak did the same by a vote of 51 to 25. Hydaburg residents accepted the reservation on a 95 to 29 vote but it was later found to have been illegally created (see 1952).

1950—The Bureau of the Census reported a total population of 128,643 of whom 33,863 were Natives.

1952—U.S. District Judge George W. Folta at Juneau found that the Hydaburg reservation of 1950 was not validly created. His decision ends the practice of creating reservations to dispose of aboriginal or possessory claims.

1953—A 400-bed, $6,000,000 hospital for only Natives opened at Anchorage.

1955—The "Fannan Report" was issued by the Department of the Interior. It exposed abject poverty, disease and neglect among Alaska's Natives.

1955—The territorial legislature provided for a Constitutional Convention with 55 delegates, to be held at Fairbanks during the following winter. In the September election of delegates, Frank Peratrovich was among those elected.

1956—In the regular territorial Primary Election, voters ratified the draft constitution for the State of Alaska. They also approved an ordinance adopted by the Constitutional Convention to abolish fish traps in the new state.

1958—Statehood Act measure passed by Congress; statehood proclaimed officially January 3, 1959.

1958—The Atomic Energy Commission proposed Project Chariot to blast out an artificial harbor at Cape Thompson in Northwestern Alaska. Eskimo leaders from 20 villages met for the first time and organized Inupiat Paitot to protest the project and protect the interests of the Eskimos. Through the protests of many organizations both in and out of Alaska, the proposed Project Chariot is finally canceled.

1959—Alaska was proclaimed the 49th State on January 3. The constitution drafted in 1955, having been approved by the voters, took effect immediately, including the abolition of fish traps. The Native villages of Angoon, Kake and Metlakatla attempted to retain the traps owned by their village corporations, but only Metlakatla was successful because of its status as a reservation created by Congress. All of its traps are within that reserve.

1959—Congress enacted Public Law 86-121 to provide funds for the construction of individual and community water and waste disposal systems in Native villages. By 1975, 88 systems had been built under this program.

1960—The Bureau of the Census reported a total population of 226,167 of whom 43,081 were shown as "Indian and other," presumably meaning Aleuts and Eskimos.

1961—An Eskimo at Barrow was arrested for shooting an eider duck out of season. A large number of other Barrow hunters appeared at the office of the wildlife agent, each with an eider duck, and asked to be jailed along with the original offender. The subsistence hunting of ducks out of season was subsequently overlooked in the Arctic.

1961—The Bureau of Indian Affairs, on behalf of four Native villages, protested a state land selection made under the Statehood Act. The villages were claiming about 5.8 million acres of land near Fairbanks, and the state had filed its claim to about 1.7 million of the same acres.

1961—The Tanana Chiefs met and formed an organization to represent the people of their area.

1962—In August the Atomic Energy Commission announced the deferment of Project Chariot at Cape Thompson.

1962—Secretary of the Interior Stewart Udall visited Alaska in September and cited settlement of historic rights and claims as the most important problem facing the Natives.

1962—The Tundra Times, a weekly newspaper, was founded to report news of Indians, Eskimos and Aleuts and to watchdog their interests. The first issue was published October 1.

1962—Athabascan David Salmon became the first Native to be ordained an Episcopal priest, in October.

1963—The U.S. Commissioner of Indian Affairs visited Alaska in January to gather information.

1963—The State of Alaska proposed a recreation area at Minto Lakes. Richard Frank, chief of the Minto people, protested because his people used the land there for subsistence hunting. The protest was heeded and the recreation area was not created.

1963—Petitions bearing the signatures of more than 1,000 Natives were sent to Secretary of the Interior Udall asking that land selections around Native villages be frozen.

1963—Howard Rock, editor of the Tundra Times, was named the top newspaper columnist in the state by the Alaska Press Club.

1963—The Council of Indian Affairs, a national organization, announced support for Alaska Natives in their land claims.

1963—Residents of Yukon Flats villages met at Fort Yukon in October to protest the proposed Rampart Dam.

1964—People on the middle Yukon River organized Gwitchya Gwitchin Ginkhye or "Yukon Flats People Speak" to express their views. Among other things, they protested a proposed dam on the Yukon River that would have flooded much of their hunting grounds.

1964—A widespread earthquake on March 27 damaged many towns and cities and wiped out a number of Native villages, including Kaguyak, Afognak and Chenega.

1964—The Cook Inlet Native Association was founded at Anchorage.

1964—Chief Andrew Isaac filed a blanket claim to the hunting and fishing areas of the Tanacross Indians.

1964—The Tyonic Indians were paid $11 million for the right to explore for oil on their reserve.

1964—The William E. Beltz State Vocational School, first of its kind in Alaska, opened at Nome on September 28.

1965—Mrs. Katherine Peter at Fort Yukon becomes the first Alaska Native to apply for a business loan under Title III of the Economic Opportunity Act.

1965—The Alaska Human Rights Commission was created by the state legislature.

1965—The governor appointed a five-member commission to report on conditions among the Natives on the Pribilof Islands.

1965—The Eskimo, Indian, Aleut Publishing Company, publisher of the weekly *Tundra Times*, filed articles of incorporation.

1966—The Arctic Slope Native Association filed claim to approximately 96 million acres on the North Slope.

1966—The Tlingit-Haida Central Council was formed during a meeting at Sitka.

1966—The Fur Seal Act of 1966, introduced by Senator Bartlett of Alaska, granted equal rights to the Natives of the Pribilof Islands.

1966—The Secretary of the Interior placed a land freeze on the public domain in Alaska until the matter of Native ownership was settled. Governor Walter Hickel sued to have the freeze lifted, winning in the District Court of Alaska but losing on appeal to the Circuit Court of San Francisco.

1966—The Alaska Federation of Natives, a statewide organization, was formed.

1966—Alaska Natives filed claim to more than 372 million acres of the state on the basis of aboriginal rights.

1966—VISTA volunteers moved into remote villages throughout the state and were funded by the Office of Economic Opportunity. Many volunteers stayed on to help the Natives fight for their rights.

1967—The Alaska Legislature voted to give Natives a royalty on minerals found on state lands if and when the federal government settled the Native Land Claims.

1968—President Johnson made a strong statement to Congress, urging prompt action on the Alaska Native Claims bill.

1968—The Indian Claims Commission ruled that Aleuts and Eskimos can now be identified as "Indians" for claims purposes.

1968—The claims entered under the Tlingit-Haida Jurisdictional Act of 1935 were settled by the court with a judgment for $7,546,053 for the loss of lands in the Tongass National Forest. The request had been for $80,000,000.

1968—Oil was struck on the North Slope by Atlantic Richfield and Humble Oil Company. The two companies, plus British Petroleum, formed a company to build a pipeline across Alaska. This was known as the Trans-Alaska Pipeline System, or TAPS.

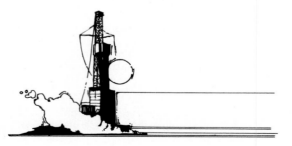

1968—The Senate Committee on Interior and Insular Affairs visited Alaska to hold hearings on Native land claims at Anchorage.

1968—When queried about Secretary Udall's Alaska land freeze, Alaska Governor Walter Hickel, seeking confirmation as Secretary of the Interior, remarked, "Anything Udall can do by Executive Order, I can undo." This alarmed the Alaska Federation of Natives, which refused to support Hickel until he promised to continue the land freeze.

1969—The Federal Field Committee for Development Planning in Alaska published a lengthy study on Native land problems. The report warned against creation of racial states within a state and recommended that land be given to individuals and communities rather than to tribes.

1970—The Bureau of the Census reported a total population of 300,882 including 51,962 "Indians and others."

1970—Plans to transfer headquarters for the Tlingit and Haida Central Council from Anchorage to Juneau were announced in February.

1970—Despite movement of many Eskimos to population centers, many outpost villages were expanding rather than shrinking, according to a survey made by the University of Alaska.

1970—A billion-dollar formula for settling Alaska Native land claims was approved by the Senate Interior Committee in April.

1970—Study in the Yup'ik Eskimo dialect was initiated in Bureau of Indian Affairs schools at Akiachak, Napakiak and Nunapitchuk on the lower Kuskokwim River when the fall term of school opened.

1970—Villages along the trans-Alaska oil pipeline haul road protested to the Secretary of the Interior that Native contractors had not been awarded contracts and that the contractors were unlikely to hire Natives. The villages of Bettles and Allakaket filed suit against Alyeska Pipeline Service Company, alleging that Alyeska had promised them jobs.

1970—U.S. District Judge George Hart Jr., in Washington, enjoins the Interior Department from issuing a construction permit to the Trans-Alaska Pipeline System across 19.8 miles of the route claimed by the residents of Stevens Village.

1971—The U.S. Corps of Engineers announced that it had abandoned any plans for a hydroelectric dam project on the Yukon River at Rampart.

1971—Congress passed the Alaska Native Land Claims Settlement Act which granted 40 million acres of land and nearly a billion dollars to the claimants.

1971—Four courses on Alaskan Native culture were offered during the fall term at the University of Alaska for the first time.

1971—The Alaska Federation of Natives sent a delegation to a meeting of the National Congress of American Indians. Laura Bergt, an Alaska delegate, renewed an old acquaintancy with Vice President Spiro Agnew and proved a successful lobbyist for the Natives.

1971—The Bethel Regional High School, to serve 200 students in a 100,000-square-mile area, opened in the fall.

1972—A videotape network for Tlingit and Haida Indians was 95% complete by the first of the year. It linked 17 villages in Southeastern Alaska with a studio at the central office in Juneau.

1972—The Episcopal Church's first woman deacon in Alaska was ordained in February. She was Jean Elizabeth Dementi of Shageluk, a Native woman.

1972—The Klukwan Village Council and Mitsubishi Corporation signed a consent agreement giving the Japanese firm the right to develop low-grade iron ore deposits in the Klukwan area.

1972—The first all-Native fire-fighting crew in history was hired by the Bureau of Land Management. It consisted of 120 men and women and in July it successfully controlled a large fire.

1972—The Athabascan Indian language was being written and spoken in a number of Interior Alaska schools with the opening of the fall school term. Previously bilingual programs had been in Yup'ik Eskimo.

1972—Mrs. Elaine Ramos, daughter of a Yakutat Tlingit chief, was named vice-president of Sheldon Jackson Junior College.

1972—Howard Bell of Nome became the first Alaska Native to vote in the electoral college balloting.

1972—Despite a national moratorium on the hunting of sea mammals, Alaska Natives retained their right to hunt for subsistence.

1972—The tuberculosis wing of the Alaska Native Hospital in Anchorage was closed because of lack of patients.

1972—The right of North Slope people to form the North Slope Borough was upheld by the Alaska Superior Court at Anchorage. The legislature subsequently placed a ceiling on the amount of taxes the borough could levy.

1972—Twelve regional corporations were formed during the year under the provisions of the Alaska Native Claims Settlement Act. The 12 regions covered the entire state.

1972—A new Alaska law required that when more than 15 students in any state school speak a language other than English, bilingual education must be added to the curriculum. The Alaska Native Language Center was established at the University of Alaska.

1973—By the March 30 deadline for filing individual applications under the Alaska Native Claims Settlement Act, about 95,000 persons had filed.

1973—Bilingual education continued to spread, with 36 rural villages participating in the state-operated schools language program and eight additional villages due to receive the program.

1973—In November President Nixon signed into law the bill authorizing construction of the trans-Alaska pipeline.

1973—Residents of the village of Angoon voted to accept a $90,000 settlement of the lawsuit against the federal government for compensation for the destruction of the village by the U.S. Navy in 1882.

1973—The first application for a village selection under the Alaska Native Land Claims Settlement Act was filed with the Bureau of Land Management by the residents of Eklutna, north of Anchorage.

1974—Ellen Lang, a Tlingit, was appointed superintendent of Sitka National Historical Park. Ms. Lang was also the first woman member of the Alaska Native Brotherhood.

1974—Inupiat University opened its doors at Barrow in the fall to offer courses of special relevance to the North Slope Natives as well as traditional curriculum.

1974—*Use of the Sea by Alaska Natives* was published by the Arctic Environmental and Data Center at the University of Alaska, Anchorage.

1974—The Tyonek Native Corporation entered into a 20-year lease of corporation acreage to the Kodiak Lumber Mills for a chip mill site.

1975—The first Eskimo to be admitted to permanent membership in the diaconate of the Roman Catholic Church was ordained at Marshall in February.

1975—Chenegans, who had lived at Tatitlek since the 1964 earthquake destroyed their village of Chenega, made plans to reestablish near the original location.

1975—Six residents of Chalkyitsik brought suit against the Alaska State Housing Authority for mismanagement in construction of six homes under the ASHA Remote Area Building Program.

1975—Afognak Natives who had been forced out of their ancestral village by the 1964 earthquake were making plans for the establishment of a model community in Afognak Bay.

1975—The U.S. Department of Justice filed trespass suits against more than 100 firms accused of trespassing on Native lands prior to enactment of the Alaska Native Claims Settlement Act in 1971. The State of Alaska intervened on the side of the defendants.

1975—The United Bank Alaska, the state's first Native-controlled bank, opened for business in Anchorage in December. The bank is controlled by a number of Native corporations.

1975—An urban survival program, designed to help Natives from outlying villages who moved to Anchorage, was opened in December by the Cook Inlet Native Associaton.

1976—Elaine Ramos, a Tlingit from Sitka and Yakutat, became the first woman and first Native vice-president of the University of Alaska on January 1.

1976—The Tanana Chiefs and the Alaska Bicentennial Commission jointly funded two photographic exhibits relating to Native Land Claims and the Athabascan Indian lifestyle 60 years ago.

1976—Information on more than 20,000 archaeological finds at 300 sites along the trans-Alaska pipeline was contained in a report compiled by the University of Alaska.

1976—Previously ruled ineligible to share in benefits of the Alaska Native Claims Settlement Act, 11 villages were reinstated by a U.S. District Court in Washington, D.C. The villages were Solomon, Uyak, Uganik, Bell Flats, Port William, Ayakulik, Salamatof, Alexander and Pauloff Harbor.

1976—A federal court at Anchorage ordered that Native women living in Alaska but married to non-Natives must not be barred from receiving general assistance from the Bureau of Indian Affairs.

1976—On January 2, President Ford signed legislation extending until January 2, 1977, the deadline for filing claims for benefits under the Alaska Native Claims Settlement Act. The deadline had been March 30, 1973.

1976—In North Slope Borough schools, eight bilingual teachers offered classes to 700 students under a program started in 1976.

1976—Olgoonik Corporation became the first village corporation in the Arctic Slope Regional Corporation to receive interim conveyance to lands it selected under the 1971 Alaska Native Claims Settlement Act. It received all but 10,000 acres of the nearly 180,000 acres it was entitled to under the terms of the act.

1976—James Mumegana Nageak was ordained in November, the first Eskimo Presbyterian minister to finish college and seminary.

1976—The first International Inuit Community Conference was held at Barrow with 52 Eskimo delegates attending from Greenland, Canada, Siberia and Alaska.

1976—More than 8,000 persons applied for Native claims benefits during the one-year extension enrollment period that ended Janaury 2, 1977.

1977—Ounalashka Corporation, the Unalaska village corporation, in January became the first village corporation under the Alaska Native Claims Settlement Act to declare a dividend for its stockholders.

1977—The United States Supreme Court upheld a controversial land trade among the state, the federal government and the Cook Inlet Region, Inc., Native corporation.

1977—In May the Museum of the Arctic was opened at Kotzebue by NANA regional corporation. The museum features arctic animals and aspects of Eskimo culture.

1977—Construction began on a 50-bed hospital at Bethel in late June. Funded by the U.S. Department of Health, Education and Welfare, the hospital was to be built in phases and completed in 1980.

1977—A circumpolar conference of Inuit people was held at Barrow in June with representatives from Greenland, Canada and Alaska.

1977—First oil through the trans-Alaska pipeline from the North Slope reached Valdez on July 28.

1977—A report published in October for the Department of Urban Development termed 90% of housing used by Alaska Natives substandard.

1977—Commercial herring fishing from Bristol Bay northward was protested by Native groups along the Bering Sea coast.

1977—The first Annual Aleutian/Pribilof Islands Conference was held at Unalaska in November.

1978—The Alaska Eskimo Whaling Commission was formed to self-regulate the taking of bowhead whales.

1978—A Haida langauge dictionary of 464 pages was published in February.

1978—The Aleut people of the Pribilof Islands won $11,239,604 in damages in an Indian Claims Commission decision. The claim was filed in 1951.

Bibliography

Ackerman, R. *The Kenaitze People*. Kenai Native Association, 1975.

Ackerman, Maria. *Tlingit Stories*. With story contributions from Austin Hammond, Sr., Laura Hotch, Charles Jimmie and Horace Marks. Anchorage: Alaska Methodist University Press, 1975.

Allen, Henry T. "Atnatanas, Natives of Copper River Alaska." In *Smithsonian Institution Annual Report for 1886*, pp. 258-66. 1889. Reprint. Seattle: Shorey Book Store, 1970.

Anchorage Daily News Staff. *The Emerging Village People*. Anchorage: Anchorage Daily News, 1967.

Arnold, Robert D. *Alaska Native Land Claims*. Anchorage: Alaska Native Foundation, 1976.

Atomic Energy Commission. *Environment of the Cape Thompson Region, Alaska*. Washington: U.S. Government Printing Office, 1966.

Attla, George, and Leversen, Bella. *Everything I Know about Training and Racing Sled Dogs*. Rome, N.Y.: Arner Publications, 1974.

Bancroft, Hubert Howe. *History of Alaska 1730-1885*. 1886. Reprint, with a new introduction by Ernest H. Gruening. New York: Antiquarian Press, 1959.

————. *Wild and Savage Tribes: The Native Races of the Pacific Coast of North America*. Vol. I. D. Appleton & Co., 1874.

Beechey, Frederik William. *Narrative of a Voyage to the Pacific and Bering's Strait*. Reprint. New York: Da Capo Press, 1969.

Bergsland, Knut. *Aleut Dialects of Atka and Attu*. Philadelphia: American Philosophical Society, 1959.

Berry, Mary Clay. *The Alaska Pipeline: The Politics of Oil and Native Land Claims*. Bloomington: Indiana University Press, 1975.

Bigjim, Frederick Seagayuk, and Ito-Adler, James. *An Interpretation of the Alaska Native Land Claims*. Anchorage: Alaska Methodist University Press, 1974.

Birket-Smith, Kaj. *The Chugach Eskimo*. Copenhagen: National Museum, 1953.

Birket-Smith, Kaj, and De Laguna, Frederica. *The Eyak Indians of the Copper River Delta, Alaska*. Copenhagen: Levin & Munksgaard, 1938.

Bodfish, Hartson Hartlett, and Allen, Joseph C. *Chasing the Bowhead*. Cambridge, MA.: Harvard University Press, 1936.

Brean, Alice. *Athabascan Stories*. Anchorage: Alaska Methodist University Press, 1975.

Brown, Emily Ivanoff. *Roots of Ticasuk*. Anchorage: Alaska Northwest Publishing Co., 1979.

Brower, Charles D.; Farrelly, Philip J.; and Anson, Lyman. *Fifty Years Below Zero: A Lifetime of Adventure in the Far North*. New York: Dodd, Mead & Co., 1942.

Cantwell, John C. *Report of the Operations of the U.S. Revenue Steamer* Nunivak, *on the Yukon River Station, Alaska, 1899-1901*. Washington: U.S. Government Printing Office, 1902.

Carrighar, Sally. *Moonlight at Midday*. New York: Alfred A. Knopf, 1958.

Cevik, Chester. *Longest Reindeer Herder*. Fairbanks: Arctic Circle Enterprise, 1973.

Chaffin, Yule M. *Koniag to King Crab: Alaska's Southwest, Kodiak from Sea Otter Settlement to King Crab Capitol*. Chaffin Inc., 1967.

Chance, Norman A. *The Eskimo of North Alaska*. New York: Holt, Rinehart and Winston, 1966.

Chevigny, Hector. *Russian America: The Great Alaskan Venture, 1741-1867*. New York: Viking Press, 1965.

Clark, Annette McFadyen. *Koyukuk River Culture*. National Museum of Man Mercury Series, Canadian Ethnology Service Paper No. 18. Ottawa: 1974.

Cline, Michael S. *Tannik School: The Impact of Education on the Eskimos of Anaktuvuk Pass*. Anchorage: Alaska Methodist University Press, 1975.

Collins, Henry Bascom, Jr.; Clark, Austin H.; and Walker, Egbert H. *The Aleutian Islands: Their People and Natural History*. Washington: Smithsonian Institution, 1945.

Committee on the Alaska Earthquake. *The Great Alaska Earthquake of 1964: Human Ecology*. National Academy of Sciences, Division of Earth Sciences, National Research Council. Washington: U.S. Government Printing Office, 1970.

Cook, James, and King, James. *A Voyage to the Pacific Ocean, Undertaken by Command of His Majesty, For Making Discoveries in the Northern Hemisphere; Performed under the Direction of Captains Cook, Clerke, and Gore, in the Years 1776, 1777, 1778, 1779, and 1780. Being a Copious, Comprehensive, and Satisfactory Abridgment of the Voyage written by Captain James Cook, F.R.S. and Captain James King, LL.D. and F.R.S.* 4 volumes. London: C. Stalker, 1788.

Coxe, William. *Account of the Russian Discoveries Between Asia and America*. London: T. Cadell, 1780.

Dall, William Healey. *Alaska and its Resources*. Boston: Lee and Shepard, 1870.

————. *On Masks, Labrets, and Certain Aboriginal Customs with an Inquiry into the Bearing of their Geographical Distribution*. 1884. Reprint. Seattle: Shorey Book Store, 1966.

Darnell, Frank, ed. *Education in the North: Selected Papers of the First International Conference on Cross-Cultural Education in the Circumpolar Nations*. College, AK: University of Alaska, 1972.

Dawson, George Mercer. *The Haidas*. 1882. Reprint. Seattle: Shorey Book Store, 1966.

De Laguna, Frederica. *The Archaeology of Cook Inlet*. Philadelphia: University of Pennsylvania Press, 1934.

————. *Chugach Prehistory: The Archaeology of Prince William Sound, Alaska*. Seattle: University of Washington Press, 1956.

————. *The Prehistory of Northern North America as seen from the Yukon*. Memoirs of the Society for American Archaeology, No. 3. Menasha, WI.: 1947.

————. *The Story of a Tlingit Community: A Problem in the Relationship between Archaeological, Ethnological and Historical Methods*. Bureau of American Ethnology, Bulletin 172. Washington: U.S. Government Printing Office, 1960.

————. *Under Mount Saint Elias: The History and Culture of the Yakutat Tlingit*. Smithsonian Contributions to Anthropology, vol. 7. Washington: Smithsonian Institution Press, 1972.

Drebert, Ferdinand. *Alaska Missionary*. Bethlehem, PA.: The Moravian Book Shop, 1959.

Driggs, John Beach. *Short Sketches from Oldest America*. Philadelphia: G.W. Jacobs & Co., 1905.

Drucker, Philip. *Cultures of the North Pacific Coast.* San Francisco: Chandler Publishing Company, 1965.

-----. *The Native Brotherhoods: Modern Intertribal Organizations of the Northwest Coast.* Bureau of Ethnology Bulletin 168. Washington: U.S. Government Printing Office, 1958.

Elliott, Henry W. *Our Arctic Province, Alaska and the Seal Islands,* Sampson, Low, 1886.

Enmonds, George T. *Report on Alaska Natives for the U.S. Congress.* Senate Document 106, Report to the Secretary of the Interior. Washington: U.S. Government Printing Office, 1905.

Federal Field Committee for Development Planning in Alaska. *Alaska Natives and the Land.* Washington: U.S. Government Printing Office, 1968.

Fedorova, Svetlana G. *The Russian Population in Alaska and California, Late 18th Century to 1867.* Translated and edited by Richard A. Pierce and Alton S. Donnelly. Kingston, Ontario: Limestone Press, 1973.

Fejes, Claire. *Enuk My Son.* New York: Pantheon Books, 1969.

-----. *People of the Noatak.* New York: Alfred A. Knopf, 1966.

Fish, Byron. *Eskimo Boy Today.* Photos by Bob and Ira Spring. Anchorage: Alaska Northwest Publishing Co., 1971.

Forsuch, Lee. *2 (c) Report: Federal Programs and Alaska Natives.* Anchorage: Robert R. Nathan Associates, 1975.

Fortuine, Robert. *Health Care and the Alaska Native: Some Historical Perspectives.* Hanover, N.H.: Dartmouth College Library, 1975.

Frost, Orcutt William. *Cross-Cultural Arts in Alaska.* Anchorage: Alaska Methodist University Press, 1970.

Gallagher, Hugh Gregory. *Etok: A Story of Eskimo Power.* New York: G.P. Putnam's Sons, 1974.

Gambell, V.C. *The School House Farthest North.* New York: Women's Board of Missions, Presbyterian Church, 1906.

Geist, Otto William, and Rainey, Froelich. *Archaeological Excavations at Kukulik, St. Lawrence Island, Alaska.* Washington: U.S. Government Printing Office, 1936.

Geoghegan, Richard Henry. *The Aleut Language; The Elements of Aleut Grammar with a Dictionary in Two Parts Containing Basic Vocabularies of Aleut and English.* Edited by Fredericka I. Martin. 1944. Reprint. Seattle: Shorey Book Store, 1964.

George, Bryon Gordon. *Notes on the Western Eskimo.* University of Pennsylvania, 1906.

Giddings, James Louis. *Ancient Men of the Arctic.* New York: Alfred A. Knopf, 1967.

-----. *Kobuk River People.* College, AK: University of Alaska, 1961.

Gillham, Charles Edward. *Beyond the Clapping Mountains: Eskimo Stories from Alaska.* New York: The Macmillan Company, 1944.

-----. *Medicine Men of Hooper Bay: or, The Eskimo's Arabian Nights.* London: Batchworth, 1955.

Goddard, Pliny Earle. *Indians of the Northwest Coast.* New York: American Museum Press, 1924.

Graburn, Nelson H., and Strong, B. Stephen. *Circumpolar Peoples: An Anthropological Perspective.* Pacific Palisades, CA.: Goodyear Publishing Co., 1973.

Green, Paul, and Abbott, Abbe. *I Am Eskimo, Aknik My Name.* Drawings by George Ahgupuk. Anchorage: Alaska Northwest Publishing Co., 1959.

Gruening, Ernest Henry. *The State of Alaska.* Rev. ed. New York: Random House, 1968.

Gubser, Nicholas J. *The Nunamiut Eskimos, Hunters of Caribou.* New Haven: Yale University Press, 1965.

Guédon, Marie Francoise. *People of Tetlin, Why Are You Singing?* Ottawa: National Museum of Man, National Museums of Canada, 1974.

Gunther, Erna. *Indian Life on the Northwest Coast of North America, as Seen by the Early Explorers and Fur Traders during the Last Decade of the Eighteenth Century.* Chicago: University of Chicago Press, 1972.

-----. *Sheldon Jackson Museum.* Sitka, AK.: Sheldon Jackson Museum, 1976.

Hall, Edwin S., Jr. *The Eskimo Storyteller: Folktales from Noatak, Alaska.* Illustrated by Claire Fejes. Knoxville, TN.: University of Tennessee Press, 1975.

Hasley, Edward H. *The McGrath Ingalik.* University of Alaska Anthropological Papers, vol. 9, no. 2. College, AK.: University of Alaska, 1961

Healey, M.A. *Report on the Cruise of the Revenue Steamer* Corwin, *1885.* Washington: U.S. Government Printing Office, 1887.

Heller, Herbert L. *Sourdough Sagas.* Cleveland: World Publishing Co., 1967.

Hill, Beth, and Hill, Ray. *Indian Petroglyphs of the Pacific Northwest.* Saanichton, B.C.: Hancock House Publishers Ltd., 1974.

Hippler, Arthur E. *Barrow and Kotzebue: An Exploratory Comparison of Acculturation and Education in Two Large Northwestern Alaska Villages.* Edited by Arthur M. Harkins and Richard G. Woods. Minneapolis: University of Minnesota, 1969.

Hippler, Arthur E., and Wood, John R. *The Subarctic Athabascans: A Selected Annotated Bibliography.* Fairbanks, AK.: Institute of Social, Economic and Government Research, University of Alaska, 1974.

Holm, Bill, and Reid, Bill. *Indian Art of the Northwest Coast: A Dialogue on Craftsmanship and Aesthetics.* Houston, TX.: Institute for the Arts, Rice University, 1976.

Hooper, Calvin Leighton. *Report of the Cruise of the U.S. Revenue Steamer* Corwin *in the Arctic Ocean by Captain C.L. Hooper, Nov. 1, 1880.* 1881. Reprint. Seattle: Shorey Book Store, 1964.

Hopkins, David Moody, Ed. *The Bering Land Bridge.* Stanford, CA.: Stanford University Press, 1967.

Hrdlicka, Ales. *Alaska Diary, 1926-1931.* Lancaster, PA.: Jaques Cattell Press, 1943.

-----. *The Aleutian and Commander Islands and their Inhabitants.* Philadelphia: The Wistar Institute of Anatomy and Biology, 1945.

-----. *Anthropological Survey in Alaska.* Washington: U.S. Government Printing Office, 1930.

-----. *The Anthropology of Kodiak Island.* Philadelphia: The Wistar Institute of Anatomy and Biology, 1944.

Hughes, Charles Campbell, and Hughes, Jane M. *An Eskimo Village in the Modern World.* Ithaca, N.Y.: Cornell University Press, 1960.

Hunt, William Raymond. *Arctic Passage: History of the Land and People of the Bering Sea, 1698-1975.* New York: Charles Scribner's Sons, 1975.

Huntington, James, and Elliott, Lawrence. *On the Edge of Nowhere.* New York: Crown Publishers Inc., 1966.

Irving, Laurence. *Arctic Life of Birds and Mammals, Including Man.* Berlin: Springer-Verlag, 1972.

Irving, W.N. "Recent Early Man Research in the North." *Arctic Anthropology* 8 (1971): no. 2.

Jackson, Sheldon. *Alaska, and Missions of the North Pacific Coast.* New York: Dodd, Mead & Co., 1880.

Jenness, Aylette. *Dwellers of the Tundra: Life in an Alaskan Eskimo Village.* Photographs by Jonathan Jenness. New York: Crowell-Collier Press, 1970.

Jenness, Diamond. *Dawn in Arctic Alaska.* Illustrated by Giacomo Raimondi. Minneapolis: University of MinnesmPress, 1957.

Jochelson, Vladimir Il'ich (Waldemar). *History, Ethnology and Anthropology of the Aleut*. Carnegie Institute of Washington Publication no. 432. Washington: Carnegie Institution of Washington, 1933.

Jones, Dorothy. *Aleuts in Transition*. Seattle: University of Washington Press, 1976.

Jones, Livingston French. *A Study of the Thlingets of Alaska*. New York: Fleming H. Revell Co., 1914.

Josephson, Karla. *Use of the Sea by Alaskan Natives, a Historical Perspective*. Alaska Sea Grant Program report no. 73-11; Alaska and the Law of the Sea. Anchorage: Arctic Environmental Information and Data Center, University of Alaska, 1974.

Kamerling, Leonard. *Kassigeluremiut: The People of Kasigluk in Pictures and Poems*. Alaska Rural School Project. College, AK.: University of Alaska, 1970.

Kawagley, Dolores. *Yupik Stories*. Anchorage: Alaska Methodist University Press, 1975.

Keim, Charles Joseph. *Aghvook, White Eskimo: Otto Geist and Alaskan Archaeology*. College, AK.: University of Alaska Press, 1969.

Keithahn, Edward Linnaeus. *Monuments in Cedar*. Seattle: Superior Publishing Co., 1963.

Kleinfeld, Judith, and Bloom, Joseph. *A Long Way from Home: Effects of Public High Schools on Village Children Away from Home*. Fairbanks: Center for Northern Educational Research and Institute of Social, Economic and Government Research, University of Alaska, 1973.

Kotzebue, Otto von. *A New Voyage Round the World, in the Years 1823, 24, 25, and 26*. London: H. Colburn and R. Bentley, 1830.

Krause, Aurel. *The Tlingit Indians: Results of a Trip to the Northwest Coast of America and the Bering Straits*. Translated by Erna Gunther. Seattle: Published for the American Ethnological Society by the University of Washington Press, 1956.

Lada-Mocarski, Valerian. *Bibliography of Books on Alaska Published before 1868*. New Haven: Yale University Press, 1969.

Lantis, Margaret. *Alaskan Eskimo Ceremonialism*. Monographs of the American Ethnological Society, 11. New York: J.J. Augustin, 1947.

-----, ed. *Ethnohistory in Southwestern Alaska and the Southern Yukon: Method and Content*. Lexington, KY.: University Press of Kentucky, 1970.

-----. *The Social Culture of the Nunivak Eskimo*. Transactions of the American Philosophical Society. Philadelphia: American Philosophical Society, 1946.

La Perouse, Jean Francois de Galaup de. *A Voyage Around the World*. London: J. Stockdale, 1798.

Larsen, Helge Eyvin, and Rainey, Froelich. *Ipiutak and the Arctic Whale Hunting Culture*. Anthropological Papers of the American Museum of Natural History, vol. 42. New York: American Museum of Natural History, 1948.

Laughlin, William S. "Eskimos and Aleuts: Their Origins and Evolution." *Science*, Nov. 8, 1963, pp. 633-45.

Lisianskii, Iurii Federovich. *A Voyage Round the World, in the Years 1803, 1804, 1805, and 1806*. 1814. Reprint. New York: De Capo Press, 1968.

Loyens, W. "The Koyukon Feast for the Dead." *Arctic Anthropology* 2 (1964): no. 2.

McCartney, A.P. "1972 Archaeological Site Survey in the Aleutian Islands, Alaska." From *International Conference on the Prehistory and Paleoecology of Western North American Arctic and Subarctic*. Calgary, Alta.: The University of Calgary, 1974.

McCracken, Harold. *Hunters of the Stormy Sea*. Garden City, N.Y.: Doubleday, 1957.

McDonald, N.C. *Witch Doctor*. New York: Ballantine Books, 1959.

MacDowell, Lloyd W. *Alaska Indian Basketry*. 1905. Reprint. Seattle: Shorey Book Store, 1966.

McFeat, Tom, ed. *Indians of the North Pacific Coast*. Seattle: University of Washington Press, 1966.

McKennan, Robert Addison. *The Chandalar Kutchin*. Arctic Institute of North America Paper no. 17. Montreal: Arctic Institute of North America, 1965.

-----. *The Upper Tanana Indians*. Yale University Publications in Anthropology, no. 55. New Haven: Yale University Press, 1959.

Marshall, Robert. *Arctic Village*. New York: Literary Guild, 1933.

Marston, Marvin R. (Muktuk). *Men of the Tundra: Eskimos at War*. New York: October House, 1969.

Martin, Fredericka I. *The Hunting of the Silver Fleece: Epic of the Fur Seal*. New York: Greenberg, 1946.

Meade, Edward F. *Indian Rock Carvings of the Pacific Northwest*. Sidney, B.C.: Gray's Publishing, 1971.

Miller, Polly and Miller, Leon. *Lost Heritage of Alaska: The Adventure and Art of the Alaskan Coastal Indians*. Cleveland: World Publishing Co., 1967.

Morgan, Lael. *And the Land Provides: Alaska Natives in a Year of Transition*. New York: Doubleday, 1974.

Murdoch, John. *Ethnological Results of the Point Barrow Expedition*. U.S. Bureau of Ethnology, Ninth Annual Report, 1887-8. Washington: U.S. Government Printing Office, 1892.

Nelson, Edward W. *The Eskimo about Bering Strait*. 1899. Reprint. New York: Johnson Reprint, 1971.

Nelson, Richard K. *Hunters of the Northern Forest: Designs for Survival among the Alaskan Kutchin*. Chicago: University of Chicago Press, 1973.

-----. *Hunters of the Northern Ice*. Chicago: University of Chicago Press, 1969.

Newell, Edythe W. *The Rescue of the Sun and Other Tales from the Far North*. Illustrated by Franz Altschuler. Chicago: Albert Whitman and Co., 1970.

Niblack, Albert Parker. *The Coast Indians of Southern Alaska and Northern British Columbia*. U.S. National Museum Annual Report, 1888. Washington: U.S. Government Printing Office, 1890.

Oliver, Ethel Ross. *Aleutian Boy*. Illustrated by Larry Lewton. Portland, OR.: Binfords and Mort, 1959.

Oliver, Simeon, and Hatch, Alden. *Son of the Smoky Sea, by Nutchuk*. New York: Julian Messner Inc., 1941.

Oman, Lela Kiana. *Eskimo Legends*. Illustrated by Minnie Kiana Keezer. Alaska Native Literature Series. Anchorage: Alaska Methodist University Press, 1975.

Oquilluk, William A., and Bland, Laurel L. *People of Kauwerak: Legends of the Northern Eskimo*. Anchorage: Alaska Methodist University Press, 1973.

Orth, Donald J. *Dictionary of Alaska Place Names*. Geological Survey Professional Paper 567. Washington: U.S. Government Printing Office, 1967.

Osgood, Cornelius. *Contributions to the Ethnology of the Kutchin*. Yale University Publications in Anthropology, no. 14. New Haven: Yale University Press, 1936.

-----. *The Ethnography of the Tanaina*. Yale University Publications in Anthropology, no. 16. New Haven: Yale University Press, 1937.

-----. *Ingalik Material Culture*. Yale University Publications in Anthropology, no. 22. New Haven: Yale University Press, 1940.

-----. *Ingalik Mental Culture*. Yale University Publications in Anthropology, no. 56. New Haven: Yale University Press, 1959.

-----. *Ingalik Social Culture*. Yale University Publications in Anthropology, no. 53. New Haven: Yale University Press, 1958.

Oswalt, Wendell H. *Alaskan Eskimos*. San Francisco: Chandler Publishing Co., 1967.

----. *Mission of Change in Alaska: Eskimos and Moravians on the Kuskokwim*. San Marino, CA.: Huntington Library, 1963.

----. *Napaskiak; An Alaskan Eskimo Community*. Tucson: University of Arizona Press, 1963.

Paul, Frances Lackey. *Kahtahah*. Illustrated by Rie Munoz. Anchorage: Alaska Northwest Publishing Co., 1976.

Peck, Cyrus E. *The Tides People: Tlingit Indians of Southeast Alaska*. Juneau, AK.: Indian Studies Program, City and Borough of Juneau School District, 1975.

Petrov, Ivan. *Report of the Population, Industry and Resources of Alaska*. Washington: U.S. Government Printing Office, 1882.

Phebus, George. *Alaskan Eskimo Life in the 1890s, as Sketched by Native Artists*. Washington: Smithsonian Institution Press, 1972.

Rainey, Froelich Gladstone. *The Whale Hunters of Tigara*. Anthropological Papers of the American Museum of Natural History, vol. 41, part 2. New York: American Museum of Natural History, 1947.

Rapaport, Stella F. *The Bear: Ship of Many Lives*. New York: Dodd, Mead & Co., 1962.

Ray, Dorothy Jean. *Artists of the Tundra and the Sea*. Seattle: University of Washington Press, 1961.

----. *The Eskimos of Bering Strait 1650-1898*. Seattle: University of Washington Press, 1975.

----, ed. *The Eskimo of St. Michael and Vicinity as Related by H.M.W. Edmonds*. Anthropological Papers of the University of Alaska, vol. 13, no. 2. College, AK.: University of Alaska Press, 1966.

Reid, William. *Out of the Silence*. Photos by Adelaide De Menil. New York: Published for the Amon Carter Museum, Fort Worth, by Outerbridge & Dienstfrey, 1971.

Report of the Secretary of the Interior. Washington: U.S. Government Printing Office, 1901.

Rudenko, Sergei Ivanovich. *The Ancient Culture of the Bering Sea and the Eskimo Problem*. Translated by Paul Tolstoy. Toronto: Published for the Arctic Institute of North America by the University of Toronto Press, 1961.

Salisbury, Oliver Maxson. *Quoth the Raven: A Little Journey into the Primitive*. Seattle: Superior Publishing Co., 1962.

Schualbe, Anna Buxbaum. *Dayspring on the Kuskokwim: The Story of Moravian Missions in Alaska*. Bethlehem, PA.: Moravian Church of America, 1951.

Schwatka, Frederick. *A Summer in Alaska: A Popular Account of the Travels of an Alaska Exploring Expedition along the Great Yukon River from its Source to its Mouth, in the British Northwest Territory and the Territory of Alaska*. St. Louis, MO.: 1893.

Senungetuk, Joseph Engasongwok. *Give or Take a Century: An Eskimo Chronicle*. San Francisco: Indian Historian Press, 1971.

Shenitz, Helen. *Alaska Good Father*. Wilkesbarre, PA.: Federated Russian Orthodox Church, 1962.

Sherwood, Morgan, ed. *The Cook Inlet Collection: Two Hundred Years of Selected Alaskan History*. Illustrated by Diana Tillion. Anchorage: Alaska Northwest Publishing Co., 1974.

----. *Exploration of Alaska 1865-1900*. New Haven: Yale University Press, 1965.

Silook, Roger. *In the Beginning*. Illustrated by Robert Mayokok. Anchorage: Anchorage Printing Co., 1970.

----. *Seevookuk: Stories the Old People Told on St. Lawrence Island*. Illustrated by Florence Malewotkuk. Anchorage: Anchorage Printing Co., 1976.

Spencer, Robert F. *The North Alaskan Eskimo: A Study in Ecology and Society*. Bureau of American Ethnology Bulletin no. 171. Washington: U.S. Government Printing Office, 1959.

----; Jennings, Jesse D.; et al. *The Native Americans: Prehistory and Ethnology of the North American Indians*. New York: Harper & Row, 1965.

Stefansson, Vilhjalmur. *My Life with the Eskimo*. New York: The Macmillan Co., 1913.

Steiner, Stanley. *The New Indians*. New York: Harper & Row, 1968.

Stewart, Hilary. *Artifacts of the Northwest Coast Indians*. Saanichton, B.C.: Hancock House Publishers Ltd., 1973.

Stoney, George M. *Explorations in Alaska 1899*. Reprint. Seattle: Shorey Book Store, 1965.

Stuck, Hudson. *Ten Thousand Miles in a Dog Sled*. New York: Charles Scribner's Sons, 1916.

----. *Voyages on the Yukon and Its Tributaries*. New York: Charles Scribner's Sons, 1917.

Swanton, John Reed. *Contributions to the Ethnology of the Haida*. Memoir of the American Museum of Natural History, vol. VIII, Part I. New York: G.E. Stechert, 1905.

Swindler, William F., and Trover, Ellen Lloyd. *A Chronology and Documentary Handbook of the State of Alaska*. Dodds Ferry,y.; Oceana Publications, 1972.

Swineford, Alfred P. *Alaska: Its History, Climate and Natural Resources*. Chicago: Rand, 1898.

Thomas, Tay. *Cry in the Wilderness*. Anchorage: Color Art Printing, 1967.

U.S. National Park Service. *Alaska History 1741-1910*. Washington: U.S. Government Printing Office.

VanStone, James W. *Eskimos of the Nushagak River: An Ethnographic History*. Seattle: University of Washington Press, 1967.

----. *Point Hope: An Eskimo Village in Transition*. Seattle: University of Washington Press, 1962.

Vaudrin, Bill. *Tanaina Tales from Alaska*. Norman: University of Oklahoma Press, 1969.

Washburn, Wilcomb E. *Red Man's Land White Man's Law: A Study of the Past and Present Status of the American Indian*. New York: Charles Scribner's Sons, 1971.

Waxell, Sven Larsson. *The American Expedition*. Translated with an introduction and notes by M.A. Michael. London: W. Hodge, 1952.

Wells, James K. *Ipani Eskimos: A Cycle of Life in Nature*. Anchorage: Alaska Methodist University Press, 1974.

Whymper, Frederick. *Travel and Adventure in the Territory of Alaska, formerly Russian America—now Ceded to the United States—and in Various other Parts of the North Pacific*. New York: Harper & Brothers, 1869.

Wickersham, James. *A Bibliography of Alaskan Literature, 1724-1924*. Cordova, AK.: Cordova Daily Times, 1927.

Workman, Karen Wood. *Alaskan Archaeology: A Bibliography*. 2nd edition. Anchorage: Alaska Division of Parks, 1974.

von Wrangell, Ferdinand Petrovich. *The Inhabitants of the Northwest Coast of America*. From "Syn Otechestva," vol. 7. Translated by James VanStone. St. Petersburg: 1939.

Young, S. Hall. *Hall Young of Alaska: The Mushing Parson*. New York: Revell, 1927.

Zagoskin, L.A. *Zagoskin's Travels in Russian America, 1824-1844*. Arctic Institute of North America. Toronto: University of Toronto Press, 1967.

Alaska Geographic® Back Issues

The North Slope, Vol. 1, No. 1. Charter issue of *ALASKA GEOGRAPHIC®*. Out of print.

One Man's Wilderness, Vol. 1, No. 2, The story of a dream shared by many, fulfilled by few: a man goes into the bush, builds a cabin and shares his incredible wilderness experience. Color photos. 116 pages, $9.95

Admiralty . . . Island in Contention, Vol. 1, No. 3. An intimate and multifaceted view of Admiralty: its geological and historical past, its present-day geography, wildlife and sparse human population. Color photos. 78 pages, $5.00

Fisheries of the North Pacific: History, Species, Gear & Processes, Vol. 1, No. 4. Out of print.

The Alaska-Yukon Wild Flowers Guide, Vol. 2, No. 1. Out of print; book edition available, $12.95

Richard Harrington's Yukon, Vol. 2, No. 2. A collection of 277 stunning color photos by Canadian photographer-writer Richard Harrington captures the Yukon in all its seasons and moods, from Watson Lake to Herschel Island. 103 pages, $7.95

Prince William Sound, Vol. 2, No. 3. Out of print.

Yakutat: The Turbulent Crescent, Vol. 2, No. 4. Out of print.

Glacier Bay: Old Ice, New Land, Vol. 3, No. 1. The expansive wilderness of Southeastern Alaska's Glacier Bay National Monument unfolds in crisp text and color photographs. Records the flora and fauna of the area, its natural history, with hike and cruise information, plus a large-scale color map. 132 pages, $9.95

The Land: Eye of the Storm, Vol. 3, No. 2. Out of print.

Richard Harrington's Antarctic, Vol. 3, No. 3. The Canadian photojournalist guides readers through remote and little understood regions of the Antarctic and Subantarctic. More than 200 color photos and a large fold-out map. 104 pages, $8.95

The Silver Years of the Alaska Canned Salmon Industry: An Album of Historical Photos, Vol. 3, No. 4. Out of print.

Alaska's Volcanoes: Northern Link in the Ring of Fire, Vol. 4, No. 1. Temporarily Out of print.

The Brooks Range: Environmental Watershed, Vol. 4, No. 2. Out of print.

Kodiak: Island of Change, Vol. 4, No. 3. Out of print.

Wilderness Proposals: Which Way for Alaska's Lands?, Vol. 4, No. 4. Out of print.

Cook Inlet Country, Vol. 5, No. 1. A visual tour of the region — its communities, big and small, and its countryside. Begins at the southern tip of the Kenai Peninsula, circles Turnagain Arm and Knik Arm for a close-up view of Anchorage, and visits the Matanuska and Susitna valleys and the wild, west side of the inlet. 144 pages; 230 color photos, separate map. $9.95

Southeast: Alaska's Panhandle, Vol. 5, No. 2. Most colorful edition to date, exploring Southeastern Alaska's maze of fjords and islands, mossy forests and glacier-draped mountains — from Dixon Entrance to Icy Bay, including all of the state's fabled Inside Passage. Along the way are profiles of every town, together with a look at the region's history, economy, people, attractions and future. Includes large fold-out map and seven area maps. 192 pages, $9.95.

Bristol Bay Basin, Vol. 5, No. 3. Out of print.

Alaska Whales and Whaling, Vol. 5, No. 4. The wonders of whales in Alaska — their life cycles, travels and travails — are examined, with an authoritative history of commercial and subsistence whaling in the North. Includes a fold-out poster of 14 major whale species in Alaska in perspective, color photos and illustrations, with historical photos and line drawings. 144 pages, $12.95

Yukon-Kuskokwim Delta, Vol. 6, No. 1. Out of print.

Aurora Borealis: The Amazing Northern Lights, Vol. 6, No. 2. One of the world's leading experts — Dr. S.-I. Akasofu of the University of Alaska — explains in an easily understood manner, aided by many diagrams and spectacular color and black-and-white photos, what causes the aurora, how it works, how and why scientists are studying it today and its implications for our future. 52 color, 49 b&w photos; 96 pages, $7.95.

Alaska's Native People, Vol. 6, No. 3. The varied worlds of the Inupiat Eskimo, Yup'ik Eskimo, Athabascan, Aleut, Tlingit, Haida and Tsimshian. Included are sensitive, informative articles by Native writers, plus a large, four-color map detailing the Native villages and defining the language areas. 304 pages, $24.95.

The Stikine, Vol. 6, No. 4. River route to three Canadian gold strikes in the 1800s, the Stikine is the largest and most navigable of several rivers that flow from northwestern Canada through Southeastern Alaska on their way to the sea. Illustrated with contemporary color photos and historic black-and-white; includes a large fold-out map. 96 pages, $9.95.

Alaska's Great Interior, Vol. 7, No. 1. Alaska's rich Interior country, west from the Alaska-Yukon Territory border and including the huge drainage between the Alaska Range and the Brooks Range, is covered thoroughly. Illustrated with contemporary color and black-and-white photos. Includes a large fold-out map. 128 pages, $9.95.

A Photographic Geography of Alaska, Vol. 7, No. 2. An overview of the entire state — a visual tour through the six regions of Alaska: Southeast, Southcentral/Gulf Coast, Alaska Peninsula and Aleutians, Bering Sea Coast, Arctic and Interior. Plus a handy appendix of valuable information — "Facts About Alaska." Approximately 160 color and black-and-white photos and 35 maps. 192 pages, $14.95.

The Aleutians, Vol 7, No. 3. The fog-shrouded Aleutians are many things — home of the Aleut, a tremendous wildlife spectacle, a major World War II battleground and now the heart of a thriving new commercial fishing industry. Included are contemporary color and black-and-white photographs, and a large fold-out map. 224 pages, $14.95.

Klondike Lost: A Decade of Photographs by Kinsey & Kinsey, Vol. 7, No. 4. Out of print; book edition available.

Wrangell-Saint Elias, Vol. 8, No. 1. Mountains, including the continent's second- and fourth-highest peaks, dominate this international wilderness that sweeps from the Wrangell Mountains in Alaska to the southern Saint Elias range in Canada. The region draws backpackers, mountain climbers, and miners, and is home for a few hardy, year-round inhabitants. Illustrated with contemporary color and historical black-and-white photographs. Includes a large fold-out map. $9.95.

Alaska Mammals, Vol. 8, No. 2. From tiny ground squirrels to the powerful polar bear, and from the tundra hare to the magnificent whales inhabiting Alaska's waters, this volume includes 80 species of mammals found in Alaska. Included are beautiful color photographs and personal accounts of wildlife encounters. *The* book on Alaska's mammals — from Southeast to the Arctic, and beyond! $12.95.

The Kotzebue Basin, Vol. 8, No. 3. Examines northwestern Alaska's thriving trading area of Kotzebue Sound and the Kobuk and Noatak river basins, lifelines of the region's Inupiat Eskimos, early explorers, and present-day, hardy residents. Contemporary color and historical black-and-white photographs illustrate varied cultures and numerous physical attractions of the area. $12.95.

Alaska National Interest Lands, Vol. 8, No. 4. Following passage of the bill formalizing Alaska's national interest land selections (d-2 lands), longtime Alaskans Celia Hunter and Ginny Wood review each selection, outlining location, size, access, and briefly describing the region's special attractions. Illustrated with contemporary color photographs depicting as no other medium can the grandeur of Alaska's national interest lands. $14.95.

Alaska's Glaciers, Vol. 9, No. 1. Examines in-depth the massive rivers of ice, their composition, exploration, present-day distribution and scientific significance. Illustrated with many contemporary color and historical black-and-white photos, the text includes separate discussions of more than a dozen glacial regions. 144 pages, $9.95.

Sitka and Its Ocean/Island World, Vol. 9, No. 2. From the elegant capital of Russian America to a beautiful but modern port, Sitka, on Baranof Island, has become a commercial and cultural center for Southeastern Alaska. Pat Roppel, longtime Southeast resident and expert on the region's history, examines in detail the past and present of Sitka, Baranof Island, and neighboring Chichagof Island. Illustrated with contemporary color and historical black-and-white photographs. 128 pages, $9.95.

Islands of the Seals: The Pribilofs, Vol. 9, No. 3. Great herds of northern fur seals drew Russians and Aleuts to these remote Bering Sea islands where they founded permanent communities and established a unique international commerce. Illustrated with contemporary color and historical black-and-white photographs. To be distributed to members September 1982. 128 pages, $9.95.

Alaska's Oil/Gas & Minerals Industry, Vol. 9, No. 4. Experts detail the geological processes and resulting mineral and fossil fuel resources that are now in the forefront of Alaska's economy. Discussions of historical methods and the latest techniques in present-day mining, submarine deposits, taxes, regulations, and education complete this overview of an important state industry. Illustrated with historical black-and-white and contemporary color photographs. 224 pages, $12.95.

Your $30 ($34 outside the U.S.) membership in The Alaska Geographic Society includes 4 subsequent issues of *ALASKA GEOGRAPHIC®*, the Society's official quarterly. Additional membership information available upon request.

Single copies of the *ALASKA GEOGRAPHIC®* back issues are available per the list here. When ordering, please add $1 postage/handling per copy. To order back issues send your check or money order and volumes desired to:

The Alaska Geographic Society

Box 4-EEE, Anchorage, AK 99509